Quantitative Research in Linguistics

Other titles in the Research Methods in Linguistics series:

Experimental Research Methods in Language Learning, Aek Phakiti

Research Methods in Applied Linguistics, edited by Brian Paltridge and Aek Phakiti

Research Methods in Interpreting, Sandra Hale and Jemina Napier

Research Methods in Linguistics, Lia Litosseliti

Quantitative Research in Linguistics

An Introduction

SECOND EDITION

SEBASTIAN M. RASINGER

BLOOMSBURY
LONDON · NEW DELHI · NEW YORK · SYDNEY

Bloomsbury Academic
An imprint of Bloomsbury Publishing Plc

50 Bedford Square	1385 Broadway
London	New York
WC1B 3DP	NY 10018
UK	USA

www.bloomsbury.com

Bloomsbury is a registered trademark of Bloomsbury Publishing Plc.

First published 2008 by Continuum

This second edition © Sebastian M. Rasinger, 2013

British Library Cataloguing-in-Publication Data
A catalogue record for this book is available from the British Library.

ISBN: HB: 978-1-4411-1722-9
PB: 978-1-4411-8010-0
ePub: 978-1-4411-1619-2
PDF: 978-1-4411-6649-4

Library of Congress Cataloging-in-Publication Data
Rasinger, Sebastian M. (Sebastian Marc), 1977-
Quantitative research in linguistics : an introduction / Sebastian M. Rasinger. –
Second Edition.
pages cm. – (Research Methods in Linguistics)
Includes bibliographical references and index.
ISBN 978-1-4411-1722-9 (hardcover : alk. paper) – ISBN 978-1-4411-8010-0 (pbk. : alk. paper)
– ISBN 978-1-4411-6649-4 (ebook) – ISBN 978-1-4411-1619-2 (ebook (epub)
1. Linguistics–Research–Methodology. 2. Linguistics–Statistical methods. I. Title.
P126.R29 2013
410.72–dc23
2013018697

Typeset by Newgen Knowledge Works (P) Ltd., Chennai, India
Printed and bound in India

For my parents

CONTENTS

FIGURES AND TABLES

Figures

Tables

ACKNOWLEDGEMENTS

As with any other book, countless people were involved in the process of this one coming into existence, to all of whom I am eternally grateful. Many thanks to, in no particular order, my former and current students and colleagues at Anglia Ruskin University, for their input, patience, and for serving as guinea pigs in my attempts to bring quantitative methods closer to them; the readers and reviewers of the first edition for their kind and useful feedback, and suggestions for improvements for this second edition; and Gurdeep Mattu and the entire team at Bloomsbury for bringing this book to life.

Any faults and shortcomings are, of course, my very own.

Sebastian M. Rasinger
Cambridge, March 2013

CHAPTER ONE

Introduction

Some things never change: the sun rises in the morning. The sun sets in the evening. A lot of linguists don't like statistics. I have spent a decade teaching English language and linguistics at various universities, and, invariably, there seems to be a widespread aversion to all things numerical. The most common complaint is that statistics is 'too difficult'. The fact is, it isn't. Or at least, it doesn't need to be.

This book is several things at once. It is, to no surprise, an introduction to quantitative research methods. As such, it is a primer: a book that is primarily aimed at those with a minimum of prior knowledge. In fact, most readers should be able to follow this book without any prior knowledge or familiarity with the contents. It is also a guidebook – one that leads its readers through the sometimes daunting process of setting up and carrying out a quantitative study from start to finish. And finally, it is a manual, as it provides its readers with hands-on practical advice on quantitative research in general and statistical methods in particular.

The original idea for the first edition of this book, published in 2008, followed an argument with some of my MA students. Having discussed the factors influencing second-language acquisition success or failure, we had started to look at the issue of learner motivation, and I came to ask (a) how we could empirically prove how motivated a learner was and (b) how we could draw sound conclusions that motivation and outcome are causally related. The result was grim. Several students, all of them language teachers with several years experience, argued that 'any good teacher is able to see that this is the case'. And, finally, one of them accused me of 'trying to measure everything – you just have a too scientific mind'. It took some not-so-gentle encouragement to persuade them that any academically sound piece work would inevitably have to use methodologically proper methods and techniques, or else. . . . Five years down the line, I am still having these discussions, but at least I have a book to refer them to. Quantitative research need not to be difficult!

The subject benchmarks for linguistics undergraduate degrees by the UK Quality Assurance Agency – the organization monitoring academic standards in higher education – state that:

> 6.13 On graduating with an honours degree in linguistics, students will typically be able to:
>
> - demonstrate an understanding of the issues involved in the basic techniques of data analysis, and evaluate and choose appropriate techniques such as *distributional criteria*, spectrographic analysis, the use of IT tools for the investigation of electronic databases, the use of computer packages for the analysis of acoustic phenomena, the use of laboratory techniques for the investigation of articulatory phenomena, *relevant statistical tests,* the use of video and audio material in the analysis of spoken interaction . . .
>
> - *demonstrate understanding of data and analyses presented by means of graphs (including tree diagrams), tables, matrices and other diagrams and present data* appropriately by these means with minimum supervision.
>
> (The Quality Assurance Agency for Higher Education. 2007. Linguistics. Subject benchmarks. www.qaa.ac.uk/Publications/ InformationAndGuidance/Documents/Linguistics07.pdf, pp. 14–15. My emphasis.)

It might be rather odd to start an introductory textbook with quotes from a policy document; yet, it shows just how important a thorough understanding of research methods is. Over the years, I have marked a number of student assignments at various universities and at various levels, which started off as excellent pieces of work, but once it came to the data analysis part it went downhill: all too often, the author just did not know how to properly handle the data they collected, analyses are flawed and basic mathematical operations simply wrong. Even worse, some continued to make the argument they had started, whether the empirical findings support it or not. Hardly anything is worse than getting (or giving!) a low mark for something that could have been solved so easily – I do speak from experience.

There is another side to this, too. Some of us may not want to conduct a quantitative study ourselves, for whatever reason; however, this does not mean that we do not need to understand the basics of quantitative research. The majority of studies in psycholinguistics and sociolinguistics – particularly those dealing with linguistics variation – are based on quantitative data and analysis; and if we want to fully understand these studies, we need to have at least some idea what all those terms, indices, figures and graphs mean. It may be unnecessary to know all the mathematical intricacies surrounding a *t*-test or Analysis of Variance (ANOVA) (see Chapter Eight), but it is for obvious reasons no good if we read in a paper that 'a *t*-test showed statistically significant differences between the 2 groups' and we do not know what either a *t*-test or statistical significance is.

There is, undoubtedly, a myriad of books on quantitative methods and statistics on the market. Predominantly, these inhabit the bookshelves of disciplines such as social and natural sciences, psychology or economics. Indeed, there are statistics books which cater specifically for linguists, too, for example Butler (1985) or Woods et al. (1986), or more recently the texts by Johnson (2008) or Gries (2009), to name but a few. All of them comprehensive pieces of work which leave little to add to. Yet, experience in teaching quantitative methods and statistics to students and professional linguists alike has shown that what many people read is not only an introduction to statistics (the number crunching bit) but also the general approach that is quantitative research: frequently it is not only the maths that is the problem, but the entire methodological setup. And hence, this book is not one on statistics alone, but an introduction to quantitative methods in general, specifically written for students and researchers in languages and linguistics.

As such, this book is written for three particular types of people, which, in some form or other, all feature in the life of its author:

- Colleagues and students who get panic attacks when asked to perform simple statistical analyses such as calculating averages and hence simply and safely refuse to approach anything vaguely related to numbers.

- The linguist who, despite being well-versed in statistical methods, insists on doing complicated calculations by hand with pen and paper and refuses to use readily available software, hence making statistics more painful.

- The undergraduate or postgraduate student or any other researcher in linguistics and language related disciplines who realizes at some point that they need a comprehensible introduction to quantitative methods in their field, in order to make their project methodologically sound.

This book has no prerequisites other than very basic numeracy skills and some basic knowledge of using a computer and standard software: being able to do basic mathematic operations such as addition, subtraction, multiplication and division, by hand or with the use of a calculator is all that is needed. And, of course, being a linguist helps! This book does not intend, nor claim, to make its reader love statistics. However, ideally, having read the book, any reader should be able to set up a simple but well-developed quantitative study, collect good data using appropriate methods, perform the most important statistic analyses, and interpret and present the results adequately; in other words, it should stop you from falling into the 'stats trap'. Alternatively, you may want to use the book or individual chapters to understand particular concepts and tools of quantitative research when reading studies using these tools. This book does not aim at elaborating or explaining the mathematical intricacies of the methods discussed. Rather, it has been written as a practical hands-on guide and should enable its readers to get going and actually *do* quantitative research from the very first pages onwards.

Throughout the book, we try and look at examples or real linguistic research, and will discuss the methods and tools employed in research such as Labov's *Language in the Inner City* (1977), Trudgill's work on sociolinguistic variation in Norwich (1974), or Johnson and Newport's studies on the 'Critical Period' in second-language acquisition (1989, 1991), all of which is aimed to help readers understanding the concepts introduced. This has the advantage that readers can read the original studies simultaneously with the relevant chapter, and increase understanding of the issues discussed. Reviews of the previous edition have criticized that the examples focus somewhat heavily on sociolinguistic and applied linguistic examples – something I entirely agree with. This, in part, reflects my own research interests, but, more importantly, a lot of the examples are comparatively easy to understand and often part of a teaching curriculum. Trying to explain statistics while simultaneously explaining complicated linguistic concepts is beyond the scope of this book.

Furthermore, with computers being omnipresent, we will introduce the appropriate steps for performing a statistical analysis using spreadsheet software, specifically Microsoft Excel. Again, this is to avoid complicated manual calculations and will give readers the opportunity to actually do statistics as quickly as possible. While this is not a textbook on using Excel, readers will need no more than basic knowledge of how to enter data into a spreadsheet software – the title of Harvey's (2003) *Excel 2003 for Dummies* might scratch people's egos a bit but it is a good starting point for those who have not previously used the programme.

The task of writing a second edition of an introductory textbook is not an easy one: on the one hand, it ought to be different, but on the other, it ought to retain its scope and depth, too. I have hence both expanded and gently updated the previous edition. The book is divided into three parts: Part One (Chapters Two to Four) introduces readers to the basics of quantitative research, by discussing fundamental concepts and common methods. Chapter Two introduces the key concepts of quantitative research and takes a close look at different types of variables and measurement as well as reliability and validity. The third chapter introduces readers to various different research designs and provides information on how to choose an appropriate design for a particular research questions. I have expanded this chapter to include a brief section on project management: knowing how to set up a project that is methodologically sound on paper is not enough – one has to actually do it. Chapter Four is dedicated to an in-depth discussion of questionnaires, their design and use in quantitative research.

Part Two (Chapters Five to Nine) covers statistical tools most commonly used in linguistic research. Specifically, we will discuss how to describe data properly (Chapters Five and Six), how to test relationships between variables using standard statistical tools (Chapter Seven), and how to check whether different sets of data are significantly different from each other, for example in pre- and post-test situations (Chapter Eight). Following popular demand, Chapter Eight now includes a discussion of ANOVAs, too. Chapter Nine provides an overview of statistical tools for the analysis of non-normal data.

Part Two has been written with the motto in mind, 'get as much as possible out of your data with as little effort as possible', and readers should be able to perform simple but thorough analyses of any data set, using Microsoft Excel or similar software. The second part contains many tasks and exercises readers are encouraged to do. Many of these tasks are discussed in detail on the spot to ensure understanding – nothing is worse than having a generic answer somewhere on the back pages but no one really knows where the solution comes from, let alone how to interpret it! Solutions for some additional exercises can be found in Chapter Eleven, together with the statistical tables necessary for the interpretation of results.

The final part, consisting of Chapter Ten, is new: it provides an overview of more advanced methods. The first section discusses Multivariate Analysis of Variances (MANOVAs), followed by a discussion of statistical meta-analysis – a method to combine (not to say, recycle) previous results in a meaningful manner. The final section introduces two pieces on statistical software: IBM SPSS (formerly 'Statistical Package for the Social Sciences') and R, with pointers to as where readers can find more information.

In Part Two, I have included 'Quick Fix' boxes which summarize the main statistical tools discussed in the chapter. You can also find cheat sheets for these tools on the companion website, together with Excel templates and short video clips demonstrating how to conduct certain statistical tools in Excel. All parts now also include a 'further reading' section at the end.

Before you start reading the book, a word of advice from my experience as both a student and a teacher of quantitative methods: do try and actually apply what you read as soon as possible. I have written the book in such a way that it should be – hopefully – relatively easy to simultaneously read and practically follow the issues discussed. So get pen and paper, or your computer, ready. As with many things in life, you will improve with practice – so start as early as you can.

PART ONE

CHAPTER TWO

Quantitative research – some basic issues

Key words: causality – concept – dependent variable – hypothesis – independent variable – latent variable – law – level of measurement – measurement – qualitative research – quantitative research – reliability – theory – type of variable – validity

This chapter discusses some of the basics of quantitative research – the main focus of this book. After an outline of the differences between qualitative and quantitative research, we will look in some detail at the concepts of measurement and different types of variables, followed by a discussion of causal relationships. Lastly, the concepts of validity and reliability are introduced.

2.1. Qualitative and quantitative data

While most people have some idea that there is a difference between quantitative and qualitative research, the general concept they have often seems fundamentally flawed. Having taught research methods courses at several universities and at several levels, the most common answer to my question 'what's the difference between qualitative and quantitative data' has usually been somewhere along the lines of 'quantitative data means much data, and qualitative data is good data'. In the worst-case scenario, this may lead to statements such as 'I want to do qualitative research because I want it to be really good' or, alternatively, 'I can't be bothered to collect all that data'.

It hence seems a good idea to begin with a brief outline of the differences between qualitative and quantitative data, providing specific examples of applications for both types, and examples for data sets that can be interpreted both quantitatively and qualitatively.

The idea that quantitative data refers to large amounts of data is only partially true. In fact, the vast majority of quantitative data analysis tools which will be discussed in this book require a data set of a decent size in order to work properly. Small amounts of data can often lead to insignificant, inconclusive or flawed results because the mathematical procedures involved in quantitative (or statistical) analyses require a certain amount of data in order to work properly – we discuss this in more detail from Chapter Five onwards. Nevertheless, the main characteristics of quantitative data is that it consists of information that is, in some way or other, *quantifiably*. In other words, we can put quantitative data into numbers, figures and graphs, and process it using statistical (i.e. a particular type of mathematical) procedures. When using quantitative analyses, we are usually interested in how *much* or how *many* there is/are of whatever we are interested in.

A typical quantitative variable (i.e. a variable that can be put into numbers) in linguistic research is the occurrence of a particular phonological or syntactic feature in a person's speech. Assume we are interested whether speakers of group A are more likely to drop the /h/ than speakers of group B. When analysing our data, we would hence count all the instances in which /h/ is produced by the speakers (such as in *hotel* or *house*), as well as all the instances in which /h/ is omitted ('*ouse*, '*otel*). What we will get at the very end is four numbers: /h/-used in group A, /h/-drop in group A, /h/-used in group B, and /h/-drop in group B – a nice and basic set of quantitative data, which could look like the one in Table 2.1.

In fact, counting occurrences of particular features (or, technically correct, the outcome of a particular variable) is the simplest form of quantitative analysis – yes, quantitative analysis can be as easy as that! Other popular quantitative variables are people's age (again, a number), people's weight (probably less important for linguistics, but quantifiable and hence quantitative), and even people's sex (how many men/women are in a particular group?). We have a closer look at the different types of quantitative data further down in this chapter.

Qualitative data, on the other hand, deals with the questions of how something is, as opposed to *how much/many*. When using qualitative data,

TABLE 2.1 Basic set of quantitative data

Group	/h/ produced	/h/-drop
A	5	18
B	36	1

we are talking about texts, patterns and qualities. Qualitative analysis in linguistics is most commonly found in discourse analytic research.

By definition, the two approaches of analysis also differ in another respect: qualitative research is *inductive*, that is, theory is derived from the research results. Qualitative analysis is often used in preliminary studies in order to evaluate the research area. For example, we may want to conduct focus groups and interviews and analyse them qualitatively in order to build a picture of what is going on. We can then use these findings to explore these issues on a larger scale, for example by using a survey, and conduct a quantitative analysis. However, it has to be emphasized that qualitative research is not merely an auxiliary tool to data analysis, but a valuable approach in itself!

Quantitative research, on the other hand, is *deductive*: based on already known theory we develop hypotheses, which we then try to prove (or disprove) in the course of our empirical investigation. Accordingly, the decision between qualitative and quantitative methodology will have a dramatic impact on how we go about our research. Figures 2.1 and 2.2 outline the deductive and inductive processes graphically.

At the beginning of the quantitative-deductive process stands the *hypothesis* (or theory). As outlined below, a hypothesis is a statement about a particular aspect of reality, such as 'the lower the socio-economic class, the more non-standard features a speaker's language shows'. The hypothesis is

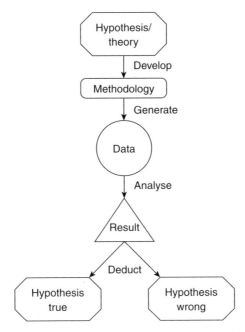

FIGURE 2.1 *Quantitative-deductive approach.*

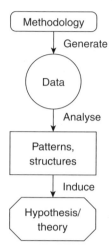

FIGURE 2.2 *Qualitative-inductive approach.*

based on findings of previous research, and the aim of our study is to prove or disprove it. Based on a precisely formulated hypothesis, or research question, we develop a methodology, that is, a set of instruments which will allow us to measure reality in such a way that the results allow us to prove the hypothesis right or wrong. This also includes the development of adequate analytic tools, which we will use to analyse our data once we have collected it. Throughout this book, I will keep reminding readers that it is paramount that hypothesis/research question and methodological-analytical framework must be developed together and form a cohesive and coherent unit. In blunt terms, our data collection methods must enable us to collect data which actually fits our research question, as do our data analysis tools. This will become clearer in the course of this and subsequent chapters. The development of the methodological-analytical framework can be a time-consuming process; especially in complex studies we need to spend considerable time and effort developing a set of reliable and valid (see below) tools.

The development of a thorough and well-founded methodology is followed by the actual data-collection process, that is, the generating of data which we will base our study on. Ideally, the data-collection stage is preceded by a pilot stage, where we test our tools for reliability and validity; in Chapter Four, we discuss piloting with regard to questionnaire-based surveys. Depending on the topic, the data-collection stage may be the most time and resource intensive of the entire process, particularly when data (or people we can get data from) is not readily available. This emphasizes the need for thorough planning in advance: imagine you are to conduct a study involving a tribe in the Amazonian rainforest. The last thing you would want is to stand in the middle of the jungle and realize that your data-collection tools are not working! In Chapter Three, I provide a very basic introduction to project management, which will give you an idea of how to balance project scope, time and resources in order to achieve the intended outcome.

Once collected, our data is then analysed using the analytic methods developed previously, ultimately providing us with our results. In quantitative research, our results will be a set (or a whole bunch) of numbers and numerical indices which describe in great detail what is going on in our data. Now comes the crucial part: based on our own results we look back at our hypothesis and compare how well or badly our results fit the hypothesis; then, we *deduce* whether the hypothesis is right or wrong.

In our simple example of socio-economic class and the use of non-standard language, we may find in our data that lower social classes show a high number of non-standard language use, middle classes show slightly less non-standard use, and upper social classes show no use of non-standard language at all. Hence, our results consist of three general observations, from which we deduce that there is a relationship between social class and language use in such a way that the lower the class, the more non-standard features occur; our original hypothesis is proven correct. However, in real life, we would usually have many more factors involved, and the relationships between them are often not as obvious as we would like them to be. In this case, the deduction process is one of carefully deriving our conclusions based on and carefully balancing the available evidence. Frequently, we may not be able to conclusively say whether a hypothesis is right or wrong, simply because circumstances are so complex.

A side note: most of us (and I do not exclude me) would like to prove whatever hypotheses we come up with correct, and frequently people perceive it as a failure if they prove their own hypothesis to be wrong. Yet, given that our original hypothesis made sense, that our methodological-analytical framework was good and thorough and that our data was of good quality (see reliability and validity discussion at the end of this chapter), there is nothing inherently bad about proving a hypothesis wrong. It might ruffle our ego a bit, but even if we show that something is *not* the case, we still contribute to the accumulation of knowledge. So, we may find that in our particular study, using our particular respondents, there is no relationship between social class and language use; if our methodological framework is reliable and valid, this is still a permissible result, even though other researchers before us came to different conclusions: it is simply that in this particular context it is *not* the case.

Much worse, however, is a situation where the results we produce simply do not make sense and appear at random. If we take the United Kingdom, it is generally true that social class and use of Standard English are linked to a certain extent, as proposed in our hypothesis (exceptions just confirm the rule). However, we might find that our results invert the hypothesis, and higher social classes use more non-standard language while lower socio-economic classes use more standard language. While we cannot immediately discard this as 'wrong', we should have a very thorough look at our methodology, our analysis and our results and try to account for this pattern. As before, it might be that our result is just a phenomenon of the particular context we looked at; however, it could also be that something has gone horribly wrong somewhere along the lines, either in the way we collected or analysed our data. Statistics using modern software can be comparatively easy – a few mouse-clicks and we get the required results – but the number on the computer screen is really just the result of certain mathematical operations. The final interpretation is still down to us, and as a general guideline, if we feed out software rubbish, we will get rubbish out.

The qualitative-inductive process, on the other hand, is significantly different. We shall just sketch it here. At the beginning is not a definite hypothesis, but an 'idea'. As before, we develop a methodology that allows us to generate and analyse data. However, whereas the results in a quantitative study inevitably revolve around the hypothesis, the qualitative analysis reveals patterns or structures which are present in our data. And it is from these patterns that we *induce* a hypothesis or theory.

Quantitative research is probably the approach most commonly found in traditional sociolinguistic, psychological and psycholinguistic and considerable parts of social research in general. Discourse analysis, and especially Critical Discourse Analysis (CDA) in the Faircloughian tradition (Fairclough 1988, 1992, 1995) is usually qualitative in nature, although a recent development towards using methods derived from corpus linguistics to support CDA has given it quantitative aspects, too (see Hardt-Mautner 1995 or Baker 2006 for an overview).

Let's look at a piece of data to illustrate the difference between quantitative and qualitative analysis. The following example is taken from Fairclough's 'Language and Power' (Fairclough 1988: 18) and represents an interview between a police officer P and a witness W.

1   P: Did you get a look at the one in the car?
2   W: I saw his face, yeah.
3   P: What sort of age was he?
4   W: About 45. He was wearing a . . .
5   P: And how tall?
6   W: Six foot one.
7   P: Six foot one. Hair?
8   W: Dark and curly. Is this going to take long? I've got to collect the kids from school.
9   P: Not much longer, no. What about his clothes?
10 W: He was a bit scruffy-looking, blue trousers, black . . .
11 P: Jeans?
12 W: Yeah.

It does not take a trained linguist to realize that the dialogue is characterized by a power imbalance, with P being clearly in control of the interaction. A quantitative analyst would try to support this hypothesis with numbers. We could, for example, look at the average turn length, the numbers of questions asked and answers given by each participant, or we could look at interruptions made by each participant. Our result would look similar to Table 2.2.

From Table 2.2, we could conclude that P indeed seems to control the interaction, as he (or she?) asks the majority of questions, while giving fewer responses, and is the only one who interrupts. We could also employ various statistical methods to strengthen this argument. All in all, we have a rather good indication that P controls the situation to a certain extent.

More conclusive in this case, however, is looking at what is going on in the conversation in terms of content and patterns – that is, a *qualitative analysis* (for a full qualitative analysis, see Fairclough 1988). P's questions seem to follow a particular predefined sequence, trying to elicit key information. W's elaboration on clothing in line 4 is interrupted by P, but the issue taken up later by P in line 9. W's attempt to leave the interview in 8 is, although acknowledged, but more or less ignored (line 9) – indicating rather strongly that this is not a chat between two friends.

In summary, our brief (and extremely superficial) analysis has shown how quantitative and qualitative approaches differ. Both can be applied to the same set of data, but in this case the analysis of *how* is much more useful than the analysis of *how much*. The choice of whether to use a qualitative or a quantitative approach is inseparably linked to the kind of research question we ask. Research questions and methods used to answer it *must* be developed together in one coherent framework – I will keep stressing this throughout the book. We have said above that while qualitative research looks at how something is, quantitative research is more interested in how much/many there is/are of the issue we are interested in. For any successful research project, we need to specify from the outset *what* we would like to

TABLE 2.2 Quantitative analysis of police interview

	Police officer	Witness
Number of turns	6	6
Average turn length in words	5.5	7
Number of questions asked	6	1
Number of responses given to questions	2	6
Numbers of interruptions made	2	0

find out and *how* we are going to find this out. In particular new researchers such as undergraduate students often come up with the idea that 'I want to look at X and I will use Y' – even though Y is an inappropriate tool to lead to any reasonable conclusions about X. This is often linked to a strong fear (or hatred) of anything related to maths, leading to a fierce rejection of anything statistical and hence quantitative – even if the only reasonable way of answering the question is a quantitative one. So let's have a look at some situations where a quantitative analysis is inevitable.

- Any study whose main argument is based on the mere counting of things. This may sound daft, but it does constitute the most basic form of a quantitative analysis. We may, for example, be interested in the following:

  ○ 'How many transitive verbs are there in "Beowulf"?'

  ○ 'How many students have taken English Language A-levels this year?'

  ○ 'How often does a politician contradict himself within one speech?'

None of these require any kind of sophisticated mathematical procedures; nevertheless, they are all quantitative in nature, as they are based on working with numbers (of words, students, contradictions). If we are choosing a research question that is essentially based on numbers, we need to work with numbers, and this has not to be difficult.

- Any study that aims at *proving* that two or more groups of people (or objects) are *distinctively* different. Typical research questions could include:

  ○ 'Men use more swear words than women.'

  ○ 'Lower social class members use more non-standard forms than members of higher social classes.'

  ○ 'This year's cohort has obtained much better exam marks than last year's cohort.'

  All of these cases are, in essence, based on simple counting, followed by a comparison: in the first case, we would count the number of swear words used by men (within the period of an hour, for example), and compare the result to the number of swear words used by women. The second example works identically: we count and eventually compare the use of non-standard forms between 2 groups. The third example is, again, based on the comparison of 2 values: exam results from this year's cohort with that of last year's.

In Chapters Five and Six we discuss in more detail how to *describe* these differences, while Chapter Eight explains how these comparisons can be made in a statistically sound way.

● Any study that aims at showing that two variables are related, that is, co-occur in a particular pattern, often in the form of 'the higher/lower X, the higher/lower Y'. These studies are based on the assumption that a change in one variable results in a change of another variable:

  ○ 'The older a learner at the start of language acquisition, the slower the progress.'

  ○ 'The lower the social class, the more non-standard forms occur.'

  ○ 'The number of loan words has steadily increased after 1300.'

  ○ In very basic terms, these questions are again based on comparisons of different numerical values, but unlike the above examples, we look at more than two groups and/or more than two points in time.

There are, of course, many more situations where we will have to use a quantitative methodology; however, to a certain extent they are only modifications of the above situations.

So, in what situations can (and should) we not use a quantitative but a qualitative method? Remember from above that quantitative research is deductive: we base our question and hypotheses on already existing theories, while qualitative research is deductive and is aimed at developing theories. Qualitative research might come with the advantage of not requiring any maths, but the advantage is only a superficial one: not only do we not have a profound theoretical basis, but we also very often do not know what we get – for inexperienced researchers this can turn into a nightmare. Prime examples of qualitative research in languages are studies in ethnography or anthropological linguistics (see, for example Duranti 1997, or Foley 1997, for introductions to the topic). Anthropology in general is interested in, broadly speaking, human behavioural patterns, and anthropological linguistics' focus is on communicative behaviour in general. Baquedano-Lopez (2006) analysed literacy practices across learning contexts, looking how literacy develops and emerges in different contexts, such as in educational settings, outside school and so on. Baquedano-Lopez's work is qualitative as the focus of her work was, essentially, on *how* literacy is, as opposed to *how much* literacy there is (i.e. the extent or proficiency – clearly a quantitative question), as well as on *patterns* and *structures*, as opposed to, for example, proportion of literacy in a given population (which again would be quantitative). Qualitative analyses can provide astonishing insights, but require the analyst to deeply engage with the data in order to develop some kind of theoretical framework for it – a mere description of what is happening is not a proper qualitative analysis. And so, in qualitative research, we often find ourselves confronted with large amounts of data which we need to make sense of, by ordering it and developing categories into which we can put different bits of our data. For those less versed, this can be difficult, especially since qualitative data can often be interpreted in different ways with no 'right' or 'wrong' answer. Quantitative methods, on the other hand, give us at least a mathematically sound result (if applied correctly) which often acts as a starting point for our interpretation: 2 times 2 is always 4, and 'all' we need is to interpret the result within our theoretical framework.

Yet, in recent years, we have seen a proliferation of research that uses mixed-methods designs, that is, use both quantitative and qualitative methods to investigate a topic; this is particularly common when dealing with topics that are so complex that a categorical separation into qualitative/quantitative would not work. Bergman (2012), Cresswell and Plano Clark (2010) and Dörnyei (2007), *inter alia*, all provide good overviews on how to conduct mixed-methods studies.

2.2. Variables and measurement

In the centre of quantitative research is the concept of a *variable*. As a general definition, a variable is a measurable feature of a particular *case*: a case is one particular 'thing' or unit that shows this particular measurable feature. In linguistics, a case may be a person, or a group of people, or a linguistic unit. As the term 'variable' implies, the values (or outcomes) of this feature can vary considerably between cases. Each case can only show one value for a particular feature. For example, the variable 'gender' when applied to human beings is generally considered to have two potential values or outcomes, 'male' and 'female', and a person can only be one or the other, that is, *either* male *or* female but not both at the same time – exceptions apply. The variable 'age' can, in theory, vary from zero years of age to indefinite (assuming that there is no naturally predefined age by which humans drop dead), and again, a single individual can only show one outcome: you obviously only have one age at a time. In a group of, for example, ten people, we may get ten different values for the variable 'age', namely when none of ten people in this group are of the same age. Linguistic variables work with the same principle: in a study on syntactic variation in spoken language we may want to look at the presence or absence of copular verbs in subject-predicate constructions, such as 'The girl is pretty' or 'He Ø fat'. For convenience's sake, we may want to define our variable 'copular presence' in such a way that it can only have two outcomes: copula present ({+Cop}) and copula absent ({–Cop}). In our examples, the first sentence,

'The girl is pretty' will take the value {+Cop}, while the second takes {–Cop}. In a fictional corpus of let's say 1,000 subject-predicate constructions, we may find 750 {+Cop} and 250 {–Cop} – but as with gender, other values are not permissible ('a bit of a copula' does not make much sense, just as someone cannot be 'a bit dead').

In a different project, we might simply be interested in the number of noun phrases (NP) per sentence in a corpus of 1,000 sentences. Here, the variable 'number of NPs' can – theoretically – take indefinitely many values:

- *'The girl is pretty'* contains 1 NP ('the girl').

- *'The cat chases the mouse'* contains 2 NPs ('the cat' and 'the mouse').

- *'The cat chases the mouse around the garden with the big trees and the green lawn'* has 5 NPs – 'the cat', 'the mouse', 'the garden', 'the big trees' and 'the green lawn'.

Closely related to the concept of *variable* is that of *measurement*. Measurement is the process of assigning a particular variable outcome to a particular case, using predefined criteria. The term and concept is well known: when measuring the size an object, we hold a ruler or a tape measure next to the object; depending on the units we work with (centimetres, metres, inches, feet), we can then assign the corresponding value to our object. If we are interested in its weight, we put our object on a scale and assign the corresponding value (in ounces, pounds or grams) to it.

Measurement, however, can also be much simpler, as it generally means to put a particular object or person (or 'case') in a predefined category. So, strictly speaking, we can also measure someone's gender: we have two clearly defined categories, male and female, and we put our case into either category, depending on how well our case fits the category.

Crucially, the categories we assign to our objects must be well defined and must not change during the process of measurement: we can only make reliable statements about an object's length in inches if, first, we have clearly defined the amount of length an inch refers to, and, second, one inch must *always* refer to exactly the same amount of length and does not vary during the measurement. In addition, our tools for measuring an object's properties should be designed in such a way that it can measure all our cases adequately. For example, with human beings, we usually get away with two categories for measuring biological sex (it gets more tricky when we look at the more culturally defined category of 'gender'): male and female, and, in the vast majority of cases, we should be able to put a human being in one of the two categories. However, if we wanted to use our two category measure for certain invertebras, such as earthworms, we would run into serious problems: earthworms are hermaphrodites, that is, they are both male and female at the same time, and when mating, can perform both 'functions' simultaneously. We have said above that for any one case we can have only one value for a particular variable, that is, we cannot put a single earthworm in both the male and female category; at the same time, putting it into the male (or female) group is also an inaccurate reflection of reality. Hence, we will have to adjust our measuring tool appropriately – in the earthworm example, we would probably add a 'both' category.

2.3. Definitions, concepts and operationalization

Some readers may argue that I pay undue interest to something straightforward. After all, most of us are able to measure someone's age, gender or weight. However, there are cases where the process of allocating a variable value to a case is not that easy. A common problem, particularly for researchers new to a field, is that it is not always clear *what* is being measured, let alone *how*. A typical example for this is the concept of 'motivation'. Over the years, I have met countless students, both undergraduate and postgraduate, who were all interested in how motivation influences second-language learners' progress. The problem usually starts when I ask the question, 'so how are you going to measure it?' We all know that motivation plays a crucial part in second-language acquisition/learning; however, in order to come to a sound conclusion along the lines of 'the higher learners' motivation, the better the outcome' we need to *measure* the different levels of motivation. But before we can even measure it, we have to clearly *define* what motivation actually *is*. A review of literature on the topic shows that motivation is a complex system of several interrelated factors, of which Stern (1983) identifies social attitudes, values and indeed other 'learner factors'. More recently, motivation is often linked to the 'learner's self' (see Dörnyei and Ushioda 2009 for an overview). As such, motivation is a *concept* rather than a variable; in fact, motivation consists of several variables, each of which has to be measured separately. In other words, we cannot reliably measure motivation as such, let alone by methods such as asking learners 'how motivated are you'. When constructing concepts, one has to ensure that they are epistemologically sound – put more bluntly, they have to make sense. For example, a concept can only be described by definitions and terms that are already known and measurable. In the above example, we need several already known and measurable learner factors in order to define our concept 'motivation'.

A different example is the concept of 'cohesion': 'Cohesion can be defined as a set of resources for constructing relations in discourse' (Martin 2001: 35). The clue is in the definition: as it is a 'set of resources', it cannot be measured directly, but we can approach it by looking at the different components that make a text cohesive.

Once we have defined the concept we want to investigate, we need to establish a set of *operation definitions*; we have to *operationalize* our concept. In other words, we need to decide how we measure the variable or variables describing our concept. To come back to our example, we would develop a set of questions (or variables) which refer to the different aspects of motivation, such as attitudes to the language, the learning process, the environment and so forth.

We shall look at a real example to illustrate the idea of concepts and their measurability. In the late 1070s, Giles et al. (1977) developed the concept of 'Ethnolinguistic Vitality' in order to provide a framework that could account for what 'makes a group likely to behave as a distinctive and active collective entity in intergroup relations' (308). It does not take too long to understand that 'group behaviour' is not something that can be straightforwardly measured, such as a person's age or weight, but is a construct that comprises various aspects and issues. Giles et al. identified three categories of variables, each to be measured independently and, more or less, objectively:

a   The group's social status, based on objective and objectively measurable variables such as income (how much money do individual group members earn), economic activity (unemployment rates), employment patterns (which jobs do they have), but also including more difficult approaches to status, such as perception of the group or the group's language (e.g. whether the group's language is an official language, such as Catalan in Spain).

b   Demographic factors, taking into account the absolute and relative size of the group as well as its density (i.e. how many group members live in a clearly defined geographic space). Again, these variables are comparatively easy to measure.

c   Institutional support, measuring to what extent the group receives formal and informal support through official and/or community-intern institutions (government, schools, churches, local authorities etc). While this last category is a rather abstract concept in itself (for details, see original work), it ultimately provides us with a quantifiable result.

Giles et al. argue that the higher a group fares in each of the categories, the higher its Ethnolinguistic Vitality is. So, the results (or scores) obtained in the individual categories allow us to fairly objectively quantify a group's vitality. In other words, we can put a comparatively reliable number to describe a rather abstract concept.

It is important that, for every quantitative study, we spend some time thinking thoroughly about our variables, how to measure them, and how to operationalize this measurement. And as such, it is paramount that we have a good grasp as to what our variables could *potentially* look like, before we develop a method to capture as much of the variation in this variable as possible. Phonology is a good linguistic example to illustrate this. Traditionally, sociolinguists and dialectologists have focused on variation in pronunciation, and have tried to explain this variation along various dimensions such as social categories or geographic areas. Sebba (1993: 23) in his study on 'London Jamaican' discusses some of the phonological differences between Jamaican Creole and London English, and identifies for one particular speaker in his sample two distinct realizations for the pronunciation of the /u/ sound in 'who' and the initial consonant in 'the': [hu:] versus [hʊ:], and [di] versus [ɗə]. If, like Sebba, we consider this phonological difference to be important, we *must* use a measure that accounts for this. In other words, we need an operation definition that allows us – in practice – to clearly classify a particular vowel as [u:]/[ʊ:] and a particular consonant as [d]/[ɗ]. At the same time, if such differences are not of interest for our study, we do not need to account for them. The trick is to develop a methodology which allows us to measure as accurately as required but does not make things unnecessarily complex.

A word of warning: some concepts, particularly abstract ones and those that comprise several variables and sub-concepts, are notoriously difficult to measure. Motivation, as outlined above, is one such concept, as are attitudes. A quantitative analysis of these takes time, effort and a lot of trial and error. Possibly more than for any other study, the thorough evaluation of previous work and in particular the methodologies used (including all the difficulties and pitfalls!) is vital. It is usually a good although resource- and time-consuming idea to support quantitative data on these issues with qualitative findings from interviews or focus groups. Often, the combination of qualitative and quantitative results provide a far better and reliable insight than one approach on its own.

2.4. Independent and dependent variables

Following our discussion of variables in general, we now turn to the relationship variables can have to each other. More specifically, we focus on *independent* and *dependent* variables. The crucial difference between independent and dependent variables is that the latter can be influenced by the former, but not vice versa.

A common independent variable in linguistic research is age. Research on second-language acquisition has shown that age influences – to some extent – acquisition success, with older learners being more likely to achieve lower proficiency in the second language than younger ones. In this case, language acquisition success *depends* on age, and is hence the *dependent variable*. At the same time, no one would argue that second-language proficiency influences a person's age – you do not become older just because your language proficiency increases!

In experimental setups, the independent variable is often deliberately manipulated by the researcher, while the dependent variable is the observed outcome of the experiment. For example, if we were interested in measuring whether word recognition decreases with increasing speed in which the word is displayed to a participant, the independent variable would be speed (as it can be manipulated by the researcher), while the dependent variable would be the outcome (i.e. the accuracy with which the words are recognized).

While in many research questions the independent and dependent variables are clear from the outset, there might be constellations where it is more difficult to define which one is which. For example, sociolinguistic research has consistently shown that social class and the use of non-standard features correlate; often, non-standard features occur more frequently in the speech of lower socio-economic classes. It is arguable that social class is the independent variable, as it influences the way people talk. However, one may consider that attitudes against the use of particular non-standard features disadvantage non-standard speakers and prevent them from certain jobs and, ultimately, socio-economic success. At the very end, it is the chick or the egg question and needs careful consideration in the interpretation of our results.

2.5. Causality and latent variables

The discussion of independent and dependent variables inevitably raises the issue of *causality*. As we have seen in the previous example, it is not always entirely clear which variable causes which outcome. *Causality* means that there is a causal relationship between A and B, that is, changes in A cause changes in B or vice versa. As we will see later on, several statistical methods can be used to measure the *relationship* between two variables; however, they do not tell us anything about whether the two variables are *causally* linked. Let's go back to our age of acquisition onset example. I suggested above that age of acquisition onset influences eventual second-language proficiency; and a lot of empirical research has shown that the older learners are when they start learning a second language, the lower their eventual proficiency scores are. From here, it is a short step to arguing that age and proficiency are in a causal relationship to each other; in fact, many people argue exactly this way. However, strictly speaking, many studies only show one thing: values for the variable 'age' and values for the variable 'proficiency' co-occur in a particular pattern, that is, the higher the 'age' values, the lower the 'proficiency' values are. In order to be able to speak of a proper causal relationship, our variables must show three characteristics:

a They must *correlate* with each other, that is, their values must co-occur in a particular pattern: for example, the older a speaker, the more dialect features you find in their speech (see Chapter Seven).

b There must be a *temporal relationship* between the two variables X and Y, that is, Y must occur after X. In our word-recognition example in Section 2.4, this would mean that for speed to have a causal effect on performance, speed must be increased first, and drop in participants' performance occurs afterwards. If performance decreases before we increase the speed, it is highly unlikely that there is causality between the two variables. The two phenomena just co-occur by sheer coincidence.

c The relationship between X and Y must not disappear when controlled for a third variable.

While most people usually consider the first two points when analysing causality between two variables, less experienced researchers (such as undergraduate students) frequently make the mistake to ignore the effect third (and often latent) variables may have on the relationship between X and Y, and take any given outcome for granted. That this can result in serious problems for linguistic research becomes obvious when considering the very nature of language and its users. Any first year linguistics student learns that there are about a dozen sociolinguistic factors alone which influence they way we use language, among them age, gender, social, educational and regional background and so on. And that before we even start thinking about cognitive and psychological aspects. If we investigate the relationship between two variables, how can we be certain that there is not a third (or fourth of fifth) variable influencing whatever we are measuring? In the worst case, latent variables will affect our measure in such a way that it threatens its validity – see below. For our example, we will stay with the age of acquisition onset debate. It has generally been argued that the age at which people acquire a second language influences the acquisition success to a certain extent; many studies have shown that the older a learner at the start of acquisition, the less their progress will be. We do not have to be experts in the field to spot a considerable problem with this hypothesis: as most people are probably aware, second-language acquisition progress is subject to a whole range of factors, among them motivation or amount and quality of input they receive. Hence, arguing that age *alone* influences second-language development is highly problematic. Any study trying to establish such a link must hence pay considerable attention to other factors and eliminate them, either through methodological modifications or through fancy statistical methods.

2.6. Levels of measurement

When we, once again, consider some of the most frequent linguistic variables, it becomes clear that they differ with respect to the values they can take. As discussed, for humans, the variable sex, for example, can only take one of two values: male or female. Age, on the other hand, can take any value from zero onwards, as discussed above. The scores of standardized language proficiency tests, such as the International English Language Testing System (IELTS), usually put examinees into a particular class or category, which is described by a particular number: an IELTS score of 1 indicates that the examinee 'essentially has no ability to use the language beyond possibly a few isolated words', while a score of 9 means that he 'has fully operational command of the language: appropriate, accurate and fluent with complete understanding' (www.ielts.org 2013).

These differences, which are explained in more detail in the following sections, refer to the *level of measurement* of a variable, and have a serious impact on the kind of statistical methods we can use, and it is critically that we, from the outset of our research, take the different levels a variable can take into consideration.

Categorical scale data

Generally, we distinguish between four different levels of measurement. At the bottom end are categorical variables. Categorical variables can have two or more *distinct* outcomes, that is, they allow us to put our case into *one* particular class or category *only*. When we look at the variable 'gender', the variable can only take one of two potential values, 'male' or 'female'. Interim answers are impermissible – one cannot be 'nought point seven male'. Similarly, the questions of whether a woman is pregnant or not can only elicit one out of two values: yes or no, as obviously you cannot be 'a bit pregnant'. A typical Equal Opportunities Questionnaire asks people to state their ethnic background, and usually provides a list of categories of which respondents have to pick one, for example, White British, White Irish, Other White, Afro-Caribbean, South-Asian, Mixed Race and so on. Again, this allows us to put respondents in one particularly category, and again, interim answers cannot be accounted for ('70% White British with 30% Afro-Carribbean' – even though this is genetically possible).

Most importantly, the outcomes of categorical variables do not reflect any kind of hierarchy: 'male' does not mean 'better' or 'more' than 'female', just as 'pregnant' and 'non-pregnant' cannot be brought into a meaningful order. We are merely *labelling* or categorizing our cases.

Ordinal scale data

Similar to categorical data, ordinal variables allow us to put particular labels on each case. However, in addition, ordinal data can be put into some kind of order or ranking system. A popular example for illustrating ordinal data is the dullness of university lectures. Students may classify lectures as 'exciting', 'ok', 'dull' or 'very dull'. It is obvious that there is an inherent semantic order to these labels, with dullness increasing from 'exciting' to 'very dull'; in other words, lectures can be *ranked* according to dullness. However, we cannot make any statement about the differences between individual labels: 'very dull' does not mean 'twice as dull as dull', but is simply an indicator that one is worse than the other.

Interval scale data

One step up from ordinal data are variables on interval scales. Again, they allow us to label cases and to put them into a meaningful sequence. However, the differences between individual values are fixed. A typical example are grading systems that evaluate work from A to D, with A being the best and D being the worst mark. The differences between A and B are the same as the difference between B and C and between C and D. In the British university grading system, B, C and D grades (Upper Second, Lower Second and Third Class) all cover a stretch of 10 percentage points and would therefore be interval; however, with First Class grades stretching from 70 to 100 per cent and Fail from 30 downwards, this order is somewhat sabotaged. In their purest form, and in order to avoid problems in statistical analysis, all categories in an interval scale must have the same distance from each other.

Interval data is commonly used in social and psychological (and hence sociolinguistic and psycholinguistic) research in the form of Likert scales, which are discussed in detail in Chapter Four.

Ratio scale data

In addition to indicating equal distances between two adjacent scores, as in interval scales, ratio scale data is characterized by having a natural zero point, with zero indicating that there is no measurable amount of whatever we are measuring. It is also possible for a ratio scale to be open-ended. For example, a weight of zero indicates that an object does not weigh anything; the amount of weight is hence zero. At the same time, an object can be indefinitely heavy.

To illustrate the difference between interval and ratio data in more language-related terms, the IELTS scores described above are usually interpreted as having equal distances, indicating a gradual increase of learners' proficiency; as such, we would interpret it as interval data. An IELTS score of 1 means that the examinee is a 'non user'. A non-user may or may not produce 'possibly a few isolated words'. A score of zero indicated the examinee has not attempted the test. It does not, however, indicate that the examinee has zero knowledge.

We could, however, think of a simple vocabulary recognition test using a ratio scale, where learners are presented with a list of 100 lexical items and are asked how many items they know. At the end, we calculate the score by simply counting the number of recognized items. A score of zero indicated that the participant has failed to recognize a single vocabulary item, that is, has 'zero' vocabulary knowledge. A participant scoring 60 has recognized twice as many items as one with a score of 30.

2.7. Continuous and discrete data

The final crucial distinction we can make is to look at whether our data is *discrete* or *continuous*. Discrete data consists of finite or countable values, while continuous data allows for infinitely many possible values on a continuous scale without gaps or interruptions. For example, the number is students in a class is a discrete variable, as the number must be an integer ('whole number'), that is, 1, 2, 5, 62 and so on. We cannot have 6.5 or 12.7 students in a class. If we consider our students' age, on the other hand, we look at continuous data, as a student might be 21.85482 years old – if we can be bothered to break it down to exactly how many years, days and hours he is old.

Please note that the discrete-continuous distinction only applies to our raw, unprocessed data, not to the results any kind of statistical analysis may bring us: if we are interested in the average seminar class-size at a university, it is highly likely that *on average* we have something like 15.7 students – it does not mean that there is a class with 0.7 student in it. We discuss the calculation of the arithmetic mean in Chapter Six.

2.8. Reliability and validity

Quantitative methods bear an advantage that should not be underestimated: natural sciences, such as chemistry or physics, require 'proper' experiments (i.e. certain research procedures or methods) to be objective and, crucially, have to be replicable by anyone who is following the instructions. In other words, anyone following this 'recipe' exactly, should get the same (or very near same) result. This is very much like baking a cake: if two people put exactly the same amount of ingredients together, mix them in exactly the same way and then bake them under exactly the same conditions (i.e. time and temperature), we should get two identical (or very near identical) cakes. Even better, we should get two identical cakes *independent* from who the baker is: it should not matter whether one is more experienced, or in a foul mood, or tired, or quite simply hates cake. This works well in basic chemistry: if we put exactly the same amounts of A and B together, at exactly the same temperature and other environmental factors, we should reliably get C – over and over again.

This is where the beauty of quantitative research lies: once we have established our methods, we probably want our methods to accurately measure the same thing again and again. Put briefly, *reliability* refers to a method repeatedly and consistently measuring whatever it is supposed to measure. In the most extreme case, if we took the same people and tested them again in exactly the same way and exactly the same environment, we should get exactly the same result if our method is reliable. In linguistic research, this is difficult to achieve: people change, the environment changes, and even if people are identical, they are unlikely to respond to the same test in exactly the same way again – be it because they have the experience of having done the test before or because they quite simply have a bad day. Nevertheless, we need to ensure that our methods work reliably, and that they remain reliable over time. At the same time, methods of measurements must be constructed in such a way that they work independently from the researcher using them: in whichever way we operationalize a variable, we need to make sure that all potential researchers using our operationalization will get same or similar data and results. That is why it is so important to define variables clearly and with as little ambiguity as possible: if we are interested in use the use of copular verbs like in the example above, we must define our variable, that is, what constitutes a copula and what does not, in such a way that any researcher carrying our the analysis knows exactly what they are looking for. Copulas are a good example: some people consider copular and auxiliary verbs as one and the same thing: English 'be' accordingly is the same in both sentences; after all, in both examples the copula has little to no independent meaning:

a   *The girl is pretty.*
b   *I am working.*

In some cases, however, it might be useful to distinguish between the two types. Crystal (1999), for example, defines copulas' primary function 'to link elements of clause structure, typically the subject and the complement' (73), while auxiliaries are 'subordinate to the chief lexical verb in a verb phrase, helping to express such grammatical distinctions as tense, mood and aspect' (30). According to these definitions, *be* in (a) is a copula, linking subject ('the girl') with the complement ('pretty'), while in (b) it helps to indicate tense and aspect (present progressive). Whether we use a broad (no difference) or narrow (difference) approach does not matter per se; the important point is that, first, our definition is the one that best fits our research questions and, second, all researchers involved in our project use the same definition. Just imagine what would happen if two people analysing the same data using different definition – their results would be incomparable and simply useless. The ability of our methods to measure the same issue reliably independent from who is the researcher is sometimes also called *inter-observer reliability*. In some context, where accuracy is crucial but despite proper operationalization it can be difficult to measure things exactly, it is common to use two people to code the data, either independent from each other, or one spot-checking the coding of the other. But even if we are the sole researcher, it is important that we use the same definition every time throughout the same study.

A quick and easy, even though by far not the most reliable way to check a method's reliability (note the paradox) is the *split-half method*: we take a sample of, for example, 100 people (for sampling, see Chapter Three), and randomly split it into two groups of 50 people each. We then administer our method to both groups. If our method is reliable, we should get equal or near equal results for both groups. We discuss the practical issues of data being 'equal' in Chapters Eight and Nine.

Another way to check reliability is the *test-retest method*: instead of testing two samples with the same method, we test the same sample with the same instrument at two different points in time. If our instrument is reliable, we should get very similar results for both test and retest. The test–retest method is problematic whenever we work with human beings: people learn from experience and tend to draw on their experience from the first test during the retest. In other words, they know what is coming, which can substantially impair the retest's significance. When can obtain a good indicator for a measurement's reliability using a correlation analysis based on the test-retest method – we will discuss this at the end of Chapter Seven.

A second factor we have to consider in quantitative research is that of *validity*. Whenever we measure something we obviously want our result to be as accurate as possible. Validity comes in several different forms and shapes; here, we will focus on the one most important one for linguistic research: *measurement validity*. Measurement validity, often just called validity, is difficult to explain, let alone to achieve: it refers to the issue of whether our method actually measures what it is supposed to measure, allowing us to draw appropriate conclusions. The copula definition example above is also an issue of validity: if we have not clearly defined our variable, how can we make sure what we measure is what we actually want?

Another typical example to illustrate validity is the design of questionnaires. Let's assume we are interested in people's attitudes towards the use of non-standard language or dialects. We are going to measure attitudes by means of a questionnaire comprising ten questions, and respondents have the choice of three answers: 'agree', 'neutral' and 'disagree'. Now imagine that we ask all our questions in a particular way or pattern, for example, 'agree' always indicates a positive opinion on dialects, while 'disagree' always indicates a negative opinion. Annoyingly, many people have the habit of answering questionnaires with a particular manner and tendency: they tend to either more agree or more disagree, or, in the worst case, have a 'neutral' opinion. If, as in our example, 'agree' always corresponds to a positive attitude towards dialects, all our questionnaire measures is respondents' tendencies to either agree or disagree, but gives us certainly no idea about what respondents' actual attitudes towards dialects are! In this case, our questionnaire is a highly invalid method. We will return to the issue of reliability and validity when we have a closer look at questionnaire design in Chapter Four.

Validity, or lack therefore, can become are rather annoying issue in a situation where we have many third and latent variables, as discussed above. If our data is not actually influenced by what we *think* influences it, but by something else, how can it we validly measure it? The best option is to conduct a pure experiment (see Chapter Three), where we as researchers have full and total control over all variables. Certain psycholinguistic questions are well suited for an experimental inquiry, and experiments are frequently used. It does not take long, though, to realize that laboratory experiments are not an option for studies require linguistic data as it occurs in real life. In these cases, only thorough planning and preparation, based on extensive research of the theoretical background involved, can help us to minimize this problem.

2.9. Hypotheses, laws and theories

Before we move on to the next chapter, we briefly need to define three core concepts in any kind of research, be it qualitative or quantitative. *Hypotheses* are statements about the potential and/or suggested relationship between at least two variables, such as 'the older a learner, the less swear words they use' (two variables) or 'age and gender influence language use' (three variables). Hypotheses can be proven right or wrong – the point of quantitative research is to do exactly that! In fact, a hypothesis *must* be proven right or wrong. For a hypothesis to be proven correct or incorrect, it is important for it to be well defined. In particular, hypotheses must be *falsifiable* and not be *tautological*: the hypothesis 'age can either influence a person's language use or not' is tautological – independent from our findings, it will always be true (age either does or does not influence a person's language use). A good hypothesis, however, *must* have the potential of being wrong.

For quantitative research, it is useful to remember that our hypothesis should relate to something we can actually measure. As with all things, it is worth spending some time to think about the phrasing of our hypothesis (or hypotheses) – it will make things much easier once we get to the stage where we develop our methodology. As a general guideline, the more specific a hypothesis is, the better. Note that 'specific' does not imply the depth or scope of the study: for obvious reasons, a 3,000 word undergraduate research essay will be different in terms of depth and scope from a project that comes equipped with £500,000 of external funding. Yet, for both it is essential to be clear about what we want to find out.

Based on the general focus of my department, many of my students are interested in issues related to language teaching and learning, and frequently, proposed topics for dissertations revolve around two aspects: learners 'liking/hating' something, and a particular teaching/learning method being 'better' or 'worse' than another. In the first stages, I usually come across hypothesis such as:

● Students like to learn in groups.

● Using electronic resources for language teaching is better than using traditional textbooks.

There is nothing inherently 'wrong' with these two examples, and both outline what could be more or less interesting research projects. The problem lies in the detail, and, in our specific case, the measurability. Let's have a closer look at the first example: while is gives us a general idea of what the researcher is after, the 'hypothesis' is far too vague and, as such, it seems impossible to find a reliable and valid measure to prove/disprove it. There is, for a start, the term 'students' – who exactly are they? What levels of study? What age? What cultural background? Everyone vaguely familiar with learning and teaching theory will know that these are three of a whole list of issues that are important; 'students' as a generic term is simple not precise enough, and a study, especially a small-scale one, is bound to fail if the group we are interested in is not defined properly. 'Native speakers of English primary school children learning Japanese', however, clearly defines the group *and* sets the scene for all methodological implications that come with it.

Then, there is the word that regularly sends shivers down my back: 'like'. We all like or hate things, but, unfortunately, 'like' is a rather difficult feature to measure. What exactly do we mean when someone 'likes' something? Do they have a preference in using one thing above the other? How strong is this preference? Where does 'like' end and 'love' (another favourite) end? A better phrasing is to work is 'prefer' or 'show a preference for' – quite simply because we can objectively measure preference. Thirdly, there is the generic 'learn' – learn what? Again, we need to specify this much more. And lastly, 'in groups' is equally vague: indications of group size is the least we should include into our hypothesis.

Despite what it may sound (or read) like, I am not being nitpicking: how can we reliably and validly measure what we have not even clearly defined beforehand? A project looking at 'how students learn' is predestined to go wrong – simply because it is too vague. For our example, a much better hypothesis could be:

English native speaker primary school children show a preference for working in groups of 3–5 when acquiring new vocabulary items compared to working in traditional full-class environment.

This hypothesis is clearly defined, it is measurable and, crucially, falsifiable: the kids may or may not prefer working in small groups, and we have quantitative evidence to prove it. Talking about falsifiability, most of us like our beautiful and carefully designed hypothesis to be proven right – it is an ego thing. However, it may be that your empirical evidence shows that your hypothesis is wrong. This might be disappointing, but is not inherently a bad thing: assuming that our hypothesis is a reasonable one, that is, emerged from what we know from previous studies, and assuming that our methodology is valid and reliable, proving a hypothesis wrong is still a noteworthy result. After all, we still contribute to knowledge by showing that a particular view on a topic does *not* work. And while we generally phrase hypotheses in a positive way (X does cause Y), if we are really too upset that our data has proven us wrong, we may want to change our entire argument in such a way that our hypothesis is that X does *not* cause Y – in other words, we would structure our study around an argument of exclusion.

Laws are hypotheses or a set of hypotheses which have been proven correct repeatedly. We may think of the hypothesis: 'Simple declarative sentences in English have subject-verb-object word order'. If we analyse a sufficient number of simple English declarative sentences, we will find that this hypothesis proves correct repeatedly, hence making it a law. Remember, however, based on the principle of falsifiability of hypotheses, if we are looking at a very large amount of data, we should find at least a few instances where the hypothesis is wrong – the exception to the rule. And here it becomes slightly tricky: since our hypothesis about declarative sentences is a definition, we cannot really prove it wrong. The definition says that declarative sentences must have subject-verb-object (SVO) word order. This implies that a sentence that does not conform to SVO is not a declarative; we cannot prove the hypothesis wrong, as if it is wrong we do not have a declarative sentence. In this sense it is almost tautological. Hence, we have to be very careful when including prescriptive definitions into our hypotheses.

A much better example for laws are sound changes: if we start with the hypothesis that during the 'Great Vowel Shift' during the Early Modern English period all long vowels moved upwards into a higher position (e.g. /e:/ became /i:/, /o/ became /u:/), we will see that, when analysing a large enough number of examples, the hypothesis is repeatedly true. Yet, we will also see that there are exceptions, that is, situations where the vowels did not move their position – mainly in combinations with particular consonants (see Baugh and Cable 2002, for an overview). So, we have a law on sound changes, but as with every rule, there are exceptions.

Lastly, *theories* are systems which combine several hypotheses and laws, all of which are in a logical relationship to each other. As such, we may want to consider the Great Vowel Shift as a theory, as it can only be fully explained as a complex interplay between various laws: most vowels moved upwards (law 1) but some did not (law 2) or moved into a lower position (law 3), based on the preceding/following consonant (laws 4 and 5) and so on.

Exercise I: Variables

1 Identify whether the following outcomes are discrete or continuous, and explain your decision:

    a Total time a London cab driver spends stopped at traffic lights in any given day

    b Number of strikes in the car industry each year

    c Number of left-handed people in the population

    d Quantity of milk produced by a cow each day

2 Determine and explain which levels of measurement are most appropriate for the following data:

    a Ratings of *excellent, very good, good, poor, unsatisfactory* for students work

    b A person's sex

    c British National Insurance Numbers

    d Percentage of all university students studying linguistics

Exercise II: Hypothesis and theory building

Design a set of hypotheses which have the following properties:

- at least one of your hypotheses should include two or more independent variables,

- your hypotheses should include variables at least two different levels of measurement,

- at least one hypothesis should contain a clear causal relationship,

- your hypotheses should be in a logical relationship to each other, that is, have the potential of forming a theory.

CHAPTER THREE

Research design and sampling

Key words: artefacts – ethics – longitudinal, cross-sectional, panel designs – population and sampling – real time and apparent time – sampling techniques – research design – representativeness – sample error – project planning and management

Having discussed the very basics of quantitative research in the previous chapter, we now have to address the question of how we are going to get from our hypothesis to reliable and valid results. In this chapter, we will focus in some detail on research design and sampling. In Part One of this chapter, we will introduce different potential research designs, such as cross-sectional, longitudinal, experimental and quasi-experimental, and discuss advantages, disadvantages and pitfalls of each method.

Part Two discusses various sampling techniques, explaining advantages and disadvantages of sampling methods. In particular, we address typical sampling problems encountered in linguistic research (e.g. lack of standardization of participants, etc.). This chapter also addresses ethical implications of linguistic research, with regard to privacy and anonymity, working with minors and minorities, and researchers' safety. New in this edition is an overview of issues to do with managing your project and how to keep a check on time, resources and scope.

Research design is best described as the actual *structure* according to which our study is organized. As such, together with the theoretical grounding, the design forms an important part of the overall methodological-analytical framework which we use to answer our research questions, and to prove or disprove our hypotheses. Research design does not, though, refer to the actual instruments we use in our investigation (such as questionnaires or interviews), although the relevance of good interplay between hypotheses, existing theory, methods and design cannot be emphasized enough; and there is a particularly strong connection between design and instruments chosen.

Research designs can be subsumed under two main categories: *longitudinal, cross-sectional* and *panel designs* structure our research in terms of a temporal order, while *experimental* and *quasi-experimental designs* allow us to investigate our question through the explicit and deliberate manipulation of variables. We will discuss each type subsequently.

3.1. Cross-sectional designs

Cross-sectional designs are probably the most frequently used in linguistic, social and psychological research. In cross-sectional designs, a comparatively large amount of data is acquired at one given point in time, providing an overview of how a particular variable (or variables) is distributed across a sample (see Section 3.6) at a particular moment in time. As such, cross-sectional research is useful for providing a *snapshot* of a status quo – it describes reality how it is right at this very moment. Cross-sectional research is characterized by two key features: first, we are dealing with a multitude of cases, that is, a number of cases (in linguistics, often people) that is significantly larger than one; the large amount of data will allow us to describe and explain the particular feature of reality we are interested in (i.e. our research question) in greater detail and accuracy. From Chapter Five onwards, we will see that many statistical tools provide us with increasingly accurate results with increasing amount of data, hence, a study based on 50 people will give us a more 'true' picture than a study based on only 5.

Second, cross-sectional data is collected within a particularly short time frame – ideally, all our data is collected simultaneously, hence ruling out any changes which might occur over time. Needless to say that in practice this can be rather problematic.

Labov's study on the 'social stratification of /r/ in New York City department stores' (Labov 1972) is an excellent example of a cross-sectional study in linguistics. Using rapid anonymous interviews, Labov was able to collect data from 264 respondents in just 6.5 hours over one or two days. His results enabled him to make conclusions about the prestige of /r/ across different social classes at a particular point in time. The advantage should be obvious: collecting all data almost simultaneously, any changes in linguistic behaviour are unlikely to occur, simply because linguistic change and changes in the sociocultural environment surrounding it are much slower processes.

Cross-sectional designs are commonly used in quantitative research, as the comparatively large amounts of data collected are particularly useful for studies which aim to either describe a status quo to an extent to which some generalizations are possible, or to detect relationships between independent and dependent variables while simultaneously ruling out that those relationships change over time. In the Labovian example above, linguistic behaviour was strongly linked to socio-economic class and the prestige different classes assign to a particular feature. If, for whatever reason, prestige changes while we are conducting our data collection, we will inevitably receive skewed results.

I am frequently asked by students about the time frame in which cross-sectional studies should take place; in other words, when does a cross-sectional design stop being a cross-sectional design? Unfortunately, a definite answer ('two days and six hours') does not exist. Yet, with a bit of common sense it should be relatively easy to determine a time frame.

First, in linguistics, cross-sectional, unlike experimental studies, are usually used to investigate the variables linked to either the linguistic features or the language user (including exogenous sociocultural variables in sociolinguistics). I assume most readers agree that linguistic change is a comparatively slow process, with changes unlikely to happen overnight or even within a few days or months. Hence, a study investigating a particular linguistic feature is unlikely to be negatively affected by change, even if data collection takes place over a longer period of time. That is, although data is collected at various points within a particular time frame, it is unlikely that the results are affected by change. Milroy's (1987) study on language use and social networks in Belfast was primarily a cross-sectional design, despite being conducted over a prolonged period of time: because the social networks she looked at were very stable, with very stable norms governing language use within those networks, language change did not occur, even though her data was not collected within a short period of time.

It is important to remember that language is hardly ever looked at without due consideration of its user. As social beings, humans move around an environment that can, quite often, undergo rather rapid changes. In other words, the context in which language is used may change halfway through a cross-sectional study, which can cause a serious impact on the results. In this case we talk about a quasi-experimental design (see below). So, in short, while there is no definite time frame for a cross-sectional study, we should carefully monitor the environment in which we collect our data for sudden changes.

Similarly, for research questions that involve, by their very nature, processes of change, cross-sectional designs are not suitable. For example, first language acquisition is a process in which children acquire are substantial linguistic competence within a very short time span, mainly between the ages of 18 months and 3 years. With change being that inherent to the subject matter, it is highly unlikely that we get reliable results with a cross-sectional design. Also, for topics where change in the defining criteria, it is more than likely that it is change and development we are interested in – again, this is something we cannot account for with a cross-sectional design, which can only provide us with a snapshot.

3.2. Longitudinal designs:
Panels and cohorts

Longitudinal designs are distinguishable from cross-sectional designs in two major respects: instead of looking at a large number of cases once, longitudinal studies look at a small(er) number of cases on several (at least two) occasions. In short, while cross-sectional studies allow us to draw conclusions about a status quo at a particular moment in time, longitudinal studies allow us to observe changes that occur over time. Also, longitudinal designs may, to a certain extent, shed more light on causal relationships than cross-sectional studies, because certain patterns may become more obvious when measured repeatedly. Please note that for longitudinal designs we still need a considerable amount of *data* for a proper quantitative analysis, for mathematical–statistical reasons. But unlike cross-sectional designs, where a large amount of data is created at one point in time by a large number of 'cases', in longitudinal designs, fewer cases produce data repeatedly.

Since they are based on the repeated collection and analysis of data, longitudinal designs are rather resource intensive, and social sciences and psychological research often try to avoid them (see Bryman 2004). Yet, for linguistic studies, longitudinal designs offer the opportunity to observe changes in linguistic behaviour over time in great detail. In fact, longitudinal designs are the *only* way to observe linguistic change.

As with cross-sectional designs, there is no definite answer as to what makes a longitudinal design longitudinal; as before, it depends on the research question we are trying to answer. We may, for example, be interested in the development of young children's vocabulary size. As a general guideline, most children utter their first word at around the age of 12 months, have an average vocabulary size of 500 words at 18 months and by their second birthday, the average child has about 500 words at their disposal. Accordingly, if we base our longitudinal study on two data collections, one at the age or 12, the second at the age of 24 months, we will be able to see a dramatic increase in vocabulary size. However, this also means that we are losing a lot of detail, as we are unable to see what exactly happens within these 12 months; we cannot detect any major intermediate stages.

Yet, some linguistic changes are much slower: the Great Vowel Shift, for example, during which all long vowels in English moved their position, is commonly agreed to have taken place somewhere between 1400 and 1700 (see, for example Baugh and Cable 2002) – that is, a massive 300-year span! As described below, Woods' work on sound changes in New Zealand seems to occur from generation to generation – still much slower than a child's vocabulary acquisition, but quicker than the Great Vowel Shift. Even though I am repeating myself, but this again emphasizes the importance of thorough research and a good familiarity with the theories that are involved in our study, and to construct our methodological framework around them.

Longitudinal studies come in two basic forms, differentiated only by their sample: panel and cohort designs. For panel designs, the sample (or panel) is drawn randomly from the population (see Section 3.6). For example, let's assume we are interested in the progression of Spanish learners of English at a particular university (our population). From this population we randomly select a small number of students, maybe ten, and we monitor their progress at three different occasions through a standardized language proficiency test as well as reflective interviews: at the beginning of January, the beginning of April, and the beginning of July. Data collected at these three occasions will allow us to draw conclusions about (a) the progression of individual students over time, and (b) general patterns of progression for the whole sample.

Cohort design work essentially similarly, but the sample we work with is slightly different. Cohorts are groups of people who share a particular characteristic which is often of temporal nature, for example year of birth, year of marriage, or time spent learning a particular language. In our above example, rather than looking at all Spanish learners of English at our university, we are only looking at students who started in the 2011/12 academic year. Cohort designs are arguably better for controlling third variables. According to Bryman (2004: 46), the crucial difference between panel and cohort designs is that while panel designs allow us to observe both cohort and aging effects, cohort studies can only identify aging effects. Whether this is an advantage or a disadvantage depends on the individual study.

An example: we are interested whether a particular phonological variable changes over time. A panel study will allow us to analyse our data on two dimensions: first, we can draw conclusions as to what extent respondents' progressing age influences their use of this particular variable (e.g. the older respondents get, the less frequently do they use the variable). Second, it also provides us with information about how respondents born in a particular year change their usage of this feature, hence allowing us to include information about generation differences. On the other hand, with all respondents born in the same year, cohort designs only allow us to observe change according to aging, as the year of birth is constant – generational differences, for example, cannot be observed.

One of the main advantages of longitudinal designs, namely the ability to measure change over time, is also one of its major pitfalls. With the entire study depending on a particular group of people over a long period of time, the research is easily compromised once members of the sample start dropping out, due to lack of motivation, relocation or, in the most extreme case, death. In other words, we may start with a sample of 20 people in 2013 for a 5-year study, but by the time we arrive in 2017 only 7 respondents remain. This may substantially impair the significance of any results we may get, and, in the worst case, endanger the entire study. Particularly in contexts where people frequently change due to the nature of the context (at British universities, for example, a typical undergraduate cohort is only here for three years), sample retention and hence longitudinal studies can be problematic.

3.3. Pseudo-longitudinal designs: *Real-time* and *apparent time*

While Labov's study used a cross-sectional design to detect relationships between linguistic and social variables at one particular point in time, cross-sectional studies may, to a certain extent, also be used to simulate longitudinal studies (Figure 3.1). In linguistic terms, we may want to design one *synchronic* study in such a way that we can infer *diachronic* development, without the hassle of having to run several repeated synchronic studies over a prolonged period of time (Bayley 2004). In particular in Labovian sociolinguistics, this is also known as *real-time* and *apparent time*. The method was first developed by Labov (1963) in his Martha's Vineyard study. We shall look at a different example here.

Woods (2000) in her study on sound changes in New Zealand in essence 'simulated time': by looking at the speech of respondents from three generations – grandmother, mother and daughter – she was able to pin down changes in vowel sounds over time, even though the majority of data was collected at the same point in time, that is, synchronically. Here, we have real-time data for the respondents, but based on the sociolinguistic theory that language is age-graded, looking at data from different generations allows us to draw conclusions about diachronic development, or apparent time, and hence language change. In other words, we are not looking at how language is changing, but how it has changed already.

Note, though, that this type of design cannot offer the full explanatory power (e.g. regarding causality) that real longitudinal designs offer, as change can only be observed across the sample, but not at the level of an

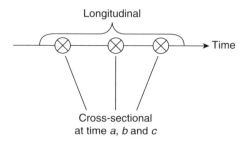

FIGURE 3.1 *Longitudinal versus cross-sectional designs.*

individual respondent. It also assumes the relative stability of all other factors – see Bayley (2004) for a comprehensive summary.

3.4. Experimental and quasi-experimental designs

Experimental designs are fundamentally different from the ones discussed so far: unlike longitudinal and cross-sectional designs, which allow us to collect and observe 'natural' data, that is, data as it occurs in its natural environment, experimental studies are based on the systematic and deliberate manipulation of one or more variables by the researcher. In their purest form, experiments are conducted in laboratories – facilities that enable the researcher to have control over all, or almost all, variables involved in a study – both overt and latent ones.

Traditionally, experimental designs are quantitative in nature and consist of the comparison between the experimental group (the one affected by the manipulation of variables) and a control group (not affected by manipulation). We shall start with a classic example from outside the field of linguistics: a pharmaceutical company, when developing a new drug against the common flu, at some point has to test the effects of this new drug. In essence, what they will do (with first animals and later humans), is to take a group of people suffering from flu and split them into two equal halves. Then, they administer the drug to the experimental group, and nothing (or a placebo) to the control group and measure the difference afterwards. If the new drug is any good, the experimental group should show some signs of improvement, while the control group does not. Statistical methods, which we will discuss in Chapters Six to Ten, help to determine whether the drug really makes a significant difference. It is important to note that in experimental designs, the assignment of any respondent into experimental or control group is completely random, that is, any respondent may end up in either group. Also, respondents usually do not know which group they belong to, as to avoid the impact of any psychological factors that this knowledge might create in a participant.

In linguistic research, too, experimental designs are based on the deliberate modification of a variable for one group. Li's (1988) study on the impact of modified input on advanced Chinese learners of English as a second language presented a set of sentences to his sample under two conditions: half of the respondents (experimental group 1, EG1) were given sentences for which meaning could be inferred from context ('cue-adequate'), the other half (experimental group 2, EG2) received sentences which were cue-inadequate (meaning could not be inferred). That is, the variable 'input' is modified in two ways: adequate/inadequate. Figure 3.2 outlined the process graphically. In step 1, as outlined, the allocation into

Step 1	Step 2	Step 3	Step 4
EG 1	Stimulus 1: cue adequate	T E	EG 1 ≠
EG 2	Stimulus 2: cue inadequate	S T	EG 2

FIGURE 3.2 *Setup of Li's study.*

EG1 or EG2 was conducted randomly, and this should ensure that EG1 and EG2 start with the same level of English language proficiency. Step 2 involved the introduction of the two stimuli – cue-adequate sentences for EG1, cue-inadequate sentences for EG2. In step 3, we test both groups for their proficiency after the introduction of the stimulus, followed by step 4, the analysis of the results: Li's hypothesis at the outset was that cue-adequate input is more beneficial to learners that cue-inadequate input; accordingly, results on step 4 should be better for EG1 than for EG2.

Note that in this example, we deal with two groups of people, divided by the two different 'versions' of the same variable 'input'. This is often referred to as *between-subject designs* – each group receives a particular type of input, similar to the drug test example. As an alternative setup, in a *within-subjects* design the same group of people receive two types of stimulus, and we compare reactions to both stimuli.

For either setting, given that all other factors are constant, for example, sentences should be of equal length and complexity, the comparison between the two sets of input should provide reliable information as to whether contextual cues help learners to understand the meaning of new words, and according to Li, it does.

There are several advantages and disadvantages of both between-subject and within-subject designs. Between-subject studies require more participants, in order to create two groups of equal sizes. Also, it must be ensured that the two groups are equal in terms of participant characteristics. A random allocation of participants into groups should avoid any participant-based bias; nevertheless, it is always worth checking: it is all too annoying to realize afterwards that group A had significantly more men than group B, while group B was significantly younger than group A – both facts which would certainly substantially skew the result. Working with one group, that is a within-subject design, avoids this problem.

On the other hand, within-subject designs put considerably more effort on participants. This can lead to boredom or fatigue – neither is a desirable feature for the reliability of our results. In addition, with increased length of the task, participant may gain practice and hence improve their results. In the worst case, this may lead to the creation of *artefacts*: that is, the results we obtain are not based on respondents' reaction to the actual content, but on their reaction to the task. In other words, artefacts are results that are based on how respondents react to a particular methodology, not on respondents' knowledge or reaction to the change in variables. As such, the phenomenon is closely related to the issue of validity, as discussed in Chapter Two.

Had Li used a within-subject design, we may imagine a situation whereby respondents indeed start to suffer from fatigue, leading to their performance decreasing across both stimuli. As a result, data we obtain may not necessarily tell us how respondents' perform with regard to adequate or inadequate cues, but simply how well or badly they react to the task. Artefacts can occur in all research designs, and the risk of creating one should not be underestimated. Hand in hand with the thorough study of previous research and methodologies used, any researcher designing a study should hence continuously ask and critically evaluate whether the method used really measures what it is intended to measure.

Quasi-experimental studies, too, are based on the change of one (or more) variables; however, there are two crucial differences to true experimental designs. First, the assignment of respondents into experimental and control group is not random, but to some extent 'naturally given'. Second, instead of a deliberate manipulation through the researcher, in quasi-experimental studies an 'external force' changes a particular variable. And since this sounds rather abstract, we will look at an example. At the time of writing this book, there is a considerable debate in the United Kingdom about the improvement of sociocultural integration of migrants, and, inevitably, the use of the English language as a means of facilitating integration as well as the provision of English language/English for Speakers of Other Languages (ESOL) classes is a major topic for politicians, media, policymakers and the general public. Imagine, for ease of comprehension, that at this moment in time there was no ESOL provision available for migrants. Now, let's also assume the government passes a law which, from next week onwards, significantly improves ESOL provision but also forces migrants to gain an English language proficiency equivalent to the Cambridge Advanced English Certificate (CAE). However, in this first instance, provision will only be provided for migrants of Pakistani descent. Hence, Pakistanis in Britain 'automatically' become our experimental group, that is, the group that will be subject to a change in a particular variable (namely ESOL provision), while all other migrants will not undergo any changes (i.e. are our control group). We would design our fictional study around two points of data collection: measuring proficiency of both experimental group and control group before the new law comes into effect, and afterwards, let's say in six months time. Similar to real experimental designs, we would obtain four scores which would allow then us to draw conclusion whether or not the new policy has any effect on migrants' English language proficiency:

- Experimental group proficiency pre-stimulus
- Control group proficiency pre-stimulus
- Experimental group proficiency post-stimulus
- Control group proficiency post-stimulus

The advantage of quasi-experimental designs is that they require relatively little effort from the side of the researcher, as the introduction of the change, or stimulus, is taken care of by other people. Yet, this is also our biggest problem: unlike in real experiments, we have no control over third variables and what is happening, and rely entirely on the observation of potential changes. In addition, since the allocation of participants into the experimental group is not random and participants will be aware of this (just imagine the media coverage!), it is likely to trigger some kind of psychological reaction (positive or negative) in them – a reaction that is not based on the ESOL provision, but the fact that they are made to participate.

3.5. Summary: Research designs

The use of a particular research design depends on several factors, but our research question and hypotheses are the most crucial aspects. Table 3.1 summarizes the main characteristics.

3.6. Sampling

Inseparably linked to the choice of a research design the question of *who* we would like to research, that is, who our participants are. On the surface, this may seem obvious and the discussion here obsolete; yet, in order to design a valid and reliable study we must have a look at the main concepts involved: the *population*, the *sample* and *sampling techniques*.

The *population* defines the group of people we are generally interested in; however, it does not necessarily mean *all* people (as in 'all people living in Britain' or even 'this universe'). More specifically, the population refers to a group of people who share certain characteristics. As such, population can equally refer to large or small groups: if we choose 'mankind' as the population we are interested in, we include all human beings living on this planet – currently around 6.6 billion individuals – with 'human being-ness' being the common feature. Similarly, we may define our population

TABLE 3.1 Summary of different research designs

Type of design	Possible application	Pros/cons
Longitudinal	Language change; development of a particular feature over time	+ real-time observation of change − but external factors difficult to control − time and risk of sample attrition
Cross-sectional	Description of current status of a particular linguistic feature	+ comparatively fast + very accurate with the right methods and framework (as no change occurs) − large sample − cannot account for any developments before time of data collection
Experimental	Influence of a particular external stimulus on a linguistic feature	+ total control of researcher − often difficult to set up − validity and reliability issues
Quasi-experimental	Influence of a particular external stimulus on a linguistic feature	+ observation of real change in comparatively short period of time (cf. longitudinal) − no control over change of variable − little control over external factors

as 'all native speakers of the English language' – compared to mankind a smaller population with just around 380 million individuals. However, populations can also be defined as much smaller groups. Over the last 20 years, sociolinguistics and linguistic anthropology has paid increasing interest in language use in minority communities. In my own research, I defined population as all first generation migrants of Bangladeshi origin who live in a particular London borough – explicitly excluding those second generation people who were already born in London. Yet again, I usually advise my undergraduate students for their final projects to go much smaller and to define their population as something along the lines of 'all students of a BA(hons) English Language degree at Anglia Ruskin University' – a population that comprises a few dozen people.

The term population does not necessarily apply to people only (or animals if you are a zoologist, or plants if you are a botanist): strictly speaking, a 'population is defined as a set of elements; an element is defined as the basic unit that comprises the population' (Frankel 2010: 85). A population can therefore also be things like 'all dating advertisements published in British tabloid newspapers', with each dating ad constituting one element.

While we have seen that populations can be of significantly different sizes and shapes, they all have one thing in common: they are usually too large to be studied in their entirety. No research project will ever be able to include every single human being living on this planet, and even with comparatively small populations such as the Bangladeshi community in East London, we are still dealing with around 65,000 people – beyond what is possible within the scope of our average project. A final-year student might struggle to interview 40-odd students for their dissertation, too – although a questionnaire-based survey here seems doable. This issue is not only limited to populations based on human respondents: one of the problems when dealing with natural language data – both spoken and written – is that data can quickly run into the hundred thousands, if not millions of words. Modern corpus analysis techniques have made dealing with large amounts of texts much easier, but for a more detailed or qualitative analysis, it often makes sense to focus on a smaller part. Studies on urban linguistic landscapes (i.e. the visual presence of languages in a particular geographic location through things like road signs, advertising, etc.), often focus on selected streets or tightly defined areas in order to make data collection and analysis more manageable. Du Plessis's (2010) study on language management in Bloemfontain, South Africa, is based, in part, on the collection of data form a single floor of a public building.

What we need then is to break down our population into smaller chunks; we need a group size we can actually realistically work with: the *sample*. A sample is a part of our population, and, crucially, the sample must be an adequate reflection of our population. In other words, our sample should have the same characteristics as our population: it is *representative* for the population. Now comes the tricky bit: the larger our population is, the more likely is it that it is also fairly diverse, or *heterogeneous*. Members, or elements, might still share the same features that make them a member of the population, but also show a number is other features in which they differ. If mankind is defined by human-beingness, there are a lot of other features that make us different! Similarly, if we move from dating ads in broadsheet newspapers to a population that also included tabloids and magazines, it is likely that the style and repertoire of the ads changes, too, as a reflection of the stratification of the readership.

On the other hand, if we have a small population, for example all second year students of linguistics at University X, it is likely that the population itself is more homogenous (in terms of, for example age, educational background, etc.). Neither homogeneity nor heterogeneity of a population are necessarily bad, indeed either can be useful depending on the research question. However, when selecting a sample, they become a major issue: since our sample ought to be a realistic reflection of the population, homogeneity or heterogeneity ought to be reflected in the sample too. That is, if our population is fairly diverse, our sample should be, too. If we have a homogeneous sample and use it to draw conclusions about a heterogeneous population, how can our results be reliable and valid?

Later on in this book, in Chapters Seven till Ten, we discuss some statistical tools which are known as *inferential statistics* (or *statistical inference*): the idea behind them is that they will allow us to look at a sample and make *inferences* as to what the population looks like. Hence, it is important that the sample is an adequate representation of the population, or else our statistical inference will lead us nowhere: imagine our population has a gender split of exactly 50%–50% of our population are male, 50% are female. If we had a sample with a 90:10 split (90% male, 10% female), how could we make accurate inferences about the population?

An example: Lakoff (1975) in her seminal study on linguistic differences between men and women looked at features typical for 'female' speech, ultimately claiming that women's language is 'powerless'. Given this result, we can infer that the population for this study are women – a fairly diverse group! When reading her study in detail, one notices (besides other methodological problems which we shall ignore here) that her conclusions are based on data collected within her own social network. The problem should be immediately obvious: how can the social network of a white female university professor be an accurate reflection of women in general? This is not to say that Lakoff's social environment was inherently homogeneous, but it seems unlikely that it was as diverse as to adequately reflecting the population – an issue many subsequent researchers have pointed out.

Figure 3.3 illustrates the relationship between population and sample: our population consists of 20 balls, 10 of which are black and 10 of which are white. We would a sample of four balls (i.e. 20% of the population). If our sample is to be representative of the population, the proportion of black and white balls should be identical (or at least very very similar): 50% of the balls in our sample should be black, 50% white. Hence, a representative sample of our population would consist of two black and two white balls.

So, what we need is an appropriate technique that allows us to draw an adequate and realistic sample from our population. There are several books dedicated entirely to the issue of sampling; here, we will discuss the most important methods and problems.

The without any doubt most valid sampling technique is *random* or *probabilistic sampling*. It is based on the assumption that all members of the population have the same chance to become a member of the sample. A probabilistic sample is basically similar to drawing lots: let's assume that our population comprises 100 people, and we have decided that we want a sample size of 25. We write all 100 names on individual pieces of paper, put them into a hat, mix them properly, and then draw 25 names out of the

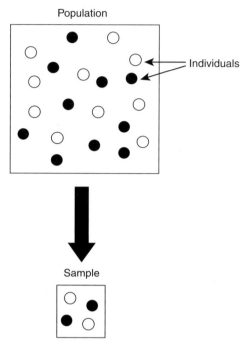

FIGURE 3.3 *Sampling.*

hat. In this case, all 100 people have the same chance to get into the sample (technically this is incorrect: with every name that is drawn from the hat the probability to be drawn increases for the remaining names: 1 of out 90 is a higher probability than 1 out of 100 – we shall ignore the mathematical details and assume that we draw all 25 names at the same time). Based on the rules of probability (see Chapter Six), our sample should now be a pretty good reflection of our population: it is unlikely that we have randomly drawn a particularly 'odd' sample (such as only very old respondents, or only men). With the researcher not being actively or consciously involved in the sampling process (apart from the drawing of names from a hat), any potential bias is eliminated.

With larger samples, the name-in-a-hat-technique can get difficult (you need a big hat for a population of 10,000!), but in essence, the technique remains the same. For a population of 5,000 and a sample size of 100, we can randomly allocate numbers from 0001 to 5,000 to the names in our population, and then randomly select 100 numbers. By not knowing individuals' names, we exclude any bias we might have (such as picking only women or names we like).

Similar to this pure probabilistic method is the *systematic sampling*: We compile an (alphabetic) list of our population, and select every fifth/

tenth/fiftieth etc. name from the list, depending on the required sample size, without paying attention to who we select.

While probabilistic sample is the only way to eliminate bias, it cannot fully eliminate *sampling error*. Sampling error is the phenomenon whereby our sample does not have the same characteristics as our population, for reasons that only skilled mathematicians can explain. We leave it here with a description of the phenomenon. An example: our population includes 100 people, 50 of which are men and 50 of which are women. Our intended sample size is 20. In order to be fully representative of the population, our sample should hence include as many men as women – 10 each. However, having drawn our random sample, we may realize that we have 15 men, but only 5 women; in other words, our sample does not quite reflect reality. This is the crux with probabilities: they only tell us what is *likely* to happen, yet they give us no guarantee that it actually will happen.

Figure 3.4 illustrates sampling error with our ball example above, based on systematic sampling of choosing every fifth ball. The example on the left-hand side shows a small sampling error: instead of a 2:2 split, we select 3 white and 1 black ball. Hence, our sample is not quite representative of our population. On the right hand side, we have a very serious sampling error, with only white balls selected. In this case, our sample is not representative of our population, simply because the black balls, even though equally represented in the population, are not represented in the sample.

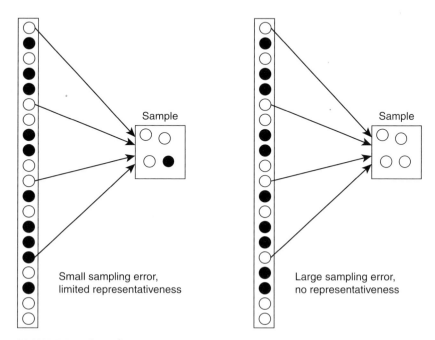

FIGURE 3.4 *Sampling error.*

It is difficult to give generic advice on what to do about sampling errors, as it very much depends on the research question. If, in our fictive example, we are interested in differences between men and women, then we would like our sampling error to be as small as possible. If gender is an irrelevant factor, we can probably live with it. What is important is that we have an awareness of the sampling error though. Depending on the circumstances, we may want to rerun our sampling.

While random/probabilistic sampling is one of, if not the most valid method, it also comes at a cost: particularly with a large population, sampling can be tedious and error-prone (although computers can take the workload off us). Also, it is unlikely that everyone we have drawn into our sample agrees to take part in our study. We might randomly select 50 people for our sample, but only 20 agree to take part. In this case, we would have to accept what is called a *non-response* leading to a *non-sampling error*. If not every member of our carefully and randomly selected sample agrees to participate, our sample loses its representativeness: it is often the case that those who agree to take part are significantly 'different' from those who do not – our sample is then skewed. We might get away with a resampling, that is, the repetition of the process to find the remaining 30 participants. However, the doubts on how representative our sample is remains.

A full probabilistic sample (pure or systematic) is often not viable, particularly when we consider small-scale projects such as student dissertations. More often than not, we have to resort to non-probabilistic sampling. I do not advocate the use of non-probabilistic sampling here, but it is important to briefly discuss this method, as it is widely used by those short of resources. To cut a long story short, in non-probabilistic sampling participants are selected in a non-random, non-probabilistic fashion. In other words, not all members of the population have the same chance to become member of the sample; sample membership is based on some kind of deliberate selection by the researcher.

The most typical type of non-random samples are *opportunity samples* (Sapsford and Jupp 1996), also known as *convenience samples* (Bryman 2004). As the terms imply, participants are chosen by the researcher on the basis of who is available at the time. For example, in my own work with the Bangladeshi community in East London (Rasinger 2007), a probabilistic sample was out of question – mainly due to limited resources the project had. Instead I recruited respondents while they were visiting a community centre in the borough by simply asking them whether they could spare half an hour to talk to me. The problems with this approach are (hopefully) obvious: first, the non-random selection does not, and cannot, exclude any bias the researcher might have. If we are honest, we have all, at some point in our lives, approached a person or not; whether or not this was a conscious decision does not matter, but the deliberate selection or non-selection of participants will inevitably reflected in the sample – in whatever way. Secondly, opportunistic samples are often highly problematic in terms of representativeness and, ultimately, the generalizability of data they generate. If a sample is selected in a potentially bias way, to what extent does it represent the population as a whole?

Yet, opportunistic sample can have their benefits, besides the obvious ones with regard to recruiting respondents. And one subcategory of non-random samples may prove particularly useful in sociolinguistic research: *snowball samples* or *social network samples* (Milroy 1987). In essence, with this method the sample is recruiting its own members. Milroy, in her study on language use and social class, for example, in the first instance contacted a few respondents from working-class areas of Belfast. Subsequently, these respondents recruited members of their social network – friends, family, etc. – and hence expanding the sample. This snowball method works well in contexts where we can be certain that social networks are comparatively homogeneous. Back in the 1980s, Milroy could rely on working-class members in Belfast mainly interacted within their own group. As such, the sample generated by the social network approach could be assumed to be a rather good reflection of the population. However, the method would have spectacularly failed if the networks were heterogeneous with regard to social class, as the sample produced would have contained members of all classes – not very representative for the desired population.

3.7. A word about ethics

Universities and other research and Higher/Further Education institutions put increasing emphasis on ethics when it comes to research involving human beings (or animals, or tissue, but these usually do not apply to linguistic research!). My own university requires all its members – staff and students – to go through a formalized ethics approval procedure; most funding bodies require this, too. In part, this is to safeguard the institution and the researchers against litigation claims from research participants, and demonstrating that ethical procedures have been followed is an important aspect in showing that due process has been followed; it is also a legal requirement in many countries (Johnstone 2000), enshrined in data protection and privacy laws, among others. Legal ethics issues aside, it is simply *ethical* to follow certain rules when working with other people. With each university having their own system (and different countries having different laws pertaining to these issues), I advise readers to familiarize themselves with the intricacies of their own organization.

Hammersley and Traianou in their introduction to *Ethics in Qualitative Research* (2012) provide an excellent attempt to define the concept:

> A set of principles that embody or exemplify what is good or right, or allow us to identify what is bad or wrong. [. . .] '[E]thical' can mean:

What is good or right, as contrasted with the *unethical* – what is bad or wrong. (ibid.: 16–17, original emphasis)

A few general guidelines apply universally with regard to ethics: first, participants in research must consent to taking part in the study, and should also have the opportunity to withdraw their consent at any time. Surreptitious data collection is, in essence, 'stealing' data from someone and is grossly unethical – both in the moral and, increasingly, in the legal sense.

In particular with research that uses actual natural speech data the issue of when to ask for consent – before or after data recording – is a crucial one: respondents who know that they are recorded from the outset may or may not deliberately change their linguistic behaviour – a phenomenon well known as the 'Observer's Paradox' (Labov 1972). On the other hand, one may decide to record informants surreptitiously, only to realize that they do not consent afterwards. There is no perfect answer to this problem. Sociolinguists and discourse analysts have spent the better part of four decades working on this issue and have developed various strategies to collect good and reliable speech data in an ethical way. Most of these approaches are based on the fieldworker getting to know their respondents as well as possible; the closer the relationship between fieldworker and informant, the higher is the probability that the Observer's Paradox decreases and the quality of data increases. It is obvious that such an approach is time and resource intensive – both commodities very few of us have in abundance. The use of a 'gatekeeper' – a person who is a member of the group we are interested in – in the data-collection process is often very useful, as it can bridge the distance between the researcher and those researched. But even then, it may take some time until everything works to a satisfactory level.

Note that some institutions may require written consent from participants, or consent that is recorded in any other way; a good template is provided by Johnstone (2000). As a general guideline, the consent form should start with a brief introduction of the researcher and the research project, so participants know who they are dealing with. It is debatable how much information about the project to include: give too much away and it might influence participants' responses (as they may try to infer what is 'expected' from them), give them to little they might not consent because they do not know what is going to happen to them. It is usually advisable to include a short explanation why they have been invited to take part. Providing contact details, so participants can get in touch with you or other researchers in the team, is also considered good practice and now included in many forms by default. The most important points, however, are the following:

1   Make participants aware of the fact that they can withdraw from the study at any time and without explanation. They

are independent human beings, and, although it is annoying when participants drop out, they have a right to do so without justification.

2 Make participants aware of any risks – psychological or physical – that are involved. Again, participants have a right to know what to expect, and it is unethical (and illegal in many countries) to expose them to risks without their consent.

3 Inform them what is happening to their data, for example, where and how it is stored and who has access to it. This also includes information about how they can obtain their own data and how to withdraw it from the study.

4 The consent form must be signed by the participant (or their legal guardian).

Make sure that the respondents are actually able to use the consent form: if your respondents are not able to read English (or whatever language you use) at the required level to understand the consent form, you may need to find other ways. This may be a translation into their own language in the case of non-native speakers; or you may audio-record your explanation and the oral consent in the case of people for which written consent is not possible (e.g. very young children, etc.).

When working with children or adolescents under the age of 18, consent must be thought from the parents or legal guardians. Over the last few years, it has become an established procedure to ask for the children's permission also – we may come across a parent who is overly keen on their child to take part in a study, but the child is less inclined to do so. It does not take much to imagine what kind of data a child produces that has been pushed by their parents into participating – we might just as well not even start.

Second, no study should harm the physical and psychological integrity of the respondents; and respondents should not suffer from any short-, mid- or long-term disadvantages because of their participation the study. The principle of the avoidance of harm is a crucial one: not only because it is 'ethical', but because harm poses a particular danger of litigation claims being brought against individual researchers or institutions. Admittedly, few linguistic projects will have serious impacts on respondents' mental or physical health (although I have come across the odd undergraduate student idea that included the use of illegal substances for their final-year project). Yet, it is quite easy to create situations in which respondents feel uneasy, intimidated or even threatened to an extent. Studies using personal narratives, for example, may trigger unpleasant memories; the nature of a task in more experimental studies may seriously increase respondents' stress levels. Similar problems may arise when working with children, the elderly, or people who are, for one reason or another, in a potentially weaker position in relation to the researcher. The pressure we are under to collect data should not result in us exploiting our position of relative power towards our participants.

Most problems can, and in fact should, be avoided by properly and comprehensively briefing and debriefing respondents. Participants who know exactly what is being asked from them are less likely to show adverse reactions than those who do not or only vaguely know what they are supposed to do. This should be done face to face and in writing (on the consent/participant information form). Also, fieldworkers should closely monitor participants during data collection and intervene if necessary. In the worst case, we should abandon our data collection and rethink our methodology.

There is, however, a third issue to the ethical implications of a study, and somewhat surprisingly, this is often ignored: while most of the ethics discussion focuses on the respondents' rights and welfare, the fieldworker is all too often forgotten. Just as for our participants the data-collection process should not infringe our own personal safety and security. This might a simple and straightforward thing: if we are collecting speech data in an urban area that has a reputation for its high–street-crime rate, we should avoid displaying our – sometimes rather expensive – equipment too openly. Füglein (2000) in her ethnographic dissertation on the use of German by second generation adolescents of Turkish descent in Germany reports that, due to her ethnographic methodology in which she acted as an insider, she was forced to participate regularly in the group's activities – even though some of them were on the verge of legality. Moreover, Füglein reports that as a young woman in an exclusively male group, she had to struggle to maintain her position and not to be considered a mere object of sexual desire. This degree of involvement seems admirable, but is probably beyond what any study justifies: it would need a pretty good project to convince me to risk going to prison for.

However, there are less extreme but not less important issues to consider. Data collection can, even if all is going well, be very stressful, and it is paramount that we are (and remain) aware of what we can physically and psychologically do. Being slightly stressed does not do any harm, but stress levels that threaten our mental well-being and sanity does; and we have to take this into account when planning our study and its methodology. A particular topic might be tempting, but if it requires us to collect large amounts of data within a particularly short period of time, we should give it a second thought. A lot of this is common sense: if you would not go down a dark alley alone late at night in your 'normal' life, why do so when collecting data? If you know that other commitments prevent you from spending more than a certain amount of time each day on your research, why do so? There is nothing wrong with stretching oneself a bit every once in a while, but no study is worth dying for (although promotion panels seem to like this kind of commitment). Strangely, especially when we are very keen on a project, we all too often forget about these things. So do remember them.

It is easy to be put off doing a particular project simply because ethics seems daunting and my references to harm, lawsuits and litigation have probably done little to disperse those fears! However, there is a way to look at ethics from a much more positive angle: a project that conforms to ethical principles is likely to be one that is well developed and planned, and will ultimately be a more successful one because of this. The ethics application at my own university consists of a range of question divided into five thematic blocks:

● What is it you want to do, and what is your rationale behind it? Why do you want to do it?

● Are you qualified to do it, that is, do you have the necessary skills?

● How are you going to do it?

● Who are your participants, and what potential harm does your project have on them?

● How will you keep your data?

Although these five blocks come in 27 daunting questions, all they ask for is your research questions and your methodology. *Anyone* should be able to answer this; if you can't, then you probably should not proceed. The last issue covers data protection and privacy, and it should be self-explanatory that data, especially raw data that allows for the identification of participants, should not be left on the train, the pub or the local park. So, ethic is nothing but good project planning, and surely this is a good thing.

3.8. Getting (and keeping) it all together: Managing your research

Most research methods textbooks spend considerable time on the basics of doing research, be it quantitative or qualitative. Most of them begin with an outline of research design issues before moving into the nitty-gritty of methodological tools and actual analysis and interpretation; and this book is no exception. What many books seem to ignore, however, is that research projects are exactly that: *projects*. They have a start date and an end date (think: paper submission deadline!), and an outcome (a paper, thesis, conference presentation, etc.). Between the start and the end date, stuff happens to make us (hopefully!) reach the outcome. Once we reached it, the project ends. This is also known as a *project lifecycle*.

Projects need to be managed, or else we will never successfully produce the intended outcome. This book is not, obviously, an introduction to project management (there are numerous of those around, see the 'Further

Reading' section at the end of this Part), but it is worth having a brief look at some of the very basics.

Any project, and this includes (academic) research projects, be it by an undergraduate student or a world-leading professor, consists of three dimensions: scope, resources and time. We will look at these in a bit more detail.

In a nutshell, the *project scope* is what the project is all about. It is defined by our research questions, by what we want to find out. In the previous chapter I have stressed the importance of clearly defined hypotheses in quantitative research, as they will define the scope of the inquiry.

Time is a straightforward one to understand: whether it is a student project or one run by an experienced academic and financed by a large research grant, time is limited: there is, somewhere, a deadline to get that paper/dissertation/report in, and after a number of weeks/months/years, funding dries up. A key problem with time is that it is usually difficult to get more of it: deadlines are very often fixed and only negotiable to a limited extent, and running over deadlines often has some repercussions (a reduced grade, blacklisting from future grant applications, etc.).

Resources are the, well, resources we need to complete the project. They can consist of things like technical equipment, or man power, or anything else we need to conduct our study.

To put it in its simplest form, scope, time and resources need to be managed so they form a balanced project. The idea is that scope, time and resources are intrinsically linked, and change in one dimension requires a change in (at least) one more. Let's have an example: imagine you are a single researcher on a project investigating heritage language maintenance in a migrant community. Your start date is 1 July, and your end date is 31 October, by which time you need to submit a paper on the topic or you will fail the course/get the sack/be denied your promotion. You have not done any work on this before and need to start from scratch – that gives you four months from start to finish. You set out to spend one month planning (includes one week of piloting), one month collecting data, one month analysing and the final month writing, so your project plan will look like Table 3.2.

TABLE 3.2 Project plan for (fictitious) project on language maintenance

Phase 1	July	Planning and pilot
Phase 2	August	Fieldwork: Collect data
Phase 3	September	Analyse data
Phase 4	October	Write up

During phase 1, you decide to collect all your data through a questionnaire-based survey. You pilot it, it goes well, so you get started with phase 2.

Scenario 1: two weeks into your data collection, you realize you don't get a sufficient response rate to allow for a meaningful quantitative analysis. However, you are being reliably informed that come September, people will return from their holidays, and many have signalled that they are willing to take part in your survey. You cannot change the overall project time, so you will need to make a decision between cutting down on the time you allocated to phases 3 and 4, or possibly cut down on the scope of the project.

Scenario 2: you are making amazing progress with your data collection and you have even started a preliminary analysis by the end of August. However, you realize that there is an extraordinarily interesting pattern emerging in the data, which your quantitative survey cannot fully capture. Again, the project must end by 31 October. Any increase in the scope of the project means that you will need to either cut down in phases 3 or 4, or you need to expand your resources – maybe you can hire a research assistant. Unfortunately, times are hard and there is no money, so it really is only a trade-off between scope or more pressure on you.

Thorough project planning can avoid a lot of problems. The above example may be a fictitious one, but far from unusual: all these things can and do happen, so make sure you build in some contingency arrangements. We often rely on the goodwill of other people to get data for our study, and people are not always available. The reason for some ethics applications asking about researchers' qualifications is not just there to annoy us: if you plan on using a particular type of software or other piece of equipment, make sure that you have access to it and know how to actually use it. Learning-by-doing may be nice, but if you are pressed for time, you probably want to get on with the doing. And talking your supervisor or Dean into splashing out a large amount of money on equipment just so you can finish writing a paper usually does not go down well. It does not mean that they won't – but it is something that should be clarified at the planning stage.

It is well worth putting the project plan with its various phases on a piece of (electronic) paper, as it can help you to see how the project develops and where potential crunch points are. A simple table like Table 3.2 will often do, or you can break it down into smaller steps: Table 3.3 is a project plan of one of my own projects. Note that I have also indicated my own unavailability.

Whatever you use, the key is that it works for you and allows you to keep track of the project.

So, to summarize: it is well worth at the start of a research project to think not only about the academic issues (theoretical framework, research design, methodology, analytic framework) but also to spend some time thinking about the management of the project. It may seem like even more work at the start, but usually helps avoiding disasters that are avoidable – that leaves more energy for struggling with the unavoidable!

TABLE 3.3 (Real) Project plan

ID	Task name	Start	Finish	Duration (working days)	Resources
1	Project name	01/07	30/04	217	
2	Set-up Phase	01/07	26/07	19	
3	Literature review	01/07	19/07	14	Renew library card
4	Contact respondents	01/07	19/07	14	Email list from Kate
5	Contact stakeholders	07/07	19/07	9	Email list from Kate
6	Develop methodology	22/07	26/07	4	
7	Holiday	29/07	14/08	12	
8	Data collection respondents	19/08	01/11	54	Questionnaire to copy services; Voice recorder from Media Services
9	Screening quant. data	09/09	20/09	9	Check SPSS version and compatibility
10	Screening qual. data	09/09	20/09	9	Check with Mark re NVivo
11	Refine stakeholders	23/09	27/09	4	Kate's list. Sharon??
12	Data collection stakeholders	04/11	20/12	34	Voice recorder from Media Services
13	Christmas break	23/12	03/01	9	
14	Main analysis	06/01	07/03	44	
15	Quantitative analysis	06/01	17/01	9	SPSS
16	Write-up quantitative analysis	20/01	31/01	9	
17	Interview transcription	06/01	21/02	34	Outsourced to transcription unit. NB: Mary to settle invoice
18	Qualitative analysis	24/02	07/03	9	NVivo
19	Final write-up	10/03	30/04	37	
20	Stakeholder report	10/03	21/03	9	
21	Paper A	24/03	11/04	14	
22	Paper B	14/04	30/04	12	

CHAPTER FOUR

Questionnaire design and coding

Key words: coding – guidelines – layout – Likert scales – measuring concepts – multiple-item questions – phrasing questions – piloting – question sequencing – response sets

It is a common scenario: a student walks into their tutor's office to discuss their project, and, with a big smile on their face, announce that they 'will be investigating X because it's easy – I just do a few questionnaires and I'm done'. Ok, this might be a slight exaggeration but questionnaires are likely to be one of the most popular methodological tools employed. Particularly students and less well-versed researchers seem to consider them the panacea that can solve all their problems. Once designed, they help accumulating vast amounts of incredibly high-quality data.

The reality, however, quite often paints a different picture altogether. While it is true that questionnaires are particularly handy if large amounts of quantitative data are needed, the problem arises at the design stage. Let's get this straight from the start:

Questionnaires are NOT a cheap and easy way to generate a vast amount of data with little to no effort!

Questionnaires must be perfect – and I do mean perfect – before they are distributed to the sample population; subsequent changes, with one part of the sample having one version and another part a different version, will invalidate the study. Questionnaires are scientific tools that require careful planning and design in order to work accurately. After all, we want questionnaires to collect reliable and valid data, and if different people have different questionnaires investigating the same issue, how can our results ever be reliable? In the worst case, we would have to run the entire data collection again – neither desirable nor practical.

This chapter serves two purposes: first, we discuss some general guidelines on how to design a questionnaire, focusing on question phrasing, ways of measuring and recording responses, and measuring attitudes using multiple-item and Likert scales. In addition, we discuss how to prepare questionnaire-based data for analysis. Simultaneously, the chapter addresses potential problems with questionnaires and the methods discussed, such as unclear phrasing of questions, loaded questions or degree of detail elicited by a particular instrument.

Before we start with the chapter properly, I need to issue a word of warning. However, carefully we design our questionnaire, however carefully we phrase our questions, and no matter how thoroughly we pilot it: we are, after all, dealing with human beings, and whatever response they provide, it is the response they give at this particular point in time. Maybe because it is an accurate reflection of their state of being at that moment, maybe because they – consciously or subconsciously – think that the response is the 'right' one, it is only ever that: a response they give at that moment in time. It is not necessarily the absolute, factual truth. If I heat water at sea level to a temperature of 100 degrees Celsius, it will change its state from liquid to gas (steam). That is a fact, and a replicable one as such. For anything involving our fellow humans, it is more complicated, and it is important that we interpret our results as such: they are only ever a reflection of our sample at the time of the data collection.

A seminal study by the late US sociologist Richard LaPiere illustrates this striking gap between what people report to be doing, and their (actual) action. Between 1930 and 1932, LaPiere travelled with a couple of Chinese ethnicity – 'a fact that could not be disguised' (LaPiere 1934: 231) across the United States.

> In something like ten thousand miles of motor travel, twice across the United States, up and down the Pacific Coast, we met definite rejection from those asked to serve us just once. We were received at 66 hotels, auto camps, and 'Tourist Homes', refused at one. We were served in 184 restaurants and cafes scattered throughout the country [. . .]. (ibid.: 232)

All in all, then, a pretty good result at a time where, as LaPiere describes, the general attitude towards the Chinese was widely considered to be negative. However, when LaPiere contacted the establishments again a few weeks later, asking them: 'Will you accept members of the Chinese race as guests in your establishment?' (ibid.: 233), more than 90% responded with 'no'. This reveals a dramatic mismatch between what people say they do, and what they actually do. And while there are ways of bridging this gap (we will look at some possible ways in this chapter), the fact remains that, ultimately, we rely on what people tell us.

4.1. Starting point: Know what you want and ask what you need

One of the main problems in designing questionnaires is that we, as researchers, know exactly what we want the questionnaire to do. Unfortunately, our respondents usually do not. Hence, it is crucial that we phrase our questions in such a way that all participants in our sample are able to (a) fully understand them and (b) answer them to the best of their knowledge. So, we should always be absolutely clear and precise with every question we ask! This may sound overly simplistic. Yet, many questionnaires designed by inexperienced researchers often contain unclear, vague or ambiguous questions.

Let's assume we are interested in people's attitudes towards learning a second language. It is tempting to simply ask questions such as: 'Do you think that learning a second language is a good idea?' After all, the question seems to aim exactly at what we want to know. Think again. Does the question really provide you with any useful information? The question as phrased above only allows for three answer options: yes, no and a neutral/ don't know option. So, in a sample of 100 respondents we might get the following distribution:

Yes	62
No	26
Don't know/no opinion	12

What we can say is that 62 out of 100 respondents (i.e. 62%) think that learning a second language is a good idea, while 26 think it is not. And that is it; it does not tell us anything else. Who should learn them? Where? When? And why? And how? Any valid research question will inevitable have to address some of these aspects; yet, our question does not provide us with the answer.

A much better, even though far from perfect question would be, 'Do you think children should be taught a foreign language in primary school?' The question elicits substantially more information: it has a clear focus on a particularly group (children of a particular age), and a particular time in their lives (in primary school), and excludes infants, adolescents and adults. Yet, the kind of information we are most likely to be interested in is not covered by the question: *why* do people have the opinion they have given? In all fairness, in this particular context a study looking at *whether* instead of *why* is unlikely to come to any interesting results. It is stating the obvious, put particularly inexperienced researchers often ignore it: before we start developing our methodology and methods, such as a questionnaire, we must have a clear and precise research question in mind! And there is a fundamentally difference in finding out *whether* someone agrees to a particular topic or *why* they do so. Again, it may seem obvious, but if we are interested in the reason behind a particular answer, we must not forget to actually ask respondents about it! As mentioned before, once respondents have returned the questionnaire, there is hardly any possibility to get additional information; hence, we must gather all the information we need during the first time.

Recent experience means that I feel I need to make this absolutely clear: the research question drives the methodology, not the other way round! It is bad practice (to phrase it in a publishable way) to build your research question around the method; there is a good chance that you create a lot of data, but data that is rubbish. Yes, we need to take methodological considerations into account when designing our research (in other words, think about whether our study is feasible), but the question defines the methodology. End of. And very often this means that questionnaires are *not* the best methodological tool to investigate your question.

Let's stay with our example question for a while. We now (hopefully) have a question that gives us a first glimpse at people's attitudes towards second-language learning in primary school. Now we need to come up with a question that reasonably well elicits respondents' reasons for giving a particular answer. At a first glance, simply asking 'Why do you think . . .' is probably the best option: as an *open question*, that is, a question which allows respondents to freely comment on, 'Why . . .' may to give us some great insights into people's opinions. On the other hand, because it is an open question it requires respondents to actively formulate their thoughts and write them down. In short, it is a lot of hassle for people to actually answer it, and all too often people (like me) tend to simply skip open-ended questions. Similarly, open questions may gather substantial amounts of unnecessary or irrelevant data; after all, we cannot control the answer a respondent is providing. Either way, for us as researchers this means we have an answer but no proper explanation for it. Thirdly, for a quantitative analysis we need to code our answers, that is, translate text into numerical values (see below). And for open question this can sometimes be tricky, especially with answers that are ambiguous.

Even though they are often an excellent source for qualitative data, we will at this point, and in fact for the remainder of this book, ignore the possibility of using (semi-)structured and open interviews to overcome this problem, and refer readers to Tagliamonte's (2006) summary on sociolinguistic interviews or Litosseliti's (2003) work on using focus groups, among others. Bear in mind: just because this book focuses on quantitative methods does not mean that qualitative methods are better or worse. They are simply *different*.

4.2. Multiple choice/multiple-item questions

A potential solution for our problem with measuring attitudes by means of a questionnaire is the use of multiple-choice questions. As the term implies, these are questions which provide the respondent with a range of possible answer options – usually at least 3. For example, in our survey investigating Modern Foreign Language teaching in primary schools, we may want to give respondents a choice of four options, of which they are to choose the one they think is most important:

Why do you think Modern Foreign Languages should be taught in primary school?

- Knowledge of other languages offers better career prospects later in life.

- Language learning enhances cognitive development.

- The extra hour of teaching keeps them in school a bit longer and out of trouble.

- Any other reason (please state).

At this point, we should note two potential pitfalls: first, since the preceding questions ('do you think that . . .?') offered three answer options – yes, no, don't know – our questionnaire should provide two multiple-item sets for the second question, a fact that is frequently ignored by inexperienced researchers. That is, we need a set of items for the 'yes' answer option (which we have done above), but also for the 'no answer' option:

Why do you think Modern Foreign Languages should NOT be taught in primary school?

- It is too difficult for children.

- It interferes with their first language.

- It is a waste of time.

- Any other reason (please state).

It is important to tell respondent at this point what to do and where to go. If we simply continue listing our questions, without telling respondents explicitly where to proceed to, they will inevitable answer the wrong questions, hence skewing our result. To be on the safe side, it is useful to tell people what to do both in the original and the follow-up question, for example:

Q1: Do you think children should be taught a foreign language in primary school?

  ❒ Yes

  ❒ No

  ❒ Don't know

  If your answer is 'yes', go to Q2; if your answer is 'no', go to Q3. Otherwise, please go to Q5.

Q2: If your answer in Q1 was 'yes': Why do you think Modern Foreign Languages should be taught in primary school?

  ❒ Knowledge of other languages offers better career prospects later in life.

  ❒ Language learning enhances cognitive development.

  ❒ The extra hour of teaching keeps them in school a bit longer.

  ❒ Any other reason (please state) _____.

Q3: If your answer in Q1 was 'no': Why do you think Modern Foreign Languages should NOT be taught in primary school?

  ❒ It is too difficult for children.

  ❒ It interferes with their first language.

  ❒ It is a waste of time.

  ❒ Any other reason (please state) _____.

The last couple of years have seen a proliferation of online survey tools: rather than on paper, respondents complete an online questionnaire. Many of these online survey providers include 'automatic guidance system' whereby respondents are sent to the appropriate question based on their previous answer automatically (so if you answer 'yes' to one question, you will be sent to the appropriate follow-up question; if you answer 'no', you will be sent to a different one). Unfortunately, while most basic features are free, you have to pay a subscription fee for most advanced features. This is something to consider at the project planning stage – see Chapter Three.

To make the question meaningful within the academic debate it is located in, items should not be chosen randomly, but emanate from previous research findings in the field: all the answer options for the example questions above are reasonable and could occur like this in real life. In many cases, particularly for small-scale projects, this will take the form of a critical review of existing literature. However, in studies of larger scale or where potential answers are not as straightforwardly predictable, the construction of multiple-choice items is often based on additional studies prior to the questionnaire survey. For example, a small-scale qualitative study with interviews and/or focus groups may help us establishing general attitudes towards language teaching; the findings of this pre-study can then be used to construct items for the large-scale survey.

4.3. Measuring abstract concepts: Attitudes and beliefs

Chapter Two has introduced concepts – a category comprising several interrelated variables, as opposed to a single variable; and by means of the example of 'learner motivation', we have outlined that concepts can be notoriously difficult to measure. Unfortunately, concepts are quite common, and especially socio- and applied-linguistic research frequently uses two concepts which are problematic: *attitudes* and *beliefs*.

In Chapter Two, we have already met Giles et al.'s (1977) concept of 'Ethnolinguistic Vitality', and we have seen that this concept can be measured using three categories of variables. A few years later, Bourhis, Giles and Rosenthal (1981) expanded the framework by including the group's own, that is subjective perception, which had so far been ignored; the approach is now known as Subjective Ethnolinguistic Vitality (SEV). Crucially, an SEV as proposed by Bouhris, Giles and Rosenthal is entirely questionnaire-based. The impact this has for the questionnaire design is obvious:

> Each questionnaire item is designed to measure group member's subjective assessment of how they rate their own group relative to a salient outgroup on important vitality dimensions. (Bourhis, Giles and Rosenthal 1981: 147–8)

Bouhris, Giles and Rosenthal's original SEV questionnaire comprises 22 questions, all of which are based on either *semantic differentials* or *Likert scales*. Semantic differentials ask respondents to indicate their response along a continuum between two opposing terms (not to say antonyms), as shown in the following example from Bouhris, Giles and Rosenthal (1981: 152):

In all parts of Melbourne where the following groups live, to what extent are they in the majority or minority?

People of Greek descent

Very small minority __:__:__:__:__:___:__: very large majority

By analysing how far to the left or right they have ticked, we can quantify respondents' attitudes towards this particular item. We will look at the actual coding of questionnaire responses at the end of this chapter.

A related and equally popular instrument for measuring attitudes are Likert scales. As before, respondents are asked to indicate their opinion/attitude along a continuum of items. However, instead of using pairs of opposing adjectives, Likert scales ask respondents to indicate agreement or disagreement with a particular issue, usually on a scale of 5 or 7, depending on degree of detail required by the researcher. Likert-scale items must be statements:

Speaking more than one language is beneficial for one's career.

5-point Likert scale with 5 indicating very strong agreement

very strongly agree	5	4	3	2	1	very strongly disagree

7-point Likert scale with 7 indicating very strong disagreement

very strongly agree	1	2	3	4	5	6	7	very strongly disagree

Frequently, we find agreement/disagreement scales like the one's above used for questions such as: 'Do you think speaking a second language is useful?' Strictly speaking, these are not true Likert scales.

Likert scale or not, for the processing and interpretation of data it is crucial to understand that our scales work on at least interval level of measurement, that is, the difference between any two adjacent answer options is identical: the difference between 'strongly agree' and 'agree' is identical with the difference between 'disagree' and 'strongly disagree' (see Chapter Two).

Note that the scale provided by Bouhris et al. allows respondents to tick one of 7 boxes; similarly, our fictional Likert scales above provide 5 and 7 answer options, respectively.

This odd number gives respondents the opportunity to indicate a 'neutral' or 'balanced' opinion if they perceive it this way, but there is also a significant risk of respondents giving a neutral answer for neutrality's sake. In contrast, a scale based on even numbers will force respondents to give an answer towards either end of the scale. This does not necessarily solve the problem. In a review of literature, Ping (2005: 1) discusses the phenomenon of the *acquiescence response set*:

> This is the tendency to agree or say 'yes' to a statement regardless of the content of the statement or their [the respondents'] actual opinion.

In the worst case, the majority of our respondents in the sample tend to agree with all items, which will inevitable substantially skew our results.

In a similar vein, *extreme response styles* are characterized by respondents' tendency to select responses at the extreme end of the scales. In a large-scale project based on data collected from 19 countries, Johnson et al. (2005) concluded that general cultural behavioural patterns are reflected in response styles: roughly speaking, respondents in individualistic and high-power distance countries are more likely to give extreme responses, and less likely to give acquiescence responses (2005: 273), while acquiescence is more frequent in cultures that value conformity. For obvious reasons, our average linguistic study will probably not allow for an in-depth investigation of the culturally typical response style; yet, it is worth spending some time thinking about our potential respondents when designing measurement scales.

One way of tackling answer tendencies, and in particular acquiescence responses, is to phrase questions in opposing directions, trying to cover both positive and negative attitudes:

Learning a foreign language in primary school is beneficial for students

very strongly agree	5	4	3	2	1	very strongly disagree

Learning a foreign language in primary school harms pupils' cognitive development

very strongly agree	1	2	3	4	5	very strongly disagree

If a respondent is in favour of foreign language teaching in primary schools, he should tend towards agreement for the first, and towards disagreement for the second question. If he agrees with both, it is likely that you have a yea-sayer.

4.4. Phrasing questions

Whenever you have been lucky enough to find someone to fill in (and ultimately return!) your questionnaire, do not bore them with information overload. After all, they want to help you, so do not punish them. Asking good questions is about being concise and precise, not about showing off your skills as a novelist. Very few questions justify a summary of research history in order to make your respondents understand it.

Similarly, unlike us, most of our respondents will not be experts in the field. Very few of them will be familiar with linguistic terminology, and enquiries about the famous 'post-vocalic rhotic r' are likely to cause just as much confusion as the question whether the complex inflectional paradigm in Spanish verbal morphology justifies pro-drop. Hence, when phrasing a question, we must bear in mind the level of knowledge our respondents possess, and in the case of non-experts this level will often be surprisingly low. On a questionnaire used during fieldwork for my own research on language use within migrant groups (Rasinger 2007), I originally used the term 'native speaker' to refer to people whose first language is not English. However, in practice, it turned out that many of my Bangladeshi respondents (some of them with limited English language proficiency anyway), did not understand the term. When, in a subsequent version, I rephrased the question and used the term 'mother tongue', the problem disappeared almost instantaneously (and yes, dear fellow linguists, I *am* aware of the problems the terms '(non)-native speaker' and 'mother tongue' pose in the first instance).

All too often, we would like our questionnaires to measure something in great detail, hence requiring the respondent to give detailed responses. However, technical/linguistic aspects discussed above aside, we have to consider whether our respondents are actually able to provide information on a great level of detail: they might quite simply not know enough about a certain topic to be able to answer it.

Another common problem are overly long and, taken to the extreme, *double-barrelled questions*. Every question asked should ask about one single issue, no more, no less. If you ask your respondents 'Do you think dialect use is a sign of low intellectual ability and should be banned at schools?', you are asking two questions: first, you are interested in respondents' attitudes towards dialect use and second, whether they think the use of dialects should be banned in schools. If, in the worst case, you provide only two-answer options (yes/no), your respondent will have to decide which of the two questions to answer. And although answers are likely to correlate, you might come across the odd person who wants dialects banned in schools, but does not think they have anything to do with intellectual ability – which answer is he to give then?

Another rather simple, yet important rule for the design of questions is the avoidance of negative constructions: 'Do you think that foreign language teaching in primary schools is not a good idea?' Put simply, 'not' as a short three letter word is prone to be read over, particularly when respondents' skim over questions (like I do, most of the time!). Also, in more complex questions, the negative can cause confusion – something we want to avoid by all means.

Similarly, questions containing more than a simple subordinate construction, such as a relative clause for clarification, should be avoided:

> Do you think that recent changes in government policy regarding the introduction of foreign language learning in primary schools, in particular, but not exclusively, those located in urban centres, which was announced yesterday, are, particularly with regard to the importance of foreign language skills for later professional success, a good idea?

This may be precise, but is bound to cause confusion with at least some respondents. If you really need to include background information in a question, and you should carefully consider whether this is really necessary, refrain from syntactic complexity and use simple constructions – even though this might be hard for a linguist:

> The government has recently announced the introduction of foreign language learning in primary schools. Foreign Language teaching is first to be introduced in inner city schools. This is based on the assumption that it will aid professional success later in life. Do you think that teaching foreign languages in primary schools in a good idea?

This contains the same information, but is undoubtedly much easier to understand.

Leading questions are questions which are phrased in such a way that they prefer a particular answer option. Leading questions appear frequently in questionnaires designed by novices such as undergraduate students, especially when the student holds a strong personal opinion on the topic he or she is investigating. Even worse, they can (and are used) to influence the results. The following example is taken from the popular 1980s British comedy show *Yes, Prime Minister*. In this scene Sir Humphrey Appleby (played by the late Sir Nigel Hawthorn), the permanent secretary and a master of manipulation and obfuscation, and Bernard Woolley, the Prime Minister's Principle Private Secretary discuss how leading questions can be used to influence survey results – in this case, about the reintroduction of National Service (conscription):

> Sir Humphrey: Mr Woolley, are you worried about the number of young people without jobs?
>
> Woolley: Yes.

Sir Humphrey:	Are you worried about the rise in crime among teenagers?
Woolley:	Yes.
Sir Humphrey:	Do you think there's a lack of discipline in our comprehensive schools?
Woolley:	Yes.
Sir Humphrey:	Do you think young people welcome some authority and leadership in their lives?
Woolley:	Yes.
Sir Humphrey:	Do you think they respond to a challenge?
Woolley:	Yes.
Sir Humphrey:	Would you be in favour of reintroducing national service?
Woolley:	Oh, well, I suppose I might-
Sir Humphrey:	Yes or no.
Woolley:	Yes.
Sir Humphrey:	Of course you would, Bernard, after all you told you can't say 'no' to that.

This is, of course, an extreme example – after all, it is a comedy. It does, however, illustrate the use of leading questions brilliantly: the entire set of questions is designed in such a way that they trigger agreement; after all, who would not be worried about teenage crime and youth unemployment. 'Yes' seems to be the logical (and I use the term loosely) answer to the majority of questions. The crucial bit happens at the end: National Service is offered as a (alleged) solution to all those problems, so again, the logical answer is agreement. (Bear in mind, this is exaggerated for comic purposes: personally, I am worried about crime and unemployment but do not agree with conscription, but that is a story for another day.)

Foddy (1993), who also uses this example, highlights the issue of people's need to appear consistent, 'presumably because it is easier to operate socially if the attitudes one holds about any particular topic are consistent with one another' (Foddy 1993: 66).

Now look at how the scene continues:

Sir Humphrey:	Mr Woolley, are you worried about the danger of war?
Woolley:	Yes.
Sir Humphrey:	Are you worried about the growth of armaments?
Woolley:	Yes.

Sir Humphrey:	Do you think there's a danger in giving young people guns and teach them how to kill?
Woolley:	Yes!
Sir Humphrey:	Do you think it's wrong to force people to take up arms against their will?
Woolley:	Yes!
Sir Humphrey:	Would you oppose the reintroduction of National Service?

('The Ministerial Broadcast', *Yes, Prime Minister*, series 1, episode 2, first broadcast 16 January 1986, BBC.) This is the same phenomenon, just in a different direction: Sir Humphrey's first four questions are likely to elicit agreement, so, as a logical consequence, question 5 will do, too: how can you be opposed to forcing to take up arms against their will and, at the same time, support National Service, which, potentially, does exactly that? The entire setup forces the respondent into a particular answer; else they appear illogical or inconsistent.

Leading questions can also be much more subtle; however, can still have the effect of provoking a particular answer. For example, lexical items in a question carry several connotations, or, in the worst case, have multiple denotations. Schnell et al. (2005: 335) list 'bureaucrat' as an example: while the term originally denotes someone working in bureaucracy, it now often comes with the rather negative connotation of 'paper shuffler'; in fact, even 'bureaucracy' is nowadays perceived as administration-gone-berserk and officialism. Philosophically oriented concepts such as 'freedom' or 'liberty' are similarly problematic: what exactly are 'freedom' and 'liberty'? If you as the reader now have to think about it for a moment, you can probably also imagine that these terms are highly problematic when used for obtaining an accurate measure in a questionnaire. Discourse analysts working on political, religious and racial discourse have repeatedly used the 'freedom fighter' versus 'terrorist' example to illustrate this point: the same referent, two very different meanings (Kennedy 1999; Ganor 2002; Hall 2007).

When designing response scales based on semantic differentials, as discussed above, lexical choice is an important issue, too. I often ask students in my master's courses and workshops on research methods to come up with a set of semantic differentials indicating character traits. Along the lines, someone suggested *brave – cowardly* as one pair. Yet, others objected and argued that they perceived *brave* not quite as strong as *courageous* or even *fearless* as opposites to *cowardly* in a semantic differential. Whatever the semantically correct answer is (most dictionaries list *brave* and *courageous* as synonyms), it is clear from the example that different people perceive words differently. Again, while this is not surprising, it is something once has to consider in the questionnaire design.

Task 4.1

Try and replicate the little survey described above. Take a group of people and ask them to come up with a list of semantic differentials, for example for character traits or anything else you can think of. Then, ask them to indicate their perception of individual items, based on how strongly positive or negative they judge items on a scale from 1 to 5. Compare the differences between individual members of the group. What can you observe? If you group is very heterogeneous in terms of gender or cultural background, are these differences manifest in the rating of items?

A final issue to consider when designing individual questions is to make sure that they are unambiguous. Again, bear in mind that while we know exactly what we would like to find out, our respondents do not; and if a questions is phrased ambiguously, respondents end up answering a 'different' question from the one we intended to ask. As before, they key to solving the problem is to phrase questions as precisely as possible, so that they do not leave any room for speculation or interpretation from the side of the respondent. Sometimes, simply moving words around or replacing them with another term may help. For example, 'To what extent do you agree with the government's policy on languages today?' can have two interpretations:

1   What does a respondent think about today's policy, meaning *current* policy?

2   What is the respondents attitude *today*, right at this moment, on the policy?

For many of us, the second interpretation may sound absurd; yet, for just as many it is a reasonable way of understanding the question. So, if we are interested in attitudes to the current policy, we should simply ask about it: 'To what extent do you agree with the government's current policy on languages?' The problem of ambiguity can also be reinforced through the use of abstract nouns or (emotive) adjectives, as discussed above.

4.5. Piloting

Once a questionnaire has been designed, it is important to test whether it actually measures whatever it is supposed to measure. We may think that the questionnaire works, but nothing is worse than handing out questionnaires to respondents, only to realize afterwards that it is flawed – I do speak from experience. Piloting it, that means, running a test with only a few participants in order to detect flaws, may seem time-consuming, but will eventually save time, effort and resources when running a well-working study. In particular, the pilot study should identify any problems with question phrasing, scope of questions, knowledge of respondents, accuracy of measures used, and should give some indication about reliability and validity.

The question is, how many respondents to test a questionnaire with? For obvious reasons, the more responses you get, the easier it will be to detect problems. At the same time, the pilot is supposed to be a mere test-run, not a complete study. Fowler (2002) suggests a pilot sample of 20–50; yet, as Burton (2000) points out, particularly for student researchers with limited resources this might be difficult to achieve. I generally advise undergraduate students to try and get out at least half a dozen questionnaires, using friends, partners, housemates and family as guinea pigs, and then having a thorough and critical look at the responses they get. While this kind of pilot does obviously not provide any real data, it is a reasonably good indicator of how the questionnaire works in general, and with a bit of critical thinking one should be able to spot the most important problems. Students on a postgraduate level, be is masters or PhD, should run a thorough and proper pilot using a pilot sample that resembles their intended real sample – even though it may be smaller.

I spent most of the chapter so far discussing the various tools which we can use to measure certain aspects using questionnaires, and I have highlighted a number of mistakes that can, and frequently do, occur. These may be quite simple: if your boyfriend ticks the 'female' box in the gender question it is a good indicator that either your question is phrased not clearly enough or you should have a chat with him. Jokes aside, I have come across a (student) questionnaire which asked respondents to indicate their age from one of the following age groups:

☐ 16–20 years ☐ 21–24 ☐ 26–30

By the third look at the very latest, you will have spotted that the list excludes respondents aged 25. And while this is obviously just a simple mistake, is can turn out to be most annoying, namely if you realize it after the questionnaires have been returned.

In addition, it is worth asking someone (if not your pilot sample) to proofread the questionnaire: some respondents may be annoyed if asked about their ethnic decent instead of their ethnic descent, and a spell checker will not detect this. In the first edition of this book, I discuss a badly designed questionnaire which includes a question on 'adeguate' [sic!] car parking facilities and coins the nouns 'congestioning' and 'closurers'. On one level, this might seem amusing, but it can also put respondents off.

These are considerably simple problems and are easy to sort out. But what about more complex issues, such as the measurement of concepts or attitudes? There is a plethora of potential problems that can come up: questions can be phrased badly, be ambiguous, scales are not accurate or run into the wrong direction, we might have leading questions without noticing it and so forth. Just because we think the questionnaire is working does not mean that it actually does work. This is not unlike proofreading your own work: we can only find that many mistakes and errors in our own pieces of writing, simply because we know what is supposed to be written; a proofreader, however, will spot what actually is written. Similarly, we are often only able to see that a particular measure does not work as well as we would like it to when we try it out and use it.

4.6. Layout

We should briefly consider the physical aspects of a questionnaire. Most standard word-processing software today comes with an abundance of functions, which allow us to design a well-structured and visually appealing and clear questionnaire. Alternatively, the technically more versed may want to use desktop publishing software, such as Adobe Pagemaker, Microsoft Publisher or Quark Xpress, to name but a few.

As a general guideline, as regards layout, less is better. Unless it absolutely necessary, it is advisable to refrain from the extensive use of different fonts, colours and other gimmicks. After all, the questionnaire is a scientific tool, not a piece of art. Fonts should be plain and of a reasonable size; anything under 11 point is usually too small. The inclusion of bold or italic style may be helpful for emphasis, but should only be used sparingly.

Questions and answer options should be laid out clearly, so respondents will not have any difficulty in recognizing which answer option belongs to which question. If you use more than one column per page, make sure the sequence of question remains clear – insert some kind of visual divide between the columns if need be. When using Likert scales, multiple-choice questions or semantic differentials, it is important that is it absolutely clear which tick box belongs to which answer – a problem that is particularly common with horizontal layouts:

Strongly agree ❑ agree ❑ undecided ❑ disagree ❑ strongly disagree ❑

In this above example, respondents easily tick 'undecided' when they actually mean 'disagree' – a mistake we have to avoid at all costs! Vertical layouts usually avoid this problem, but, obviously, take up substantially more space:

- ❑ Strongly agree
- ❑ Agree
- ❑ Undecided
- ❑ Disagree
- ❑ Strongly disagree

If the questionnaire includes open questions, which ask respondents to write their opinion instead of ticking a box, enough space should be provided to do so. Be careful though: providing too much space may imply that respondents have to write a lot and will scare them off.

Right at the top, each questionnaire should have a *unique identifier*, such as a number, which will allow you later to find a particular questionnaire again and again. Imagine you are inputting data from 100 questionnaires. Right in the middle of it, the door bell rings and you leave your desk to answer it. Unfortunately, the draught you create by running towards the door in addition to the draught created by opening the door (and the already open window in your office!) blows most of the questionnaires off your desk. Without a unique identifier, it can be almost impossible to reconstruct which questionnaire you have processed already. In the worst case, you would have to start inputting data from scratch!

4.7. Number and sequence of questions

Related to the issue of questionnaire layout is the aspect of question ordering. Considerable amounts of research have focused on the impact of the sequence of questions; without going into any details, when designing the order of our questions we should bear the following in mind: generally, the order of questions should guide respondents through the questionnaire – without guiding them into a particular answer direction! As a student, I was once told that a good questionnaire is like a story, with an introduction, a middle part culminating in a 'climax' and an ending. Right at the top of the questionnaire (or on the cover sheet) should be a very short introduction, explaining what the survey is about. As before, keep it simple and avoid overly technical language: after all, the introduction should give respondents an idea of the topic. As with the phrasing of actual questions, avoid anything that is controversial or leads the respondent into a particular direction. Also, the introduction should include clear instructions as to what respondents are to do with the questionnaire after filling it in ('return it to the researcher' or 'put it into the self-addressed and stamped envelope and post it').

Simple and 'easy' questions should come first, that is, any questions which require minimal effort from the respondent should be at the beginning (age, gender, etc. are typical starter questions). Then, questions should become gradually more complex and detailed, allowing the respondent to become familiar with the topic. Questions relating to the same issue should be grouped into a particular section. That said, in particular when interested in concepts such as attitudes, it might be worth distributing questions across the entire questionnaire, so as to avoid response sets. You may want to consider splitting a block of eight questions measuring a particular attitude into two groups, and place these groups at two different places. At the end, there may be some more general questions – often these can also be open-ended ones.

Lastly, there remains the – particularly popular with students – question of how long a questionnaire should be, that is, how many questions should it involve. The answer is simple: just as many as it needs, no more, no less. At the beginning of the chapter we have discussed the importance of asking both the right questions and asking them right. As a general rule, with every question we design we should ask ourselves, it is absolutely necessary to ask it? Has its content not already been covered elsewhere? Should a previous question be rephrased to better reflect the content? What does the answer tell us, in relation to our overall research question? For example, it is usually unnecessary to ask respondents for both their current age and their year of birth. Similarly, if a respondent indicates that he lives in London, the question which country he lives in is redundant. Note, however, that this does not work the other way round – again, make sure you ask the question according to the answer you would like to know. From my own experience as a university teacher, a good quarter of questions are superfluous in questionnaires designed by less experienced researchers. Yet, there are usually considerable gaps in terms of what should be but is not asked.

4.8. Coding

The last section of this chapter discusses some basic approaches to coding questionnaire data. So far, our questionnaires are little more than a collection of questions, answer options and, once filled in, ticked boxes. In order for our questionnaires to provide useful data for analysis, we have to translate our tick boxes and answer spaces into something meaningful and analysable. And as this book is exclusively concerned with quantitative research, we need to translate our data into something we can quantitatively analyse: scores and numbers.

Variables which require respondents to fill in a number themselves are de facto self coding: if the question is 'How old are you?' and the answer is '34', we can simply transfer this answer to our software (I assume at this point that the majority of readers will refrain from conducting statistical procedures by hand). Similarly, questions like 'what is your year of birth' or 'how many children do you have?' do not need to be coded as such, as the answer is already a number which we can input directly – the coding comes with the answer.

The situation gets slightly more difficult with the question about respondents' gender. Usually, we would provide respondents with a question ('Are you . . .') and two answer options to tick from ('male' and 'female'). Unfortunately, our answer is now a word or text – inherently qualitative data. What we have to do now is to translate text into numbers, in other words: we code it. In our gender example, this is simple: we assign the number 1 to the answer 'male', and the number 2 to 'female' (or vice versa, although the former is most frequently found) and enter our data accordingly. Similarly, answers to 'yes' and 'no' questions would also coded with 1= 'yes' and 2= 'no' (or with any other 2 values, but 1 and 2 make the most sense). Remember from Chapter Two that gender is a nominal variable, that is, it is a mere label and severely limits the statistical tools we can use. A data matrix for 5 respondents (RPS) including their year of birth (YOB), current age (AGE), gender (SEX) and knowledge of a language other than the mother tongue (L2; 1=yes, 2=no) will look like Table 4.1. Note that RSP should be anonymous or replaced by pseudonyms; I have used pseudonyms here to illustrate gender coding.

The coding of other variables works accordingly: each item is assigned a particular numerical value, which we can then use for further processing. If, instead of asking for their current age, we ask respondents about which age group they belong to, each group is assigned a particular value – ideally the values should be sequential and reflect the age (see Table 4.2).

- ❐ 16–20 years → 1 (or 3, but not 2)
- ❐ 21–24 years → 2
- ❐ 25–30 years → 3 (or 1, but not 2)

TABLE 4.1 Data matrix for 5 respondents

RSP	YOB	Age	Sex	L2
Mike	1983	24	1	2
Emily	1988	19	2	1
Tony	1977	30	1	1
Ralph	1985	22	1	2
Kirsty	1983	24	2	1

TABLE 4.2 Age-group coding

RSP	Age	Age group
Mike	24	2
Emily	19	1
Tony	30	3
Ralph	22	2
Kirsty	24	2

We have to bear in mind that respondents frequently skip questions or decide, for whatever reason, not to provide an answer. However, some statistical software packages such as SPSS get easily confused if an entry is missing; yet, they allow you to specify a value that indicates that an entry is missing (see for example Field 2000). Hence, it is worth allocating a 'missing value'-value, which tells the software that a value for this variable does not exist for a particular respondent (as opposed to you having forgotten to fill in the value). At the same time, the missing value indicator should not coincide with any potential real value. For example, a missing value for 'gender' could be '3', as we naturally only have to answer options to code, and any answers other than 1 (male) and 2 (female) are impossible. However, if we define the missing value for age as 99, we will run into trouble if we come across a very old respondent. It is hence advisable to use missing values that are well outside any potential real answer. '999' usually does a good job. In our matrix, a missing value would look like Table 4.3, with Emily not providing any information about her age.

The coding of multiple-choice questions, semantic differentials and Likert (or other) scales works just like the above, by allocating a numerical value to an item or a point on the scale (if the numerical values are not already given on the questionnaire anyway) (Table 4.4).

TABLE 4.3 Age-group and gender coding

RSP	YOB	Age	Sex
Mike	1983	24	1
Emily	999	999	2
Tony	1977	30	1
Ralph	1985	22	1
Kirsty	1983	24	2

TABLE 4.4 Attitudes towards language teaching

RSP	L2 PRIM	L2 CAR
Mike	1	2
Emily	3	3
Tony	4	5
Ralph	2	1
Kirsty	1	2

'Why do you think Modern Foreign Languages should NOT be taught in primary school?' (L2PRIM)

- ● It is too difficult for children.   = 1
- ● It interferes with their first language.   = 2
- ● It is a waste of time.   = 3
- ● Any other reason.   = 4

'Speaking more than one language is beneficial for ones career.' (L2CAR)

very strongly agree	5	4	3	2	1 very strongly disagree

So, in summary, the data matrix for Mike will look like this:

RSP	Age	Age group	YOB	Sex	L2 PRIM	L2 CAR
Mike	24	2	1983	1	1	2

In other words, Mike was born in 1983 (YOB=1983) and hence is a 24-year-old (AGE=24) man (SEX=1), falls into the age group of 21–24-year olds (AGEGROUP=2), and thinks that foreign language teaching in primary school is too difficult for children (L2 PRIM=1), and he disagrees that speaking a foreign language benefits the career (L2 CAR=2).

At this point, a word of warning: in particular when coding Likert scales, it is important to ensure that questions, answers and coding scores correspond and measure what they are supposed to measure (see validity discussion in Chapter Two). For example, as explained above, for the measurement of more complex concepts, such as attitudes, we will usually use more than one question, and frequently, we will ask questions that run into opposing directions in order to avoid response sets. In our example for tackling acquiescence responses, we have used two questions to measure attitudes towards foreign language learning. The attentive reader will have spotted that the answer coding for each question is different, in that the answer scores run into opposing directions:

(1) Learning a foreign language in primary school is beneficial for students

Very strongly agree	5	4	3	2	1 Very strongly disagree

(2) Learning a foreign language in primary school harms pupils' cognitive development

Very strongly agree	1	2	3	4	5	Very strongly disagree

This is neither a mistake nor randomness: what we want to measure is how strongly someone supports language teaching in primary education. And, at the end, we would like to have data where high-overall scores indicate agreement, and low-overall scores indicate disagreement. As described above, a respondent supporting language teaching would agree with (1) but disagree with (2), while someone against it would disagree with (1) and agree with (2). In other words, respondent A (supporter) will score something like (1)=5 and (2)=4, with an according overall score of 5+4=9. Respondent B, accordingly, scores (1)=2 and (2)=1, giving him an overall score of 3. Our overall scores immediately correspond with respondents' attitudes: high score means high levels of support, and low-overall scores translate into low levels of support.

If our Likert scales for both questions were identical, respondent A would score (1)=5 and (2)=2, and B (1)=2 and (2)=5. If we look at the overall scores A gets 7 and B, well, 7 again. And this result obviously does not tell us anything about attitudes. So, it is crucial to always bear in mind what each question is supposed to do, and to construct questions, answer options and coding scheme accordingly.

4.9. A 'real' questionnaire

I have spent considerable time – an entire chapter in fact – discussing questionnaires and their design from a rather theoretical point of view. It seems about time that we look at a real questionnaire and some of the tools we have discussed (and those we are going to discuss later in this book) in some detail. And since it is difficult to come up with a linguistic topic all readers are equally familiar with, the questionnaire I have designed focuses on something we are all familiar with: this book.

As the author of this book, I am primarily concerned with three issues: first, who are the readers of the book (i.e. you); second, what do the readers think of the book; and third, what effect has the book had on your understanding of quantitative methods. The questionnaire is designed to provide some insights into all of these questions. This questionnaire is far from perfect; in fact, I have included some minor (or possibly major!) flaws in order to support the arguments made so far. So let's have a closer look at it (note: it is helpful if you read and try to complete the questionnaire first, and then read the discussion).

We start with a brief look at the layout first: apart from the first two questions, which appear next to each other, all questions are listed in one column and are adequately numbered. This obviously takes up space but has the advantage of being clearly arranged and avoids confusion. Also, when designing this questionnaire I was aware that the eventual paper format of the book will be smaller than the standard A4 – a two columns design and smaller font size combined with a smaller overall page format would have had an adverse effect on clarity. In 'real' life, print-runs with several hundred questionnaires are expensive, so it is well worth thinking about these issues in advance.

Right in the top right corner, you will find the unique identifier for the questionnaire ('00001'). Remember to include one on any questionnaire you develop as they are an enormous help once you get to the data entry stage. This is followed by a brief introduction, which tells the respondents what the questionnaire is about and what to do with it after completion. For most basic questionnaires, such as this one, this is plenty of information, and we do not need to include any more, as this may confuse the respondent. It is up to you whether you put the introduction in a box, but some kind of visual distinction between the introduction and the actual questions is usually a good thing.

The introduction is followed by section A of the questionnaire. If you read it, you will see that this section is primarily concerned with the reader. Note: I have labelled this section 'A' for explanation purposes in this book only. In a 'real' questionnaire this may cause confusion. Section A consists of eight questions aimed at providing as much detail about the readership as possible within the scope of this survey. Questions 1 and 2 are questions which should be included in every questionnaire: question 2 allows us to detect any differences between genders, which is always useful information. It is also an 'easy' question which does not require any effort from the respondent. Note that in question 1 I specifically ask for the year of birth, not the current age – this will allows us to detect potential cohort effects (see Chapter Three). Since date of birth is a 'static' measure (which never changes, unlike age), we may, for example, make inferences about the differences in previous knowledge between different cohorts: maybe readers born before a certain year have a better knowledge of quantitative methods than those born after that year.

Questions 3, 4, 5 and 6 provide us with additional information about the respondents. Particularly from a marketing point of view, it is useful to know what the primary market for the book is. Note that the answer options provided in 3, 4 and 6 are not randomly chosen but are based on our expectations and previous research: it is unlikely that a student of nuclear physics will buy a book which is aimed – clearly visible from the title – at linguists. At the same time, the 'other' option allows us to detect anything we did not expect. In question 6, we have not included the 'other' option, as the four options given should suffice: readers bought the book because they need it for their studies (options 1 and 2), because they need to improve their knowledge of quantitative methods for a project (question 3), or because they have a general interest in the topic. All four answer options have been phrased rather broadly, so one of them should apply; if none of them applies, it is unclear why the book was bought in the first place. There is one problem with question 6: it implies that the reader who is completing the questionnaire has actually *bought* the book; hence, it cannot capture instances where a reader was *given* the book, for example as a present, in which case none of these options necessarily apply. This is an inaccuracy which, in a real-life survey, we would have to address – the easiest way is to include another 'other' option.

Questions 7 (a) and (b), the last in this section, finish our survey of the readership; yet, it is also the first question that provides us with information about the book: while question 7(a) collects information about previous knowledge, (b) provides data on how knowledge has changed during the reading process. It is a long way to go before we could argue that the book has a *causal* impact on readers' knowledge, but this gives us a first idea. Question 7 is particularly interesting when analysed in conjunction to question 6: if in 6 a respondent has chosen one of the last two options, and in question 7 indicates an improvement of knowledge, the argument that improvement in knowledge is linked to reading the book is strengthened. If in question 6 the answer is 1 or 2, it may be the course, not the book that has caused the change. So, with two simple questions we can get a lot more information than provided by the questions individually, but bear in mind that 'information' does not mean 'statistically sound proof'.

We have seen that the 8 questions in section A can provide us with substantial information about the readers of this book. Most importantly, not only has each question been phrased to address one particular issue, but individual questions also interlink: using appropriate statistical methods (as discussed in the second part of this book), and given a sample of a reasonable size, we may use this section to show that, having read the book, the perceived knowledge of quantitative methods of female undergraduate students of linguistics improves more so than that of their male counterparts'. That is a lot of information for 8 questions! Here is a brief guideline as to how to perform this basic analysis.

1   Code and input all your data into a spreadsheet software. Enter them in such a way that variables (i.e. the individual questions) are displayed in columns, and individual cases (i.e. respondents) in rows. Code variables in such a way that positive attitudes/ opinions are assigned high numerical values, and negative opinions low numerical values: for questions 7(a) and (b), with 5 answer options, 'very good knowledge' equals 5, 'no knowledge' equals 1. Code questions 2, 3, 4 and 6 by simply numbering them – they are nominal variables, that is, only act as a descriptive label of a particular group. They will ultimately help us to break down (or filter) our data into smaller chunks.

2   Question 7 (a) and (b) provide information about readers' (perceived) knowledge at 2 points in time: pre- and post-reading. In a separate column, calculate the difference in knowledge. The maximum difference we can obtain is 4 (change from no knowledge to very good knowledge: 5–1=4), the minimum difference is zero (no change at all).

(See Chapter Five for how to calculate sums and differences.)

We may get a matrix looking like Table 4.5.

3   In Excel, use the 'Filter' option to filter your data so you get all undergraduate linguistic students only. In the Menu bar, go to 'Data' > 'Filter', choose 'Auto filter' and select the appropriate options.

Our filtered data (only undergraduate linguistic students) looks like Table 4.6.

4   Conduct a t-test to test the difference between male and female respondents, based on the filtered data.

(See Chapter Eight for how to perform a t-test.)

5   If the t-test shows a difference in knowledge change between male and female respondents, our hypothesis that having read the book, female undergraduate linguistic students' knowledge improved more than their male counterparts' knowledge.

TABLE 4.5 Fictional data set for questionnaire

RSP	Sex	Job	Subject	Pre	Post	Diff
Alf	1	1	2	3	4	1
Bert	1	1	1	3	4	1
Charlie	2	2	1	1	5	4
Dolly	2	1	3	2	4	2
Emily	2	1	1	1	4	3
Fred	1	2	1	3	5	2
Gemma	2	1	1	1	3	2
Harold	1	1	1	2	2	0
Ivan	1	1	1	3	3	0
Juliet	2	1	1	1	2	1

TABLE 4.6 Filtered data set for questionnaire

RSP	Sex	Job	Subject	Pre	Post	Diff
Bert	1	1	1	3	4	1
Harold	1	1	1	2	2	0
Ivan	1	1	1	3	3	0
Emily	2	1	1	1	4	3
Gemma	2	1	1	1	3	2
Juliet	2	1	1	1	2	1

Section B of the questionnaire focuses on the book itself. It consists of two main questions: question 8 used 5-point Likert scales to measure respondents' opinion of the book; question 9 uses semantic differentials based on a 5-point scale. In both questions, high numerical values correspond to positive, low numerical values to negative attitudes. Also, all answer options have a positive phrasing: 'well' (a), 'help' (b), 'right' (c) and so forth. This is mainly because of the limited length of the questionnaire: in a longer version, it would be advisable to ask questions with an inverted rating, too, as to avoid response sets (see discussion above). The one-directional character here is not necessarily a bad thing, as long as we are aware of the potential problem. It is a trade-off between accuracy and resources (here: length) available. In terms of data processing, an overall positive attitude towards the book measured in question 8 will result in a high numerical value (with a maximum possible score of 5×5=25 for 5 'total agreement' answers), while a low attitude is reflected by a low-overall score (to a minimum of 5 for 5 'total disagreement' answers).

Note again how the individual questions are related to each other, and also show links to the previous section: 8b and 8e are directly related as they both aim at measuring knowledge improvement. Yet, the focus of 8b is the book, while the focus of 8e is the respondent. Note also that 8e relates back to question 7; in fact, 8e and 5 measure the same thing, namely change in knowledge. However, 7 is more accurate as it provides detailed information about both pre- and post-reading knowledge, while 8 just shows potential change. So, is question 8 redundant? At the first look, yes. Why ask the same question twice? However, 8 can act as an internal reliability and validity check: for example, a respondent may not indicate a change in knowledge in question 7, but then indicates a moderate improvement in 8. This could be a problem related to the respondent, or an issue related to the questionnaire: the items in question 7 are comparatively broad, and we might imagine a respondent who has 'some knowledge' before reading the book, and gains more knowledge through reading the book, but is still far from confident enough to say he has 'good knowledge' afterwards. We take up this issue of checking validity and reliability at the end of Chapter Seven, when we discuss Pearson's correlation coefficient as a measure.

There is no 'right' or 'wrong' way of handling this problem, and in this particular example questionnaire, it does not really matter. In a longer and more complex survey, this would need to be addressed though: through rephrasing the questions or answer items, or through looking back at evaluative research, for example, focus groups, etc.

The final question is the only open-ended one in the questionnaire. The reason is simple: it is almost impossible to provide a complete set of all possible answers respondents might give us. At the very end, we would always have to offer an 'other' category, too. A much better solution to cover the breadth of possible answers is to use an open-ended question. This does not mean that we cannot perform a quantitative analysis: it is more than likely that answers fall into particular categories, such as 'content', 'layout' or 'use of examples'. Once individual answers have been categorized, we can then perform a quantitative analysis.

In summary, we have seen that even a short and basic questionnaire can give us reasonably good insights into our research questions. Yet, it is obviously only a snapshot – for a more detailed analysis we would have to modify and extend it.

Sample Questionnaire

00001

> Thank you for buying 'Quantitative Research in Linguistics: An Introduction'. We hope you have enjoyed reading this book. In order to improve subsequent editions, we would like to you ask for your opinion. Information collected by this questionnaire will be treated confidentially. Please complete this questionnaire and return it to:
>
> Dr Sebastian Rasinger, Anglia Ruskin University, Department of English, Communication, Film and Media, Cambridge CB1 1PT, UK.

A

(1)   Your date of birth _____   (2)   Are you: male   ❏
                                                              female   ❏

(3)   Are you: an undergraduate student   ❏
                 a postgraduate student   ❏
                 Faculty/Academic   ❏
                 Other   ❏   please specify: _____

(4)   What subject area are you primarily studying/working in?
      ❏   Linguistics
      ❏   Modern Foreign Languages
      ❏   Sociology
      ❏   Psychology
      ❏   Other   please specify: _____

(5)   How many years have you been studying/working in this subject area?
      _____ years.

(6)   Why have you bought this book?
      ❏   It is core reading for my course.
      ❏   It is additional reading for my course.
      ❏   I need to use quantitative methods for a project.
      ❏   I am interested in the topic.

(7)   How would you rate your knowledge of quantitative methods:
      (a)   Before reading the book: (b)   After reading the book
            ❏   Very good knowledge   ❏   Very good knowledge
            ❏   Good knowledge   ❏   Good knowledge
            ❏   Some knowledge   ❏   Some knowledge
            ❏   Little knowledge   ❏   Little knowledge
            ❏   No knowledge   ❏   No knowledge

B

(8) Please indicate your agreement/disagreement with the following statements on a scale from 1 to 5, whereby 5 indicates total agreement and 1 indicates total disagreement.

(a)	The book is well written.	5	4	3	2	1
(b)	The book helped me to understand quantitative methods.	5	4	3	2	1
(c)	The scope of the book was right.	5	4	3	2	1
(d)	Examples helped me to understand the methods discussed.	5	4	3	2	1
(e)	My knowledge of quantitative methods has improved.	5	4	3	2	1

(9) On the following scales, please circle the answer that best reflects your opinion.

(a) I found the book . . .

5	4	3	2	1
Very helpful				Not helpful at all

(b) Having read the book I feel . . .

5	4	3	2	1
Very confident				Not confident at all

(c) The topics in this book should be discussed . . .

5	4	3	2	1
In much more detail				Much more superficially

(10) How, in your opinion, could the book be improved?

_____

_____

_____

Thank you for completing this questionnaire.
Now please send it to the address provided at the top.

4.10. Summary: Questionnaires

Despite the problems we have discussed in this chapter, questionnaires bear the enormous advantage of generating comparatively large amounts of high-quality data with little effort once the questionnaire exists. However, we have also seen that designing a good questionnaire requires much thought and planning. It is important that the research questions asked, the hypotheses made and the questionnaire used to answer them (and methodology in general for that matter) form a coherent unit, and there are situations in linguistic research where questionnaires quite simply will not do the job. Take, for example, a study that quantitatively investigates changes in pronunciation patterns. One way of investigating this is by means of a questionnaire, asking respondents whether they produced a particular word one way or the other. However, this will tell us very little about the extent to which a particular pronunciation is actually *used*. Recordings of real-speech data would be a much more appropriate method.

PART ONE

Further reading

General reading

There has been an explosion of titles on research methods in linguistics over the last few years, some with a quantitative, other with a qualitative methods, but many with a focus on both.

Litosseliti, Lia. (2009), *Research Methods in Linguistics*. London: Continuum.
An edited volume published in the same series as this book, provides a good overview of the different methodological approaches commonly used in linguistics.

Wei, Li and Melissa G. Moyer (2008), *The Blackwell Guide to Research Methods in Bilingualism and Multilingualism*. Malden, Oxford: Blackwell.
At first sight not very different from the Litosseliti volume, but, as the title implies, focuses exclusively on methods in bilingual/multilingual research.

Macaulay, Ronald K. S. (2009), *Quantitative Methods in Sociolinguistics*.
Houndmills, Basingstoke New York: Palgrave Macmillan.
Slim little book outlining the most seminal variationist (quantitative) pieces of sociolinguistic research. It is not detailed nor very 'deep' but nevertheless an excellent intro.

Tagliamonte, Sali (2006), *Analysing Sociolinguistic Variation*. Cambridge: Cambridge University Press.
On the other end of the spectrum from Macaulay: this is a comprehensive discussion of variationist sociolinguistic methods, including a detailed discussion of the VABRUL software.

On survey research/questionnaires

Foddy, William (1993), *Constructing Questions for Interviews and Questionnaires: Theory and Practice in Social Research*. Cambridge: Cambridge University Press.

> An entire book on how to develop questions. Looks quite daunting at first sight but is very comprehensive and includes a lot of interesting discussion on the theoretical background, too.

Marsden, Peter V. and James D. Wright, eds (2010), *Handbook of Survey Research*. 2nd ed. Bingley: Emerald Group Pub.

> A 900-page volume on survey research that leaves little to add to. It is a handbook, so not really good for those looking for a quick and basic intro, but a very useful resource for those writing methodology chapters for PhD theses etc.

On ethics

Oliver, Paul (2010), *The Student's Guide to Research Ethics*. 2nd ed. Maidenhead: Open University Press.

> One of the few interesting and readable introductions on research ethics aimed at, unsurprisingly, student researchers. A successful attempt to take the fear aspect out of ethics.

Hammersley, Michael and Anna Traianou (2012), *Ethics in Qualitative Research: Controversies and Contexts*. London, SAGE.

> Another good intro, which gives both background and practical advice. Yes, it says 'qualitative research' in the title, but a lot is obviously also applicable to quantitative.

On project management

Burke, Rory (2010), *Fundamentals of Project Management: Tools and Techniques*. Ringwood: Burke.

> A good general introduction to project management but with a strong industry focus, so it is slightly difficult to transfer it into an academic context.

Lock, Dennis (2007), *Project Management*. Aldershot: Gower.

> Similar to the Burke book but included a brief discussion of academic research projects at the beginning.

PART TWO

CHAPTER FIVE

A first glimpse at data

Key words: absolute and relative frequency – bar charts – cumulative frequencies – classes – line charts – percentages – pie charts – scatter-plots – sums

So far, we have discussed some of the basic concepts and methods of quantitative research methods. At this point, readers should be able to plan a basic quantitative research project (Chapter Two), design it appropriately (Chapter Three), and, in case of a questionnaire-based survey, develop a questionnaire and code the data (Chapter Four). So, in theory, you should now sit in front of your computer with a pile of coded data in front of you. In this chapter, we will look at how to carry out a very basic evaluation of our data. The chapter will introduce readers to:

- calculating and interpreting absolute and relative frequencies,
- plotting and interpreting different types of graphs.

There comes the point of no return in any quantitative project: data has been collected, coded and entered into our spreadsheet software. We are ready to go.

We must – finally – come to one of the things most dreaded by many language researchers: we are going to look at – deep breath – statistics and some basic maths.

To help us overcome our inherent fear of numbers, and to make it sound familiar, we will use one of the first and probably most significant works in modern sociolinguistics: William Labov's 1970s studies in the Black English Vernacular (Labov 1972, 1977), a detailed description of the vernacular used by black speakers in inner-city areas in the United States, including most linguistic sub-disciplines from phonology, over morphosyntactic structures, to discourse patterns. One of the many features of the BEV

TABLE 5.1 Consonant cluster use

Consonant Cluster	BF simplified	BF total	AO simplified	AO total
/-st/	29	37	18	23
/-ft/	7	9	0	2
/-nt/	8	16	14	29
/-nd/	8	14	8	14
/-ld/	8	15	2	4
/-zd/	5	8	3	4
/-md/	2	3	0	1
other	4	4	1	4
TOTAL	71	106	46	81

Source: Adapted from Labov (1972: 16).

identified by Labov was the simplification of consonant clusters involving /d/ and /t/ in casual speech. Table 5.1 illustrates the distribution of cluster-usage of two New Yorkers: BF, a black working-class man, and AO, a white man. Table 5.1 shows the number of simplified clusters, compared to the total use of the clusters.

5.1. Taking it easy: Sums

I have – obviously – already done the first step in analysing the data, by putting the sums at the bottom of each column ('total'). While this is not strictly speaking statistical analysis, sums usually give us some idea about what is going on. Without further analysis, we can immediately see that there are more simplified clusters in BF's speech: 71 simplified clusters as opposed to only 46 simplified clusters AO produces. In the next section, I will issue a detailed warning as to why this result is problematic, though!

Doing statistics using Excel: Sums

*Please note: Excel instructions throughout this book are based on language settings that use a full stop to indicate decimals – such as English. If it is customary in your language to indicate decimals with a comma (i.e. '2,5' instead of '2.5'), you need to replace the commas given in the Excel formulae here with a semicolon.

*Doing sums using the Microsoft Excel spreadsheet software is dead-easy, although other programmes provide the same or very similar features. To do sums in Excel, select the cell in which you want the sum to be displayed (the 'target cell'; in the table above, use the cell at the bottom of each column) and click the 'Auto-Sum' icon on the tool-bar, which looks like the Greek letter Σ ('sigma'). Excel will automatically add up the values in all the cells above our target cell, until it comes to an empty cell. Alternatively, navigate to the formula via the 'Insert' menu, then 'Function' as choose 'Sum'.

If you want to add up values from different cells, you can select these by highlighting them the usual way, and pressing 'enter'. You do the same if you don't want the result to be displayed in a cell adjacent to your data.

To enter the formula manually, type '=' followed by the cells you want to add up, with a '+' sign in between. For example,

$$= A1 + A2 + C5 + F7$$

will give you the sum of the values in the cells A1, A2, C5 and F7.

(See companion website for a short clip on basic arithmetic operations in Excel.)

Task 5.1

Using a spreadsheet software, a calculator, or just your brain, calculate the sums for each cluster (i.e. each row). What do these results tell us? Are they useful? Why? What is problematic?

5.2. Absolute and relative frequencies

The table above with its sums at the end of each column looks like a helpful tool for making statements about consonant cluster simplification for the two speakers. Looking at it again, though, we realize that something is rather odd about it. Yes, BF does simplify more clusters than AO (71 compared to 46), but then, while there are 106 clusters in BF's data, Labov only found 81 clusters in the speech produced by AO. So, if we think about it for a second or two, it should become obvious that the comparison is somewhat unfair and our conclusions skewed and premature. What we need is some kind of standardization, a proper basis to compare the results.

Whenever we simply count something (consonant clusters in speech, students in a class, pages in a book), the number we obtain is the *absolute frequency* – the result of the mere counting. The numbers displayed in Table 5.1 are the absolute frequencies. That is, they present, in absolute numbers, the occurrences with which each cluster was produced. In other words, what Labov did was to count *how often* and *how* BF and AO produced a certain cluster. For example, in BF's data, /-st/ occurs 37 times, of which 29 occurrences are simplified; AO produces 18 simplified /-st/ in 23 total occurrences.

While the absolute frequencies can indeed be useful to some extent, if we want to compare the two speakers we need some sort of comparable measure. What we really need to know is how often a certain cluster is simplified in a fixed number of occurrences. This leads us to the *relative frequencies* (rf). As the term implies, the relative frequency indicates how often something occurs relative to something else. In our example, we want to know how often the simplified version occurs in relation to *all* instances of a particular cluster being produced, for example, how many /-st/ clusters are simplified out of *all* /-st/ clusters found in the data.

The relative frequency for our example is the quotient of simplified cluster over all clusters, that is, we divide the number (or absolute frequency) of simplified clusters by the number of all clusters:

$$rf = \frac{\text{Simplified clusters}}{\text{All clusters}}$$

$$rf = \frac{29}{37} = 0.7834$$

The relative frequency tells us that in every cluster we find 0.78 simplified clusters – this is somewhat abstract. However, if we multiply the result by 100, we obtain the percentage.

$$0.7834 \times 100 = 78.34\%$$

So, for /-st/ we can say that 78% of all /-st/ clusters produced by BF are simplified; coincidentally, the relative frequency for AO is almost identical with 0.7861 (78.61%). To refresh our knowledge of Latin, 'per cent' comes from the Latin 'per cento' – literally meaning 'in every hundred'. So 78% simplification means that 78 in every 100 clusters are simplified. And because the relative frequency is standardized, as it is based on 100, we can easily and reliably compare different percentages – unlike the problem we had with the absolute frequencies.

Task 5.2

Calculate the relative frequency for all clusters and both speakers, including the total scores. What can we say?

If you have done the last task, you will have (hopefully!) found that overall (looking at the TOTAL row), BF simplifies about 67% of all consonant clusters analysed by Labov, while AO only showed simplification in around 57%:

$$\text{rf(BF)} = \frac{71}{106} = 0.67 \times 100 = 67\%$$

$$\text{rf(AO)} = \frac{46}{81} = 0.57 \times 100 = 57\%$$

Now we have a more reliable figure to work with, as it allows us to easily and directly compare the results: for both respondents we now know how many out of 100 clusters are produced simplified; and this works even though we do not even have 100 clusters for AO. Nevertheless, as we will see in subsequent chapters, we should not trust this result unconditionally. But for the moment, it does the job very well.

When talking about relative frequencies it is important to distinguish between percentages and *percentage points*: percentage refers to the relative frequency, as described above. Percentage points refer to the difference between two relative frequencies. It is important to understand this concept. For example, imagine that in 2006, 80% of 100 students on an EFL course pass the course with a 'good' mark. In 2007, the number of students who pass with this mark is only 70% (i.e., 70 students). That is, we have a decrease of 10 *percentage points* – not 10%! If the rate had decreased by 10%, we would calculate:

$$10\% \text{ of } 80 \text{ students: } 80 \times 0.1 = 8$$

That is, a decrease by 10% would mean that the number of students finishing the course with 'good' only decreases by 8 students, not by 10. Analogously, in the Labovian example above, the interpretation is that the difference between AO's and BF's simplification is 10 percentage points – not 10%! I hope it is obvious that a mix-up in terminology can lead to considerable confusion and misinterpretation when reporting results.

A tool very similar to relative frequencies, and one that is often wrongly, if at all, used, are *ratios*. A ratio indicates how many of X there are in relation to Y; in other words, we compare the values of two items. In our example, we may want to now know the ratio of simplified clusters between BF and AO.

$$\text{Ratio} = \frac{\text{Frequency of simplified clusters AO}}{\text{Frequency of simplified clusters BF}} = \frac{46}{71}$$

In other words, for every 71 simplified clusters BF produces, we find 46 simplified clusters produced by AO (and vice versa). Yet more simplified, if we actually calculate the ratio, that is, divide 71 by 46, we find that the ration is approximately 1 to 1.5: for every simplified cluster of AO we find 1.5 simplified clusters for BF:

$$\text{Ratio} = \frac{71}{46} = 1.54$$

It is important to understand that relative frequency/percentage and ratios are different things, even though they are calculated in similar ways: percentage allows us to compare two absolute frequencies with relation to 100, while ratios give us the relations of two absolute frequencies with each other.

With comparatively little effort and minimal mathematical skills, we now have a rather good overview of what our data looks like:

● how many items or cases are there in any category, or for any respondent (sums, absolute frequencies),

● how many items/cases are there in relation to the entire sample/ category (relative frequencies),

● how categories behave in comparison to each other (ratio).

QUICK FIX

- Absolute frequency: the number based on simply counting things.
- Relative frequency: absolute frequency of a specific event/outcome divided by absolute frequency of all events/outcomes.
- Percentage: relative frequency multiplied by 100.
- Ratio: quotient of event X over event Y.

You may remember that in Chapter Two when discussing the differences between quantitative and qualitative research, I wrote that quantitative (or statistical) methods require comparatively large amounts of data to work properly. Now that we have discussed our first statistical tools, we should have a closer look at this. In the Labov example, we have seen that 71 out of 106 of BF's consonant clusters are produced in a simplified manner, or, in terms of relative frequency, $\frac{71}{106} = 66.98\%$ of all clusters are simplified. Imagine now that our data only contained 10 consonant clusters. Because a cluster can only be either simplified or not (i.e. it is a discrete variable), we can only have an integer as the number of simplified clusters: 1, 2, 3, 4, etc., but not 6.5 simplified clusters. If we now calculate the relative frequencies, all we obtain are percentages which are multiples of 10: 10%, 20%, 30% etc:

$$\frac{2 \text{ simplified clusters}}{10 \text{ clusters overall}} = 20\%, \frac{6 \text{ simplified clusters}}{10 \text{ clusters overall}} = 60\%$$

and so forth.

In other words, every single simplified cluster will contribute 10 percentage points to the relative frequency: 1 simplification in 10 clusters means 10% simplification, but 2 out of 10 means 20% already – that is one-fifth! That is, we do not get a very accurate picture of what is going on. Compare this to the original example where we had 106 clusters: if 1 cluster out of the 106 is simplified, the relative frequency of simplified clusters is:

$$\frac{1 \text{ simplified clusters}}{106 \text{ clusters overall}} = 0.94\%$$

With two simplified clusters we get, accordingly, a relative frequency of 1.89%, with 4, we get rf=3.77% and so forth. That is, we move in much smaller steps, and the result we get is much more detailed.

The impact a small sample size has on relative frequencies immense, and it can be misleading and result in the wrong kind of exaggerated interpretation of data. A reasonably large sample size is therefore important for the interpretation of any quantitative result – the smaller the sample, the less reliable and valid it our result. We will pick up this issue at a later point again.

5.3. Classes, width and cumulative frequencies

Our adventures into the world of quantitative analysis so far have provided us with some cheap and cheerful tools for data analysis. Frequencies, both absolute and relative, should give us some idea of what is going on in our data set. Yet, particularly when we are working with large samples, our data can look somewhat chaotic and intimidating, and often it is worth, if not necessary, to do some tidy up work in order to get something substantial out of it. Imagine we are auditing student numbers on 20 undergraduate courses, and for the last academic year, we get the following distribution of student numbers per course:

12	14	19	18	15	15	18	17	20	27
22	23	22	21	33	28	14	18	16	13

It is obvious that a data matrix like this is not particularly helpful. If nothing else, we need to bring our data in some kind of order, which will then allow us to make some statements. The easiest thing to do is to group our data into larger categories, or classes, such as small, medium and large courses. We can then see how many of our courses are small, medium or large in terms of student numbers.

In a first step, we have to decide on the number of *non-overlapping classes* we want or need. Since we have 20 cases, it seems reasonable to divide them into 5 classes (very small, small, medium, large, huge). The trick is to get it right: the more classes we have, the more chaotic and less good an overview we will get; the fewer classes, the less detail we obtain. At the very end, it is up to our judgement of what we need and want.

Second, we need to determine the *width of each class*. For this, we subtract the smallest value in our data from the highest value, and divide the result by the number of classes we like to use:

$$\text{Approx. class width} = \frac{\text{Largest data value} - \text{Smallest data value}}{\text{Number of classes}}$$

In our case, the approximate class width is:

$$\text{Class width} = \frac{\text{Largest data value} - \text{Smallest data value}}{\text{Number of classes}} = \frac{33 - 12}{5} = 4.2$$

Since a width of 4.2 is a pain to work with (and rather odd as there are no 0.2 students – students are discrete entities!), we decide on a class width of 5.

Third, we have to set the *class limits*, that is, the lowest and highest boundaries for each class. Note that classes *must not* overlap – each value must belong to only one class! For our example, we set the following class boundaries, based on a class width of 5, as just discussed:

Very small	10–14 students
Small	15–19 students
Medium	20–24 students
Large	25–29 students
Very large	30–34 students

The rest is easy: we simply put our values into the class they belong into, and then get an overview of how many courses are of which category.

TABLE 5.2 Frequency table

Size	Class interval	f	rf	crf
Very small	10–14	4	0.20	0.20
Small	15–19	8	0.40	0.60
Medium	20–24	5	0.25	0.85
Large	25–29	2	0.10	0.95
Very large	30–34	1	0.05	1
Total		20	1	

Task 5.3

Finish the example discussed so far by constructing a table which indicates course size using the five classes.

Task 5.4

Using the table you have just constructed, calculate the relative frequency for each class.

If everything went to plan, your table should look like Table 5.2. f stands for absolute frequency, rf for relative frequency. Please ignore the crf column at the right end for a moment.

Doing statistics using Excel: Frequencies

I assume most of you found constructing the frequency table tedious, especially the part where you had to count the frequencies of individual classes. Luckily, Excel can do this for us:

1. In column A, enter your data, each value into one cell.
2. In column B, enter what is called the 'bins array': this is nothing but the *upper* limit of each class. In our example, these would be 14, 19, 24, 29 and 34. Again, each in its own cell.
3. In column C, next to the bins array in column B, highlight as many cells as there are in the bins array. For example, if your bins array is in cells B1 to B5, highlight C1 to C5.
4. With C1:C5 highlighted, enter the following equation:
   =frequency(DATA, bins_array), whereby DATA is our data, for example A1:A20, and bins_array is, well, the bins array, here B1:B5)

5. Press Control-Shift-Enter – just Enter will not work!

6. In the highlighted area in column C we should now have the frequencies for each class.

If you are struggling with the equation, follow steps 1 to 3 and then go to Insert, Function, and use the equation wizard.

(To see how to construct a frequency table in Excel, see the clip on the companion website.)

It should be obvious that our processed data is much more useful than the raw data presented at the beginning of this section. Table 5.2 allows us to make concrete statements, such as '40 per cent of our courses are small, that is, have between 15 and 19 students'. As before, working with numbers and figures does not have to be scary. It is little things which can make our lives as researchers much easier.

You have probably spotted that I have cunningly inserted another column into Table 5.2, which I labelled 'crf'. This column represents the *cumulative relative frequencies*. Cumulative frequencies are nothing but the running total of frequencies across all classes. In other words, we subsequently add up the frequencies (absolute or relative) of each class. If we look at the crf column in Table 5.2, we can see that the first cumulative relative frequency value is identical to the 'normal' relative frequency value for the 'very small' class. However, moving down one row into the 'small group' class, the crf is 0.6: the sum of relative frequencies of both 'very small' (rf=0.2) and 'small group' (rf=0.4) class. So what does the cumulative frequency tell us? As a reminder, the rf for the first group tells us that 0.2 (or 20%) of our courses have between 10 and 14 students; 0.4 (40%) of our courses have between 15 and 19 students. The crf for the two groups of crf=0.6 indicates that 60% of all our courses have between 10 and 19 students. We could also say that 60% of all our courses have fewer than 20 students – it all depends on what story we would like our statistic to tell. Accordingly, the next crf is 0.85: 85% of our courses have fewer than 25 students (or between 10 and 24 students – depending on how we argue).

The last comment is an important one: even with simple tools such as cumulative frequencies, we can get our data to 'say' what we want it to. For example, facing increasing financial pressure, many higher education institutions now take a very close look at whether a particular course is financially viable and introduce minimum student numbers. Let's assume we set our 'viable' student number for a course at 20. With a Table such as 5.2, one can easily argue that 60% of courses do not meet this target – pretty bad in times of tight finances.

However, we all know that large student numbers on a course have a negative effect on the quality of teaching and learning. Let's take a look at

TABLE 5.3 Inverted frequency table

Size	Class interval	rf	crf
Very large	30–34	0.05	0.05
Large	25–29	0.10	0.15
Medium	20–24	0.25	0.40
Small	15–19	0.40	0.80
Very small	10–14	0.20	1

Table 5.3. All we have done is to invert the table, putting the 'very large' class on top, and recalculate the cumulative relative frequencies. Now we can, just as easily, argue that 40% of courses already have 20 students or more; moreover, 15% have even more than 25 students – surely this has a negative impact on teaching quality.

Yet, both arguments are constructed from the same data. When Huff (1991) describes 'How to lie with statistics', it may sound overly dramatic. Fact is, however, that the presentation of data plays a crucial role in the argument we construct from it.

Before we move on to the next section of this chapter, let's use our course size example for a last time. This time, we would like to class our data in three groups: small, medium and large.

Task 5.5

Construct a frequency table for the course size example, using three classes.

As in the previous calculation, our minimum and maximum values are 12 and 33, but this time the class width is:

$$\text{Class width} = \frac{\text{Largest data value} - \text{Smallest data value}}{\text{Number of classes}} = \frac{33 - 12}{3} = 7$$

Accordingly, our class intervals are:

Small	12–19
Medium	20–26
Large	27–33

TABLE 5.4 Frequency table with four classes

Size	Interval	f	rf	crf
Small	12–19	12	0.6	0.6
Medium	20–26	5	0.25	0.85
Large	27–33	3	0.15	1
		20	100	

And, finally, our frequency table should look like Table 5.4:

Even though it is based on the same data as Tables 5.2 and 5.3, we can use 5.4 to yet again spin a slightly different story, particularly when we only refer to the labels: now, 60% of our courses are 'small' and 85 per cent of them are of medium size or smaller – even though the maximum permissible size for 'medium' is a whopping 26 students! Similarly, if we invert the table as we did before, 40 per cent of our courses (15+25=40) are medium sized or larger. I would go as far and argue that just by playing around with class numbers and widths, we could support as many arguments as we could think of – all based on one and the same data set! It may take you some time to become fully familiar how the presentation of data influences the way we can develop our arguments, but it is a valuable tool you should take on board – either when constructing your own argument, or deconstructing others'.

Task 5.6

Familiarize yourself with the presentation of data: using the data set discussed in this chapter, try and manipulate class widths and numbers. Recalculate the cumulative frequencies. Think of arguments your new presentation(s) can support.

5.4. Visualize: Graphs and charts

Creating a table is usual a first good step towards a thorough data analysis: data is presented in a clearly laid-out way; and even basic software allows us to sort and filter our data in whatever way we like (if you are unfamiliar with how to sort/filter data, most software should have an in-build help function, to which I refer you here). Yet, sometimes we need something even more visual than tables: graphs or charts.

Graphs and charts often suffer a fate similar to that of questionnaires (see Chapter Four): they are often overused and ill-designed. While modern software offers the chance to create all sorts of fancy graphs in flash colours and extravagant shapes and forms, the information content of many graphs is poor if not non-existent. In essence, we can apply the same guidelines we use for questionnaires: first, do we really need a graph/chart, and second, what *exactly* is it supposed to tell us and our readers? The first question is comparatively easy to answer: a graph should be used to *complement* and *support* whatever argument we make. As such, a graph should never be on its own, that is, without an explanation. A common mistake found in the work of student researchers is that their essays and dissertations include dozens of elaborate graphs, but lack even the most basic explanation as to what the graphs tell us. However, a graph should never be on its own and uncommented, but should be included in and part of the overall argument. This also means that any graph we include should also come with a brief introduction in order to tell readers what it actually displays.

The second question requires a bit more thought. First and foremost, since we would like our graph to support our argument, we have to be clear about what our argument actually is – this may sound daft, but I have come across many instances where argument and graph did not match (or worse, contradicted each other). In metaphorical words, we must think about what story our graph should tell. We will look at some instances of bad graph-argument matches later.

Let's have another look at Labov's example of cluster simplification in two speakers (Table 5.5). Note that I have now also included the relative frequencies (in percentages) for the proportion of simplified clusters. The argument we are likely to make (and indeed, Labov made) is that BF uses more simplified clusters than AO – a brief look at the table confirms this, with 67% of simplified clusters produced by BF, compared to 57% by AO.

If we decide to illustrate this information graphically, we have several options: a *bar chart* (Figure 5.1a) displays our data in bars, or blocks, whereby the higher a bar is, the higher the data value is. In Figure 5.1a, the bar for BF is higher than that for AO – even without looking at the exact value we can see that BF scores higher. Note that in Figure 5.1a, the data displayed is the relative frequencies, as the (vertical) y-axis shows the percentage.

We could also display the absolute frequencies (Figure 5.1b) – there is very little difference, but, as is the case with absolute frequencies, it is somewhat more difficult to judge without the baseline of 100.

TABLE 5.5 Cluster simplification: absolute and relative frequencies

BF simplified	BF simp %	BF total	AO simplified	AO simp %	AO total
71	67	106	46	57	81

Source: Adapted from Labov (1972).

(a)

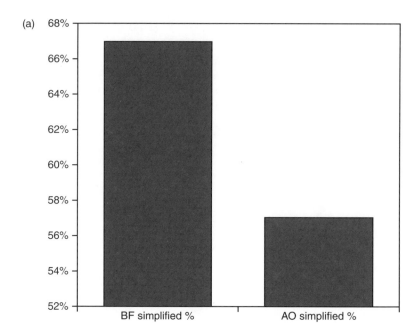

(b)

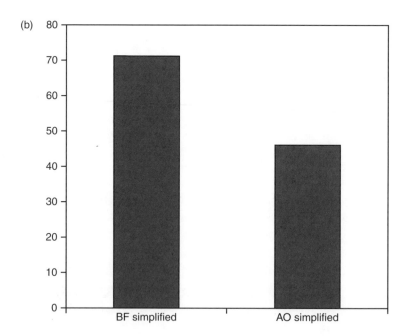

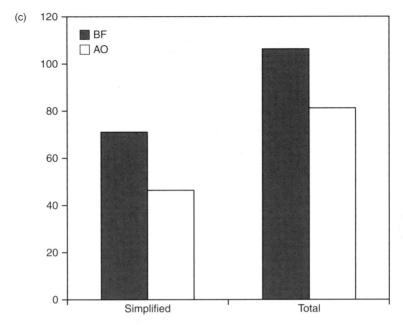

FIGURE 5.1 *Bar chart.*

What both Figures 5.1a and 5.1b are missing is information that tells us more about the extent of simplification – so far, all we have got is the relative frequency bars in Figure 5.1a. Figure 5.1c, the last bar chart we are going to look at, provides us with a direct comparison of absolute frequencies for both AO and BF, and for both simplified clusters and total number of clusters. In short, Figure 5.1c displays all absolute frequencies.

While the bar chart provides us with good visual information as to which speaker produces more simplified consonant clusters, it only tell us how any clusters show simplification *within* each speaker: the 67% bar for BF in Figure 5.1a means that 67% of BF's clusters are simplified, and accordingly, 57% of AO's are. Figure 5.1c gives us a direct comparison of absolute frequencies; without any difficulty we can see in Figure 5.1c that first, simplification occurs more frequently in BF's speech, but also that AO produces more relevant consonant clusters overall, in comparison to AO. With practice and improved graph-reading skills you will also be able to see from Figure 5.1c that the proportion of simplified clusters is slightly higher in BF's than AO's speech. For this, you need to compare the bars for BF with each other and the bars for AO with each other; you will see that the relative difference in height is slightly higher for BF.

However, in some cases we may want to know (and see) who contributes how much to the overall number of simplified clusters – information the bar charts above do not give us. In this case, we need a *pie chart* – names after its distinct shape (Figure 5.2).

Figure 5.2 is based on exactly the same data as Figures 5.1a, 5.1b and 5.1c: 71 simplified clusters for BF and 46 for AO, respectively. Yet, the graph provides this information is a different form. Again, we can immediately see that BF (grey slice) shows more simplifications than AO. However, each slice represents the proportion of simplification in relation to the *overall number* of simplifications *across* both speakers. Accordingly, the percentages given refer to the relative frequency of simplification for all simplified clusters: 71 simplified clusters for BF calculates as 61% of all simplified clusters – 117 overall across both speakers (71+46=117).

It is important to fully understand which argument each graph supports: the bar charts as in Figures 5.1a, 5.1b and 5.1c allow us to display differences within (and to a certain extent across) speakers, while the pie chart looks at the distribution of values across speakers only. In other words, we cannot make any statements about the degree of simplification *within* a particular speaker when we only have a pie chart.

We do not need to change the type of graph we use in order to tell a slightly different story. In fact, especially with bar charts, all we need to do is to invert rows and columns. Another example: both Wolfram (1969) and Trudgill (1974) have worked on the influence of social class onto the use of non-standard variation, in Detroit, United States and Norwich, United

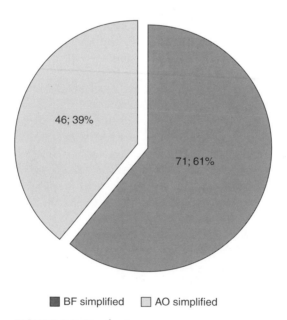

46; 39%

71; 61%

■ BF simplified   ☐ AO simplified

FIGURE 5.2 *Pie chart.*

Kingdom, respectively. In Table 5.6 I have condensed their results for one non-standard feature into one table, indicating the relative frequency this particular feature has been used across three socio-economic classes: lower middle class (LMC), upper working class (UWC) and lower working class (LWC).

Figures 5.3 and 5.4 show bar charts which use exactly the same information, yet, they support different arguments.

Task 5.7

Look at the 2 bar charts in Figures 5.3 and 5.4. What argument does each one support?

Even though the two charts show identical information, as they are based on the same data, their emphasis is different. Figure 5.3 allows a more direct comparison between the two cities, with the bars for Detroit and Norwich being adjacent across all categories. Hence, we are immediately able to see that speakers belonging to the two working classes in Norwich

TABLE 5.6 Relative frequencies across three socioeconomic groups in two cities

	Detroit	Norwich
LMC	10	2
UWC	57	70
LWC	71	97

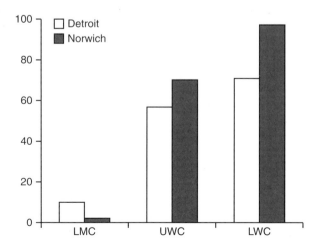

FIGURE 5.3 *Bar chart showing feature distribution across LMC, UWC and LWC.*

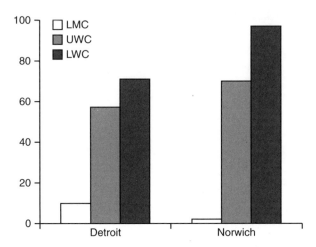

FIGURE 5.4 *Bar chart showing feature distribution between Detroit and Norwich.*

show a higher proportion of our linguistic feature than their counterparts in Detroit. For the LMC, this is inverted, with speakers in Detroit showing a higher frequency. In addition, we can see a general trend whereby the use of the linguistic feature under investigation is increasing the lower the socio-economic class is, and this trend occurs in both cities. So, Figure 5.4 would be a graph we would use to support this line of argument. Note that Figure 5.4 also gives us this information, but the bars are not next to each other, making it a bit more difficult to see.

Figure 5.4, on the other hand, focuses more on social class differences *within* one city. Similar to Figure 5.3 it also allows us to infer a general trend whereby the use of our linguistic variable increases the lower the socio-economic class of the speaker is. Yet, the focus is on what is happening within each city, not across. It has to be emphasized here that neither graph is 'right' or 'wrong' to display this kind of information, however, I hope it is obvious that one is better than another in order to illustrate a particular point.

Another type of chart frequently found in linguistic research is a line graph. Line graphs are particularly useful for displaying increases or decreases, or temporal sequences. Figure 5.5 is a line chart for our Detroit/Norwich data set.

Similar to Figure 5.3, Figure 5.5 shows the increase of the feature with decreasing socio-economic class particularly well: the line moves up steeply between LMC and UWC, indicating that there is a stark increase in the use of this particular non-standard feature; and, as outlined before, this is a parallel development on both sides of the Atlantic. We can also see something else: the gradient of the Norwich line is slightly steeper than that for Detroit; this means the differences in non-standard use between

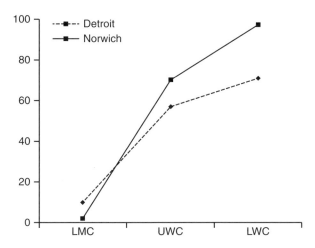

FIGURE 5.5 *Line graph showing feature distribution between Detroit and Norwich.*

the social classes are much more pronounced in Norwich than in Detroit, where the gradient is flatter.

The line graph also shows us another fact which is not as obvious in the bar charts: from UWC onwards, the differences between Detroit become more pronounced; in fact, Norwich overtakes Detroit in the use of the non-standard feature for the two lowest classes. As a general guideline, where two (or more) lines in a line chart cross, something interesting happens – if this happens in your data, it is usually worth investigating it a bit further. Let's look at another example. Figure 5.6 is a line graph adapted from data by Hirsh-Pasek and Golinkoff (1996: 137). The data is based on an experiment trying to investigate young children's ability to identify verb argument structure (transitive/intransitive) using the Preferential Looking Paradigm (ibid.). Children are presented with an audio stimulus, that is, a sentence containing a verb they know, as well as two visual stimuli on two separate screens, one matching the audio-stimulus and one non-matching. Children's understanding of verb argument structure are being inferred through their visual fixation time at either the matching or the non-matching screen, whereby a longer fixation of the matching screen indicates understanding. Knowledge of the syntactic properties of the verb also allows them to make certain predictions of what they are likely to see in terms of visual stimulus. Figure 5.6 shows the results for four conditions: boys and girls and matched and non-matched stimuli; the *x*-axis displays children's age in months, the *y*-axis shows visual fixation time in seconds.

Figure 5.6 makes it easier to understand the overall pattern of the data presented in Table 5.4. First, we can see that children's performance at the age of 19 months in comparatively similar, with fixation times for all four groups around 2.5 seconds, independent from whether audio and

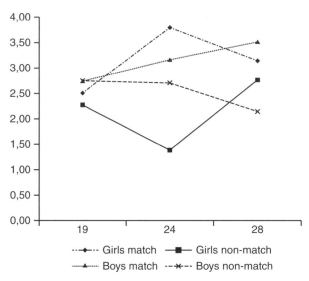

FIGURE 5.6 *Line graph showing fixation times for boys and girls.*

TABLE 5.7 Fixation time in seconds

Age in months	Girls		Boys	
	match	non-match	match	non-match
19	2.50	2.28	2.73	2.74
24	3.80	1.39	3.16	2.70
28	3.14	2.77	3.51	2.15

Source: Adapted from Hirsh-Pasek and Golinkoff (1996: 137).

visual stimuli match or not. Second, we can see a considerable development between 19 and 24 months, and this development concerns both stimulus type and children's sex: at 24 months, girls' match and non-match fixation times vary dramatically with 3.8 and 1.4 seconds fixation time, respectively. In other words, the difference in fixation time has increased to 2.4 seconds. For boys, this development is less pronounced: match fixation time increases to 3.16, unmatched decreases to 2.7 – a difference of a mere 0.5 seconds (Table 5.7).

A third striking observation can be made at 28 months: boys' fixation times move progressively apart for match and non-match conditions, indicating gradual development. At 28 months, match and non-match fixation times differ by 1.36 seconds. For girls, on the other hand, the results are somewhat confusing. Instead of following the previous development of increasing fixation time for match, and decreasing fixation time for non-match conditions, as was so distinctively the case at 24 months, fixation times for both conditions converge: non-match fixation times increase, while match times decrease, leaving a difference of 0.4 seconds.

However, when we look at the children's performance with regard to unknown words, the picture is slightly different. Figure 5.7 shows how the development for the match condition for unknown words is almost parallel between boys and girls. Even though fixation times for the match condition are shorter for both boys and girls at the age of 19 months, and even drop slightly by 24 months, the considerable rise in fixation times at 28 months for match conditions show that children have a high understanding of verb argument structure even for unknown verbs. Hirsh-Pasek and Golinkoff conclude that:

> [i]n general, then, by the age of 28 months, children [. . .] can use a verb's argument structure to predict verb meaning. In fact, these 2 1/2-year-olds did better (considering the girls' nonsignificant performance on the known verbs) with unknown verbs than with known verbs! (1996: 139)

Task 5.8

Write a short concise summary of Figure 5.7 that goes beyond what has already been mentioned. Then, using all available information, write a short paragraph supporting Hirsh-Pasek and Golinkoff's conclusions.

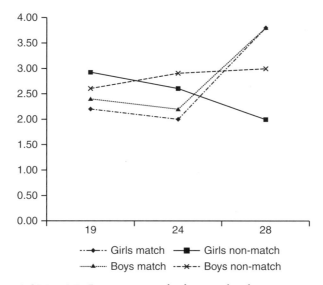

FIGURE 5.7 *Fixation times for boys and girls.*

Task 5.9

Using any of the data discussed in this chapter so far, create different types of graphs, and write a short and concise summary of what exactly each graph tells you.

The last chart type frequently used in linguistics is the *scatter-plot*. We will meet scatter-plots again in Chapter Seven and discuss them in more detail. In brief, scatter-plots allow us to plot two variables for one case at the same time, providing us with a visual representation of how the two variables are related. In Chapter Three we have outlined Li's experiment on the impact of different input types on learners' performance. For each learner, we have two scores: pre- and post-stimulus. Table 5.8 is a fictive data set for ten people and two pre- and post-scores.

In our scatter-plot, we now plot our data in such a way that each respondent is represented by one data point, and this data point indicates score A on the *x* and score B on the *y*-axis (or vice versa). Figure 5.8 is the scatter-plot for our data.

Without looking at our original data, what we can see immediately identify a general tendency: the higher the score A (*x*-axis) for a particular respondent is, the higher score B (*y*-axis) is for this particular respondent. If this was data derived from an experiment similar to Loschky's, we could infer that the introduction of the stimulus has positively influenced participants' scores – before we actually start analysing our data properly. In technical terms, we speak of a *positive correlation* between the two variables – we look at the details in Chapter Seven.

TABLE 5.8 Fictive set of pre- and post-test scores

Respondent	Score A	Score B
Amelie	23	48
Bertie	19	45
Chris	18	36
Dan	29	59
Elizabeth	12	60
Frances	32	47
Graeme	17	22
Harold	22	36
Ian	27	55
Juliet	24	47

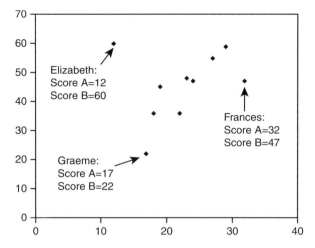

FIGURE 5.8 *Score A and Score B scatter plot.*

Creating charts in Excel:

1 Highlight the cells containing the data you want to display.

   a For the bar chart in Figures 5.1a, 5.1b and 5.1c highlight the 'BF simp %' and 'AO simp %' columns respectively. Note that you need to highlight the column header as well (i.e. highlight 'BF simp %' and 'AO simp %' – not only the numbers).

   b Accordingly, for the pie chart highlight the appropriate absolute frequencies.

2 Click on the 'Insert' Tab in the menu bar.

3 Select the appropriate chart type.

4 To create different graphs such as Figures 5.3 and 5.4, check the appropriate option ('row' or 'column' in the second step when asked 'Series in . . .'.

5.5. Summary

The aim of this chapter was to familiarize readers with some of the most basic techniques of presenting their data in an orderly and concise fashion. I would go as far and argue that the methods discussed in this chapter should be applied to all data sets, simply because they are easily produced and provide much useful information we may need for further analysis. For some, even though very few projects these steps may even be enough.

A clear and tidy data set is a first step towards a thorough analysis: once we have a rough idea what is going on, it is much easier to investigate individual issues further. It is also important in terms of readability and comprehensibility: I guess that most of us have come across a study where the data presented (in tables and/or graphs) had little to do with the explanation we were given. For the reader, this is annoying at best; for the author, it can mean anything from a rejection of the journal article to a bad mark in a student assignment.

Yet, it is important to know exactly *how* to present our data: just having dozens of tables and graphs, put together in a random fashion is precisely not the way of doing it. The presentation of our data is essential to our argument and should hence be part of it, with words, tables and graphs forming a coherent unit with individual parts supporting each other.

Task 5.10

The following table is taken from O'Barr and Atkin's (1980) study into whether women's language is 'powerless'. It is based on the recordings of witness statements. The data is based on six respondents: three women (A, B and C) and three men (D, E and F), and includes the absolute frequencies for eight features considered to illustrate powerlessness. It also provides the total number of utterances/answers given by each witness.

You can download the data set from the companion website.
Using everything you have learned in this chapter,

a   provide an analysis of the data, and

b   discuss whether the data indicates that 'women's speech is powerless'.

	Women			Men		
	A	B	C	D	E	F
Intensifiers	16	0	0	21	2	1
Hedges	19	2	3	2	5	0
Hesitation forms	52	20	13	26	27	11
Witness asks lawyer questions	2	0	0	0	0	0
Gestures	2	0	0	0	0	0
Polite forms	9	0	2	2	0	1
Use of 'Sir'	2	0	6	32	13	11
Quotes	1	5	0	0	0	0
# of answers in interview	90	32	136	61	73	52

Source: Adapted from O'Barr and Atkins (1980: 100).

CHAPTER SIX

Describing data properly – central location and dispersion

Key words: central tendency – mean – median – mode – normal distribution – percentiles – quartiles – range – standard deviation – standard error – skewed distributions and skewness – variance – z-scores

While the previous chapter as provided us with some very easy and basic ways of describing and presenting our data, this chapter is the first focusing on real statistical analysis of data – it does not mean that it is more complicated though! We start with an explanation of the main and most basic means of describing quantitative data: the *measures of central location* arithmetic mean, median and mode, as well as the *measures of dispersion* variance, standard deviation and z-scores. With this, we also introduce the concept of *normal distribution*.

6.1. Statistics: What and why?

In good linguistic fashion, we shall start this chapter with a brief look at the meaning of the word 'statistic' or 'statistics'. The Oxford English Dictionary defines *statistic* (singular) as:

> that branch of political science dealing with the collection, classification, and discussion of facts (especially of a numerical kind) bearing on the condition of a state or community. In recent use, the department of study that has for its object the collection and arrangement of numerical facts or data, whether relating to human affairs or to natural phenomena.

While *statistics* (plural) refers quite simply to:

numerical facts or data collected and classified. (ibid.)

Let's look at this in a bit more detail. In general, a statistic (or statistics) is any *orderly summary of numbers*, for example, results of an election, league tables, etc. We may, for example, take a collection of scores, such as students' exam marks, and sort them from highest to lowest (or lowest to highest – depending in preference), and we would have the most simplest of statistics:

Student exam marks, unsorted, 'raw' data

55	68	41	58	76	23	62

Student exam marks, sorted from lowest to highest – a very simple statistic

23	41	55	58	62	68	76

Student exam marks, sorted from highest to lowest – another simple statistic

76	68	62	58	55	41	23

This is obviously an extremely simply approach to looking at data, far from a proper in-depth analysis. However, even a simple step such as sorting data can help us to get an overview of what our data looks like – much more so than the chaotic collection of unprocessed, raw data.

Doing statistics using Excel: *Sorting*

You can sort data in Excel both my column and by row, even though the former is the default function.

1. Highlight the data you want to sort. If your data contains more than one column (i.e. more than one variable), make sure you highlight the entire data set – otherwise Excel will only sort the column you have selected. This will lead to data for individual cases being broken up. Note: the same applies if you sort rows.

2. In the menu bar, go to 'Home' and then 'Sort&Filter'.
3. If you select a sort function straightaway, it will sort according to the column the cursor is in. Alternatively, click on 'custom' and select which column you would like to sort by and whether you would like ascending or descending order.
4. If you want to sort by row, click 'options' and select 'Sort left to right' under 'Orientation'.
5. Click ok.

However, simply ordering and sorting data is usually not enough. As we outlined in Chapter Two, quantitative analysis is ultimately concerned with *how much* or *how many* there is/are of whatever we are interested in, and, accordingly, all statistical tools are based around this.

What we need for a quantitative analysis, then, is some kind of *numerical measurement describing some characteristic of a sample*. We may want to know, for example, how many students scored better than 60% in the exam. In this case, a statistic is pretty much what we did in the previous chapter when we calculated cumulative frequencies, where we received a numerical, quantifiable answer, such as '10 out of 20 students, that is 50%, obtained results of 60% or over'. Again, this is fairly simple.

Statistics also refers to a *collection of methodological tools* that help to systematically and exemplarily and empirically collect, process and display information. In the course of this and the following chapters, we will look at several of those tools, and discuss which ones are the most useful ones for a particular purpose.

So far, we have mainly discussed statistics as a *descriptive approach* to looking at data, that is, an approach that is concerned with quantifying and summarizing information in order to describe and display an issue in the most effective and optimal manner. In other words, based on the data collected from our sample we try to describe reality. The various different tools of *descriptive statistics* are the focus of this chapter.

However, statistics also serves two other functions, which we will discuss in subsequent chapters: first, *statistic inference* allows us to generalize, that is, to infer information about the population by looking at the sample. In plain English, by analysing the data from our sample using appropriate tools we can conclude more or less well what is going on in the population. And second, statistical methods can help us *identifying (causal) relationships*, that is, how two or more phenomena are related, for example, how X influences Y.

Ultimately, thorough description, inference and insights about relationships between variables help us making decisions: in Chapter Three, when we discussed research designs, we had a look at Li's study on the impact of various types of input on learners' progress. If we obtain quantitative evidence that a particular type of input is particularly beneficial to learners' development, while another is not, we have good reason to change our teaching style towards this particular type of input. The important point is that we have numerical, hard evidence that method A is better than method B – much better than just guessing. Yet, the problems with quantitative analysis lie in the details: there is a plethora of tools and methods around, and especially for those less experienced it is easy to choose the wrong ones, leading to flawed analyses and conclusions. Hence, in this book we will not only introduce the most common tools, but also have a closer look at when to apply them.

6.2. Measures of central tendency

We start with three basic tools of descriptive statistics: the *measures of central tendency mean*, *median* and *mode*. As the term implies, all three tell us something about the 'centre' or the 'middle' of our data, giving us some idea where about our data is located. The advantage is that we have one numerical measure (or one value) that can tell us a lot about our data, so we do not have to look at the entire data set in detail when we try to describe it. This is particularly useful when we have large samples: using the measures of central tendency, we can summarize a large data set with just a few numbers:

> The analysis of 200,000 graduates has shown that the mean degree qualification mark between 1990 and 2000 was 58.7%, with a mode of 53.3% and a standard deviation of 6.3.

For anyone familiar with the meaning of these three measures – mean, mode and standard deviation, which we will all discuss in this chapter – can get a lot of information out of this, without looking at all 200,000 results individually. In fact, they would not have to look at the individual results at all!

6.2.1. The arithmetic mean and the trimmed arithmetic mean

The probably most popular statistical tool is the *arithmetic mean*; most of us will probably know it as the 'average' – a term that is, for various reasons we will ignore for the time being, not quite accurate. The mean tells us the 'average value' of our data. It is a handy tool to tell us where about our data is approximately located. Plus, it is very easy to calculate – I have heard of people who do this in their head! In order to calculate a reliable and meaningful mean, our data must be on a ratio scale. Think about it: how could we possible calculate the 'average' of a nominal variable measuring, for example, respondents' sex? One is either male or female, so any results along the lines of 'the average sex of the group is 1.7' makes no sense whatsoever.

To calculate the mean, we add up all the scores for a given variable in our data set, and divide the sum by the number of scores/cases in the set. An example: we have a sample of 6 people (we will henceforth use the technically correct nomenclature N for number of scores/people/items in the sample), so N=6. Their individual age in years is:

| 25 | 30 | 35 | 40 | 45 | 50 |

In order to calculate the mean, we add up all five individual scores and divide it by N:

$$\bar{x} = \frac{\sum \text{Age}}{N} = \frac{25+30+35+40+45+50}{6} = \frac{225}{6} = 37.5$$

Note that the $\bar{x}$ stands for the mean, and Σ, the Greek letter sigma, indicates a sum (i.e. 'add up all individual age scores'). In our example, the mean age is 37.5 years.

It is important to understand that the mean, just like any other measure we are going to discuss in this chapter, is only a summary of the data: 37.5 years is a summary that best describes the 'average' age of the people in our sample, but, as you can see, not a single person in our sample is actually 37.5 years old. Figure 6.1 shows both the individual ages plotted and the arithmetic mean indicated by the fat line at 37.5 on the y-axis. As you can see, the mean is somewhere in the middle between all individual values; it is the value that best represents all other values in the sample. Yet, not a single value is actually identical with the mean.

Let's apply the arithmetic mean to a set of real data: Table 6.1 shows the percentage of non-standard pronunciation of the cluster (-ing) as -/in/ (as in *I'm goin*) across five social classes in Norwich.

Task 6.1

Calculate the mean non-standard pronunciation of (-ing) in Table 6.1.

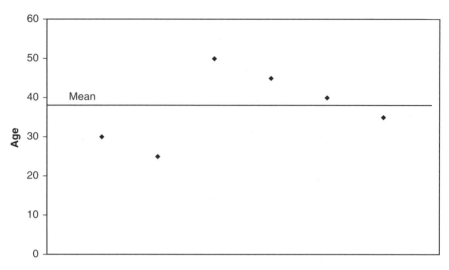

FIGURE 6.1 *Arithmetic mean.*

TABLE 6.1 (ing) distribution across five social classes

Social class	(ing) %
Middle middle class	31
Lower middle class	42
Upper working class	87
Middle working class	95
Lower working class	100

Source: Adapted from romaine (2000: 69).

Doing statistics using Excel: *Mean*

Calculating the mean with Excel is simple:
   Input your data with variables (here: class and percentage of non-standard features) in columns and instances in rows, as in Table 6.1.

- Click into the cell you want the mean to appear. Note: it does make sense to have it nearby the data it refers to, for example, below the 100 % in Table 6.1.
- Select menu 'Formulas' > 'Insert Function'. Search for 'average' (*sic!*)

- On the next screen, if Excel has not already done it for you, highlight the cells that contain the data you are interested in obtaining the mean for.
- Click ok, and you mean should appear in the cell you selected.
- Alternatively, expand the menu of the AutoSum button (by clicking on the tiny arrow at the bottom). Select 'Average'.

For those well versed with Excel: the formula for the mean is

=average(DATA), whereby DATA stands for the data you would like to select. If your data appears in column A, rows 1 to 5, the formula will be

=average(A1:A5) meaning 'calculate the mean for all value in cells A1 to A5'.

Hopefully, you will have found that the mean is $\bar{x} = 71\%$, that is, on average, 71% of (ing)-clusters are pronounced with a final /g/ drop; in yet other words, almost three in four (ing) endings are pronounced without the final /g/. This should not have been too difficult, and with a simple bit of maths we have obtained quite a good indicator as to what our data looks like.

But is this really true? Look at the next (fictive) example given in Table 6.2, where, again, we have the /g/ drop in (ing) clusters across five social classes (i.e., $N=5$).

Task 6.2

Calculate the mean of the following sample.

If your maths is correct, you will have found that the mean is again 71:

$$\bar{x} = \frac{68 + 70 + 71 + 72 + 74}{5} = 71$$

TABLE 6.2 Fictive example of /g/ drop

Social class	(ing) %
Middle middle class	68
Lower middle class	70
Upper working class	71
Middle working class	72
Lower working class	74

Yet, undoubtedly the sample is rather different from the first one! In the first data set, we had values ranging from 31% to 100%; here, data only ranges from 68% to 74%. In other words, we may have data sets which are substantially different, but their mean is identical! That is, if someone told us 'Speakers in Norwich drop 71% of all /g/ in (ing) endings', all this tells us is a general tendency, but it is far from sufficient information to draw any deeper conclusions from.

Another problem we may encounter with the mean is that is rather sensitive towards outlying values, and small sample sizes aggravate this problem: if we calculate the means for the two data sets (a) and (b) given below, we see that although they only differ in one score, their mean is substantially different. Look at examples (a) and (b) which only differ in a single value:

| (a) | 16 | 18 | 20 | 22 | 25 | $\bar{x} = 20.2$ |
| (b) | 16 | 18 | 20 | 22 | 65 | $\bar{x} = 28.2$ |

Even though the two sets are identical for all but one value, there is a considerable difference in the mean. So, maybe the mean is not as reliable a tool as we thought? A cheap and cheerful solution for this problem is the use of the *trimmed mean*. In essence, we 'trim' our data set by chopping off bits at both ends. This leads to the exclusion of outlying values. Assume we have the following set of data:

62 56 70 63 25 58 60 59 79 57 65 52

Task 6.3

Sort the data and calculate the mean.

For our example, we would like a 5% trimmed mean, which means that we remove the lowest and highest 5% of our scores. We have 12 scores/values, and would like to trim it by 5%, so:

$$12 \times 0.05 = 0.6$$

Since we cannot remove 0.6 of a value (as it is a discrete variable!), we have to remove one on each end. Our sorted data looks like this:

| 25 | 52 | 56 | 57 | 58 | 59 | 60 | 62 | 63 | 65 | 70 | 79 |

Hence, we remove the highest (79) and the lowest (25) value, and recalculate the mean without the removed scores. You should find that the trimmed mean is $\bar{x}(t)=60.2$. Compare this to the original mean (see Chapter Eleven for solution). You will see that it is slightly different. Note that it is *absolutely essential* that we remove scores from both ends!

The discussion of the arithmetic mean and the impact of outlying values leads us straight back to our problem of sample size: the smaller our sample, the fewer data we have got, and the more sensitive our data becomes towards extreme values. Consider the following two sets of data; first, calculate the mean for the entire set, then remove the extreme value, that is, 24 for set (a) and 20 for set (b)

(a) 1   3   3   4   5   6   7   7   8   9   24
(b) 1   3   3   20

For (a), the mean is $\bar{x}=6.73$ and for (b), $\bar{x}=6.75$. However, if we remove the largest value from both sets, we get $\bar{x}$ (a)=5.3 and $\bar{x}$ (b)=2.3. In other words, the removal of one single value has a much more dramatic impact on the mean for the smaller sample, as here every single value contributes comparatively more to the calculation of the mean. This is similar to the problem we discussed in Chapter Five when exploring relative frequencies. Smaller samples are much more sensitive to individual values and should therefore approached with due care. In relation to trimmed means, with small data sets it can be problematic to remove scores, which will make the set even smaller, hence affecting the reliability of statistical tools.

Doing statistics using Excel: *Trimmed Mean*

Fortunate for us, Excel includes an inbuilt function to calculate the trimmed mean. The function is:

=trimmean(array, per cent) whereby 'array' refers to the data array we would like to calculate the mean for, and 'per cent' refers to the percentage we would like to trim our mean by. Hence,

=trimmean(A1:A10, 0.05) calculates the 5% trimmed mean for the data in cells A1 to A10.

6.2.2. The median

As we have seen, the mean can be a bit problematic in some circumstances. Another useful measure of central tendency, although often ignored, is the *median*. The median simply divides our data set into two equal halves, giving us the 'middle' value. Look at the following data, indicating respondents' scores in a test in per cent; for convenience, I have sorted the data already:

45   51   56   62   66   78   89

Our data set consists of seven scores, and the median is the *middle-most score* of them all. If we start counting from both ends, after three steps we end up at the 62, which is right in the middle of our data – it is our median! A median of 62 tell us that half of our respondents scored more than 62%, while the other half scores less.

With data sets with odd numbers of scores, finding the median does not require any major mathematics skills apart from counting. But what about sets with even numbers, such as the following:

45   51   56   60   62   66   78   89

Here we do not have a middle value, as eight can be divided into two equal halves of four. Luckily, another simple solution is at hand: in the case of even numbers of scores, we take the *two middle-most values* and divide them by two (in other words, we calculate their mean). In our example, the two middle values are 60 and 62, as they are both four positions in from either end. The median is hence:

$(60+62)/2 = 61$

We interpret this median as half of our respondents scoring more and less than 61% respectively. One of the advantages of the median is that it is unaffected by extreme values; as the next example shows, both data sets have identical medians even though their outlying values are different.

(a)   45   51   56   60   62   66   78   89
(b)   14   51   56   60   62   66   78   99

As with the mean, the median is a very handy tool to give us some idea of what is going on in any data set, but also, as before, it is not unproblematic, as the next example shows:

23   25   37   59   62   67   76

Here the median is 59 (as the middle-most score), but it should be obvious that it is not always a very insightful piece of information: while the median is unaffected by any extreme values (unlike the mean), is does not tell us anything about what is going on *within* one of the two halves of our data. In this example, if it represented exam scores, we could happily argue that half of our students received a mark better than 59% (which is a comparatively good result), but this neglects the fact that the other half all failed the exam (if, as in most British universities, the pass mark is 40).

Doing statistics using Excel: *Median*

Calculating the mean with Excel is almost identical to calculating the mean. The difference is that instead of *average*, the formula is called *median*

=median(DATA), for example =median(A1:A5)

Something else we need to know about the median, and that is its relation to the mean. Both mean and median provide us information about the 'middle' or 'centre' of our data, and that is why many people confuse them. However, they are two separate measures! Even more confusing, in some data sets, namely those that are normally distributed (see below), mean and media will be identical; quite regularly, however, they are not. The following data has a mean of 47.5 but a median of 35. So, while 47.5 is one way of summarizing our data (along the lines of 'our average value is 47.5'), we can also say that half of our scores fall above and the other half below 35. If we look at the graphic representation of this data in Figure 6.2, we

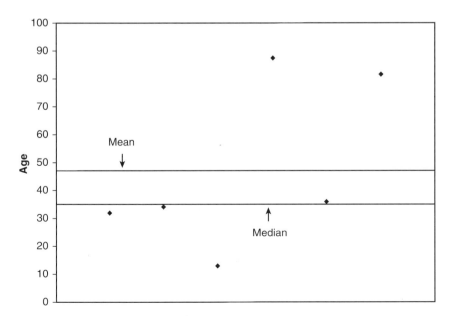

FIGURE 6.2 *Median in relation to the arithmetic mean.*

see that while the median divides our data in two equal halves, with three values above and three below the median, more values fall below the mean than above – this supports the points made earlier about the mean and the impact of outlying values.

6.2.3. The mode

The last of our measures of central tendency is the *mode*. The mode is simply the score that occurs with the highest frequency in a data set – not more, not less. For example, in the following data set, the mode is 4, as it occurs three times:

1   4   5   9   4   3   1   6   7   4

If in our data we have two scores which occur with the same frequency, we talk about a *bimodal* set of data, like we have here, where the modes are 2 and 4:

7   5   1   4   2   4   2   9   6   8

If more than two scores occur with the same frequency, we talk about *multimodal* data.

Doing statistics using Excel: *Mode*

Calculate the mode just as you calculate the mean and the median, the function is *mode*:

=mode(DATA), for example =mode(A1:A5)

Note: with multimodal data, Excel will only display one of the modes – usually the lowest. Other software packages are able to display multiple modes.

→Go to the companion website to see a clip on how to calculate the measures of location in Excel.←

The mode is a useful tool for analysing categorical/nominal data. As discussed at the beginning of this chapter, we cannot use the mean, nor the median, for variables such as gender – one is either male or female, and accordingly, we cannot have a mean that says 'the mean gender is 1.3, which indicates it is slightly more male'. This is where the mode comes handy, as it does nothing else but counts the frequencies of individual scores. In a data set consisting of 1s (for men) and 2s (for women), the mode tells us which occurs more frequently, and we get an instant overview of whether we got more men or women in our sample.

Usually, the mode is really only of importance if its frequency is particularly high: for example, in data set of ten scores, as above, a particular score may occur twice, but this is not necessarily of any significance. If, on the other hand, a particular score occurs again and again, then it is definitely worth looking into this a bit more. It is also worth mentioning that the mode can be significantly different from the mean and median; in fact, median and mean can be almost identical while the mode is far 'off' both other measures.

6.2.4. *Quartiles, quintiles and percentiles*

A set of descriptive tool that is all too often neglected is *quartiles*, *quintiles* and *percentiles*. To cut a potentially long story short, quartiles, quintiles and percentiles work equivalently to the median in that they allow us to split our data in chunks of equal sizes: *Quartiles* divide our data into 4 equal parts, *quintiles* into 5 equal parts, and *percentiles* into 100 equal parts. Annoyingly, a survey of statistics literature shows that there is no consensus as to how to calculate quartiles – you may find different approaches if you look elsewhere. To some extent, quartiles, quintiles and percentiles are similar to the frequency distributions we discussed in Chapter Five, when we brought our data into order by using classes. In the course size example in Chapter Five, we ordered our data in such a way that it fitted five pre-defined classes (very small, small, medium, large, very large). Back then, we defined the class width and boundaries ourselves. When working with quartiles, we know that we will have four classes (or five for quintiles), but the upper and lower boundaries are given by the data itself.

In this book, we calculate quartiles as follows:

- *First quartile* (i.e. lowest 25% of values): $Q1=0.25*(N+1)$ whereby N is the sample size.

- The *second quartile* (Q2) divides the lowest 50% from the highest 50% and is hence nothing else but the median!

- For the third quartile, multiply $(N-1)$ by 0.75, so $Q3=0.75*(N-1)$

Example: number of journal articles published by a group of eight linguists

2 4 6 8 10 12 14 16; $N=8$

The first quartile is calculated as Q1=0.25*(8–1)=1.75. We round this up to 2: the first quartile lies between the second and the third value, so, roughly, Q1=5. In other words, values below 5 fall into the lowest 25% of the data set.

The second quartile is the median, that is Q2=(8+10)/2=9.

And Q3=0.75*7=5.25, again, we round this up to 6. This indicates that values above 12 fall into the top quarter of the data set. Accordingly, we can dissect our data into the following quartiles:

2	4	6	8	10	12	14	16
Q1		Q2		Q3		Q4	

Based on the quartiles, we can make statements such as the following:

- The lowest 25% of linguists have published 4 articles or fewer.

- Linguists in the fourth quartile (top 75%) have published 14 articles or more.

- And do not forget: with a median of 9, 50% of our linguists have published more and 50% have published fewer than 9 articles.

Quintiles work accordingly:

Q1 = 0.2*(N+1): lowest 20% Q1=0.2*7=1.4 → 2nd value, here: 4.

Q2 = 0.4*(N+1)

Q3 = 0.6*(N+1)

Q4 = 0.8*(N+1)

And lastly, for percentiles, we multiply (N–1) with the appropriate fraction, that is, 0.1 for the lowest 10% and so on.

Quartiles, quintiles and percentiles can give us a good overview of how our data is distributed; however, it is really only useful with samples of 12 or more for quartiles, and 20 or more for quintiles. We can see above that the first quintile, that is, the lowest 20% for our example, runs up to a score of 1.4 – a value that is not even in our sample. Dividing an already small sample into even smaller parts makes little sense.

Doing statistics using Excel: *Quartiles* and *percentiles*

The Excel formulae for quartiles and percentiles (there is not one for quintiles) are:

=quartile(DATA; q), with q denoting the quartile we are interested in, for example

=quartile(A1:A5; 1) to obtain the first quartile for data in the area A1 to A5.

=percentile(DATA, p), with p denoting the percentile of interest, for example,

=percentile(A1:A14, 3) for the third percentile of data in A1 to A14.

Note that Excel does not give us the position (as with the manual calculation above) but the actual value. You will see that there is a slight discrepancy, as Excel is slightly more accurate in the way it is doing the calculations.

6.2.4. *Summary: Mean, median and mode*

With the measures of central tendency we have, despite all potential pitfalls, three useful tools for a basic data analysis. As a general guideline, it is usually worth considering all three as opposed to looking at them individually. This allows us to identify any interesting features of oddities in our data early on. We may have, for example, a set of data where mean, median and modes are worlds apart; if we looked at such data from only one approach, we are bound for trouble.

Yet, as we have seen, none of the three tools is perfect. In particular, being measures of central tendency, they do not tell us much about how data is *distributed*. For this, we need to look at the *measures of dispersion*.

QUICK FIX: MEASURES OF CENTRAL LOCATION

- Mean: also wrongly known as the 'average'. Central value that best represents the data. Excel command: =mean(DATA).
- Median: divides the sample into two equal halves. Excel command: =median(DATA).
- Mode: value that occurs most frequently in a set of data. Excel command: =mode(DATA).
- Quartiles: divided data into four equal parts. Excel command: =quartile(DATA, QUARTILE).
- Quintile: divided data into five equal parts. Excel command: =quintile(DATA, QUINTILE).
- Percentile: divided data into 100 equal parts. Excel command: =percentile(DATA, percentile).

→Go to the companion website for a simple Excel template for calculating basic descriptive statistics.←

Task 6.4

Using the seminar size example from Chapter Five, replicated here (see table below), calculate

● Mean, median and mode

● Quartiles

Briefly comment on your results. Solutions in Chapter Eleven.

Data: Seminar size in students

12	14	19	18	15	15	18	17	20	27
22	23	22	21	33	28	14	18	16	13

6.3. Measures of dispersion

Above, when discussing the mean, we have seen that two different sets of data can have the same mean, and it is then obviously problematic to draw any definite conclusions or comparisons. Also, the median, although unaffected by outlying values, is only useful to a certain extent. However, there is a solution. The *measures of dispersion*, as the term implies, tell us how dispersed, or diverse, our data is. In Table 6.3 below, we find again the non-standard pronunciation of (ing), both the 'real' data based on Romaine (2000) as well as my fictive example. If you cannot remember and do not want to calculate it yourself, the mean was 71% for both real and fictive data.

TABLE 6.3 Social distribution of (ing). Romaine (2000) and fictive values

Social class	(ing) 'real'%	(ing) 'fictive'%
Middle middle class	31	68
Lower middle class	42	70
Upper working class	87	71
Middle working class	95	72
Lower working class	100	74
Mean	71	71

In this section, we focus on how to describe our data in more detail, and we look at three measures of dispersion: range, standard variation and variance.

6.3.1. Range

As always, we start with the easiest: the range. Unsurprisingly for the linguistically versed, the range gives us the – well – range of our data. In other words, it gives us the difference between the lowest score (or *minimum*) and the highest score (*maximum*) of a variable. To calculate the range, subtract the minimum score from the maximum score, and voila! Let's calculate the range(s) of our data above. You are more than welcome to do this yourself.

For the original data, the minimum score is 31% (middle middle class), the maximum score 100% (lower working class). The range, accordingly, is 69 percentage *points* (*not* 69%!):

MAX–MIN = 100–31 = 69

For our fictive example, minimum and maximum are 68% and 74%, respectively, so we have a range of a mere six percentage points. It is obvious that the two sets of data, although they have the same mean, are substantially different, with a difference in range of 63 percentage points (69 – 6 = 63).

Doing statistics using Excel: *Minimum, maximum, range*

The formulae for the maximum and minimum are, respectively,

=max(DATA), for example =max (A1:A5)

=min(DATA), for example =min(A1:A5)

In order to obtain the range, set up a formula that subtracts the minimum from the maximum value: for example, if the maximum is displayed in cell A6 and the minimum is displayed in cell A7, then the equation for the range is:

=A7–A6

→Go to the companion website to see a clip on how to calculate the measures of dispersion in Excel.←

Minimum, maximum and range are good indicators of how dispersed data is, and they work very well when taken in combination with the measures of central tendency in order to give us a first idea of what our data looks like. They are particularly good of spotting outlying values. I personally recommend to always calculate these six measures and to have a thorough look at them; with a bit of practice one can easily spot a lot of issues – especially when they are put into the theoretical context of the research questions: if we are interested in the attitudes towards taboo language, and we find that our mean age is 78 years, with a range of 6 years, we may have a problem with a biased sample (assuming that older people perceive swear words generally more negatively). Similarly, if for a sample of $N=20$ your mean is 11 and the maximum is 60, it is worth looking into this in more detail – 60 might well be an outlier. Minimum, maximum and range are good basic measures to tell us the extent of dispersion of our data, but for any further and deeper analysis, we need something a bit more statistically sound: the variance and the standard deviation are slightly more advanced measures which can help us to draw conclusions about our data. And, they are fairly easily calculated, too!

6.3.2. *Variance and standard deviation*

The *variance* is a measure of dispersion that tells us how much our data on average (*sic!*)[1] deviates from its mean. In other words, the variance is summary measure derived from looking at the difference between each data point (i.e. individual score/value) and the mean. Variance is usually denoted by σ^2. Consider the following simple data set, showing the number of successful funding bids for five linguists:

2	4	6	8	10

By now, it should not cause too much difficulty to calculate the mean as $\bar{x}=6$, that is, the mean is 6 successful bids. Without much ado, we can see that the median is 6, too. Figure 6.3 shows the distribution of values, and also shows us the deviation from the mean. The variance is a mathematical tool to describe this deviation in a single number.

In order to calculate the variance, we first subtract the mean from every single data point, square the difference, and add up all the squares differences. Then we divide it by $N-1$, that is, sample size minus 1. What sounds very abstract in theory is rather simple in practice – especially when we do this in conjunction with looking at the graph:

1   Calculate the deviation from each data point from the mean and square (multiply with itself) the result: $(2-6)^2$ $(4-6)^2$ $(6-6)^2$ $(8-6)^2$ $(10-6)^2$.

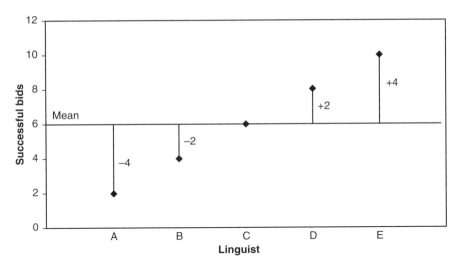

FIGURE 6.3 *Example: Linguists and bid success.*

This gives us:

$(-4)^2$ $(-2)^2$ $(0)^2$ $(2)^2$ $(4)^2$ and accordingly, once squared:

  16   4   0   4   16

2 Add up all the squared values, that is,

   $16 + 4 + 0 + 4 + 16 = 40$. This value is called the *sum of squares.*

3 Now, we divide the sum of squares by the sample size minus 1, that is, $N-1$. In essence, the subtraction of 1 eliminates any bias that a small sample in comparison to a large population could bring up – we shall ignore the technical details here. In our example, $N=5$, so we divide the sum of squares by 4 ($5-1=4$):

   $\sigma^2 = 40/4 = 10$.

Our variance, or *mean squared deviation from the mean*, is 10. Now comes the annoying bit: since we have squared all the differences, we have also squared the units of measurement. That is, our variance is 10 squared funding bids. This obviously makes little sense, although the variance as a mathematic construct is used in several statistical tools which we will come across – we shall ignore the details here. Again, the solution is easy: a much more comprehensive measure is the *standard deviation*. And the standard deviation (σ or SD) is nothing but the square root of the variance:

$$\sigma = \sqrt{\sigma^2}$$

In our example, the SD is hence:

$$\sigma = \sqrt{10} = 3.16$$

The advantage of the SD is that we get our original units of measurements back. That is, our SD is 3.16 funding bids. The standard deviation for one sample is often difficult to interpret on its own; as a guideline, the smaller the SD is in relation to the mean, the less dispersed the data is, that is, the closer individual values are to the mean. In our example, the mean is 6 and the SD is 3.16, so this is rather difficult to judge. Yet, the standard deviation is an important tool for some of the statistical methods we discuss later, such as the z-score below.

Doing statistics using Excel: *Variance* and *standard deviation*

Calculating standard deviations and variance is a great tool for annoying students, but can be tedious and error-prone when we have to do it ourselves, especially with large data sets. Luckily, Excel can do it for us.

The formulae for the variance and standard deviation are, respectively,

=var(DATA), for example =var(A1:A5)

=stdev(DATA), for example =stdev(A1:A5)

Let's have a look at the SD in practice. Above, we have already calculated the mean of the non-standard pronunciation of (ing) for both the real and the fictive data set.

Task 6.5

Using pen and paper or Excel, calculate the standard deviation for both data sets.

If you have not made a mistake somewhere in your calculations, your SD for the real data should be $\sigma=32$ and for the fictive data $\sigma=2.24$ (detailed solutions for manual calculation in Chapter Eleven). We now have a statistically sound proof for what we have already seen from calculating the range and the visual inspection of the data: the real data is much more dispersed the fictive one, that is, its values are further from the mean.

6.3.3. Z-scores

So far, we have a collection of some rather useful tools to describe our data. Yet, it is about time that we think a bit about how we can use these tools to do more than just describing data. In particular, we should have a brief

TABLE 6.4 Exam scores for 20 groups

Group		Group	
Student	Mark	Student	Mark
A	90	G	35
B	50	H	40
Charles	78	Ian	70
D	30	J	75
E	62	K	55
F	50	L	55
Mean		Mean	
SD		SD	

look at how the mean and the standard deviation can be used to compare individual values across two data sets. Let's assume the following situation (see Table 6.4), adapted from Lewis (1967): exam scores for two groups of students.

Task 6.6

Calculate mean and standard deviation for both groups.

Charles scores 78 points, while Ian scores 70 points. I guess, spontaneously the vast majority of us would argue that Charles performed better than Ian. Let's consider this in more detail. The mean score for group A is $\bar{x}$ (A)=60, the mean score for group B is $\bar{x}$ (B)=55; the standard deviations are σ(A)=21.6 and σ(B)=15.8, respectively. That is, group A's scores are more dispersed. Now, look at the differences between the individual's score and the group mean: Charles deviates 18 points from the mean (78–60) and Ian 15 points (70–55). Again, it would be easy to conclude that Charles, having a higher mark both in absolute terms (78 being higher than 70) and in terms of deviation from the mean (18 being higher than 15) has done better. But is this really the case?

We have seen that the SD for group A is higher. One way of solving our problem is to take this into account: we compare Charles's and Ian's scores in terms of standard deviations from the mean. In technical terms, we need the *z-score*, also known as the *standard score*. The generic formula for the z-score is:

$$z = \frac{X - \bar{x}}{\sigma}$$

whereby X denotes the individual data point we are interested in, $\bar{x}$ denotes the mean of the sample, and σ the standard deviation, as before. Accordingly, for Charles, the z-score is

$$z = \frac{78-60}{21.6} = 0.83$$

For Ian, the z-score is

$$z = \frac{70-55}{15.8} = 0.95$$

This means that Charles's score is 0.83 standard deviations above the mean, while Ian's score is 0.95 standard deviations above the mean. In other words, Ian is nearer to the top of his group B's top than Charles is to group A's. So we could argue that Ian has performed better.

Doing statistics using Excel: *Z-score*

The Excel formula for calculating the z-score is =standardize(X, mean, Standard_dev), whereby X is the value you want to calculate the z-score for, mean is the arithmetic mean of the sample, and Standard_dev the, well, standard deviation of the sample.

A word of warning: working with z-scores and standard deviations is only reliable with data that is normally or fairly normally distributed – otherwise, our results do not make much sense. In the next section, we look at the issue of normal distributions in more detail.

QUICK FIX: MEASURES OF DISPERSION

- Range: simply the difference between the highest and the lowest value in our data.
- Variance: mean squared deviation from the mean. Note: units of measurements also end up squared! Excel command: =var(DATA).
- Standard deviation: square root of variance. Gives us original units of measurements. Excel command: =stdev(DATA).
- Z-score: or standard score. Allows us to compare scores from different groups of data. Excel command: =standardize(X, mean, Standard_dev).

6.4. The normal distribution

Having spent this chapter looking at different ways to describe data, we shall finish our discussion by looking at how to describe data in more general terms. In particular, we should have a closer look at how data points in a data set are distributed. In Chapter Five we have looked at frequencies, that is, how often a particular score appears in the data. We can also refer to this as a *frequency distribution*. Oddly enough, when we look at properties of living organisms, for example, height or IQ of humans, we will find that these properties are all distributed in a similar pattern: we have a high frequency of scores which are close to the mean, and the more we move away from the mean in either direction, the lower the frequencies become. Sometimes, frequencies are distributed in such as way that mean, median and mode are identical. As a fictive example, we could say that the mean height of a human being is 6 feet, and that 50% of the sample are smaller and taller than 6 feet respectively (median). In addition, we would find that 6-feet-tall people occur with the highest frequency in our sample (mode). We call this the *normal distribution*. Plotted as a graph, it looks a bit like a bell, which is why it is often referred to as a *bell-shaped distribution*. A third term is *Gaussian distribution*, after the mathematician Carl Friedrich Gauss, who discovered it. Note that the two ends of curve never touch the x-axis (the horizontal one) but only approaches it in infinitively small numbers. Figure 6.4 shows the normal distribution as a typical curve.

Since this may sound a bit abstract, it is about time to introduce another property of the normal distribution: we have said above that in a normal distribution, data is distributed symmetrically (hence the nice symmetric bell shape), and mean, median and mode correspond. Now, let's have a

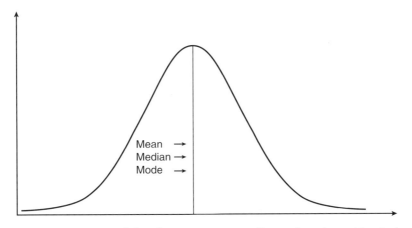

FIGURE 6.4 *Normal distribution – mean, median and mode are identical.*

look at the area *under* the curve. Because it is symmetrical, and because of mathematical reasons too difficult to go into here, the area between the mean and the first standard deviation is always, in both directions, 34% (34.13% to be precise). That is, if we move one standard deviation from the mean to either side, then we have covered about two-thirds (68.26%) of all our scores. The area between the mean and two standard deviations covers about 47.5%, so in a normal distribution 95% of all our data points lie within two standard deviations from the mean.

A concrete example helps here. A sample of exam marks from 100 students (N=100) has a mean of 60% and a standard deviation of 5%, and our data is normally distributed. Based on the above, because we have a standard deviation of 5%, we can then say that 34% of all our students have received between 60% and 65%, while another 34% have marks between 55% and 60%. In yet other words, 68% of all our students have received marks between 55% and 65%. Accordingly, from what we know about two standard deviations, 95% of our students have obtained marks between 50 and 70%. Note how this is yet another way of approaching and describing data, just like what we did when discussing relative frequencies in Chapter Five and quartiles in this current chapter. Also, like the measures of location, the measures of dispersion, especially the standard deviation, is a useful tool to summarize our data in one simple number.

Based on the above, we can easily obtain a rough estimate of where a particular student is located in the distribution: in the above example, a student with a mark of 71% falls above two standard deviations (as 71% is larger than 60%+2 standard deviation, that is, 60%+5%+5%), and we can immediately conclude that she falls into the top 5% of the marks!

Sadly, though, very often data is not normally distributed but *skewed* to the left or the right. In these cases, mean, median and mode do not overlap. Figures 6.5 and 6.6 show right and left-skewed distributions, respectively.

Having a (fairly) normal distribution is crucial for many statistical methods which only really work with normally distributed data. For example, using z-scores to determine a data point's relative position on a distribution relies heavily on the distribution being symmetrical, that is, data must be distributed equally under the two tails of the curve (left and right of the mean). If the distribution is skewed, and the mean and the median are different, we do not have an equal distribution of scores or values. Look at Figure 6.7: with mean and median being different, the areas left and right of the mean are of unequal size. The standard deviations remain at equal distance from the mean. If we look at the two points labelled z(*a*) and z(*b*), they are both at approximately the same position, just about left (z(*a*)) and right (z(*b*)) of the first standard deviation. However, it is obvious that the areas between the mean and standard deviation and the mean and SD and the z-scores are not of equal size. Hence, even though it looks like the

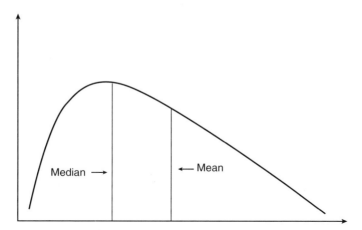

FIGURE 6.5 *Right-skewed distribution.*

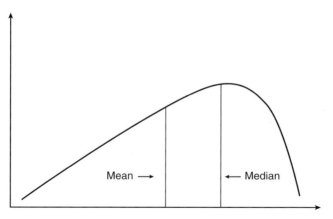

FIGURE 6.6 *Left-skewed distribution.*

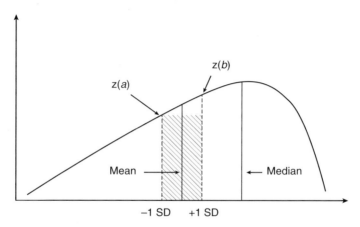

FIGURE 6.7 *Z-score in skewed distributions.*

two points are of equal distance from the mean, in relative terms they are not. And magic 34% rule also fails.

QUICK FIX: IS MY DATA NORMAL?

There is a plethora of cunning tests around that allow us to check whether our distribution is normal – none of which is available in Excel. There are, however, ways of approaching the issue.

1. Calculate the mean and median. If they are very similar, there is a good chance that your data is normally distributed.
2. We know that is a normal distribution, 68% of our data is within plus/minus one SDs, and 95% of data is within plus/minus two SDs. Does this approximately relate to your data?
3. Calculate the skewness: Excel has a function called SKEW which we can use: =skew(data). Interpret the result as follows:

   - If the result is 0 (or extremely close), then there is no skew.
   - If the result is larger than 0, then we have a positive or right-skew distribution (e.g. the tail is to the right)
   - If the result is smaller than 0, then our distribution shows negative of left-hand skew.

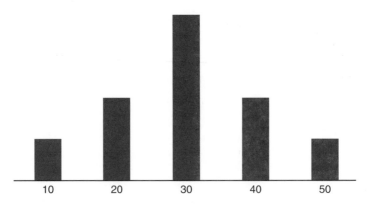

FIGURE 6.8 *Normal distribution. Skew= 0.*

In Chapter Nine, when introducing non-parametric data, we will pick up the issue is normal versus non-normal distributions again and introduce an addition measure to check for normality.

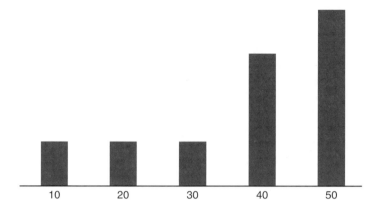

FIGURE 6.9 *Left-hand/negative skew. Skew= –0.64.*

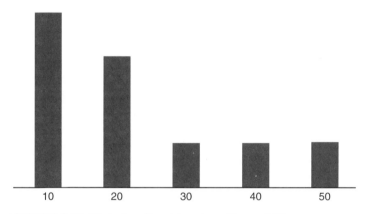

FIGURE 6.10 *Right-hand/positive skew. Skew= 1.31.*

6.5. The standard error

There is another measure of dispersion which is worth mentioning: the standard error (SE). I have deliberately taken it out of the discussion above, as the SE is often confused with the standard deviation, and, while it is a measure of dispersion, it works on a slightly different level. It is frequently included in other statistical tools, such as the *t*-test, which we will discuss in Chapter Eight.

We said above that the standard deviation provides information on how much the data in our sample is dispersed, with smaller standard deviations indicating values being less dispersed and distributed more closely around the mean. So far, we have only focused on samples, that is, a small part of the population. Sometimes, however, we would like to draw conclusions about the entire population, and use the sample to make inferences about what our population might look like. Also, we may want to use data from *several* samples, not just one. Based on data from several samples, we can then calculate the population mean (or an approximation of the population mean), assuming that all samples are randomly drawn from the same population. Assume we are interested in the size of the active vocabulary (measured in words) for 12-month-old children acquiring English as a first language. Also assume that we have a population of 100 12-month-old children (due to low birth rates in recent years we have a very small population), and we draw five random samples of five people each, giving us an overall sample size of 25 (=25% of the population). For each sample, we calculate the mean and the standard deviation. Table 6.5 displays the results for our five samples.

We can also calculate the population mean, either by calculating the mean of the individual sample means, or by calculating the mean for the scores of 25 children. Either way, the population mean is $X = 7.28$ words – bear in mind that this is an approximation only, as we have not included all members of the population but inferred the mean via the samples (remember: this is why it important that your sample is an adequate reflection of the population). If we look at the means for the individual samples, we see that samples A, B, C and E a relatively close to the population mean, while D is considerably higher – indicating that for some reason, sample D has linguistically more advanced children (which may, even with random sampling, happen – see Chapter Three). So, in order to fully understand our population mean, we need an indicator that tells us how dispersed the individual *sample means* are around the *population mean*. This is where the *standard error* enters the stage: one way of seeing the SE is that it is the standard deviation of the sample means. It is calculated the same way as the sample standard deviations, but in the first step of the manual calculation,

TABLE 6.5 Mean and standard deviation for five fictive samples

	Sample A	Sample B	Sample C	Sample D	Sample E
	1	2	2	6	1
	3	4	5	10	4
	5	6	8	12	6
	7	8	10	14	8
	9	10	11	20	10
Mean	5	6	7.2	12.4	5.8
SD	3.16	3.16	3.70	5.18	3.49

instead of subtracting each data point from the sample mean, we subtract each sample mean from the (approximate) population mean. This approach can be used when we have many samples – the more, the better. For our example in Table 6.5, the SE is 2.97 – this is fairly close to the population mean of $X = 7.28$. In Excel, the formula for the example is =stdev(5, 6, 7.2, 12.4, 5.8).

Unfortunately, we do not always have the chance to obtain data from many samples: sometimes, we have only one sample, and hence one sample mean, but we would still like to know how good or bad our sample and sample mean fits the population. And even worse, sometimes we only have a very small sample. In this case, we can use the sample standard deviation and the sample size N to calculate the SE: SE is the result of the sample standard deviation divided by the square root of sample size:

$$SE = \frac{STDEV_{sample}}{\sqrt{N}}$$

Let's say in our vocabulary size example (see Table 6.15), we only have one sample, sample A:

	Sample A
Mean	5
SD	3.16
N	5

The SE for our sample is then accordingly:

$$SE = \frac{3.16}{\sqrt{5}} = 1.41$$

Please note that this is an approximation only. Field (2000: 9–10) provides an excellent definition for how to interpret the SE:

[The standard error] is a measure of how representative a sample is likely to be of the population. A large standard error (relative to the sample mean) means that there is a lot of variability between the means of different samples and so the sample we have might not be representative of the population.

In our example, for sample A we have a mean of 5 and an SE of 1.41, so this is a good indicator that our sample mean is not too far off the population mean. This is coherent with what we said when we looked at all five samples from our population; and a sample mean of 5 is again fairly close to the approximate population mean of 7.28. For sample D, with a mean of 12.4 and a standard deviation of 5.18, the SE is

$$SE = \frac{5.18}{\sqrt{5}} = 2.32$$

This is higher than the SE for sample A and indicates than sample D is likely to be less representative of the population than A.

By its very nature, the sample size is a good way to illustrate the relationship between population and sample size: I have so far repeatedly said that most quantitative tools work best if we use them with a reasonably sized sample – relative frequencies show a higher level of detail with larger samples (Chapter Five), the arithmetic mean becomes less affected by extreme values and so forth. If you think about it for a moment, it should become clear that the larger the sample in relation to the population, the more representative it becomes. If we have a sample of ten people standing for a population of 100,000, there is considerable room for error (viz. the SE!); if on the other hand, we have a sample of 50,000, error is less likely. If this is true, we should find mathematic proof for it; and indeed, there is. In our fictive example, we assumed a population of 100 children, and our sample size was 5. For sample A, we calculated the SE as:

$$SE = \frac{3.16}{\sqrt{5}} = 1.41$$

If we now imagine that our sample was bigger, let's say 20 children, the sample should become more representative, as it now includes 20% of the population as opposed to 5%. And a higher degree of representativeness should be reflected in a lower SE. Let's try this:

$$SE = \frac{3.16}{\sqrt{20}} = 0.71$$

With a sample four times the size of our original one, the SE would be reduced by one half! Do bear in mind, though, that with a larger sample it is likely that we have a slightly different standard deviation – I use this here just as a matter of illustration.

6.6. Summary: Descriptive statistics

In the last two chapters we have met several useful tools for describing data. At this point, readers should be able to carry out a basic but thorough descriptive analysis of a given data set, and you should be aware of problems surrounding various statistical tools. I strongly recommend undertaking a through descriptive analysis of any data set acquired. With time (and practice), you will develop a 'feel' for data in all its forms and glory, and you will start spotting potential problems. Also, it is worth familiarizing yourself with a spreadsheet software – not having to worry about doing statistics by hand is a major step forward!

CHAPTER SEVEN

Analysing data – a few steps further

Key words: probability – chi-squared test – observed and expected frequencies – Pearson correlation – degrees of freedom – partial correlation – regression – significance – type I/type II error

So far, we have focused on both tidying up and describing our data. For smaller pieces of research, such as an undergraduate essay, this may well be enough. However, what most of us are really likely to want is a thorough data analysis that goes beyond mere description: we would like to explain and understand what is going on. Most likely, we are interested in how two or more variables are related, for example, does age of acquisition onset influence second language development, or do men really use non-standard forms more frequently than women.

We start this chapter with a very brief outline of probability theory, before moving on to explain two ways of measuring the relationship between variables: the chi-test and Pearson correlation.

7.1. Probability: The basics

Probability (n). the extent to which something is likely to happen or be the case; the appearance of truth, or likelihood d being realized, which a statement of event bears in the light of evidence.

OED

As the term implies, *probability theory* is concerned with how probable (or likely) a certain event is to occur. It is an important factor whenever we are interested in how certain (or uncertain) we can be that any conclusions we draw are correct or incorrect – issues we will address later in this chapter. One of the key terms in probability theory is that of the *event*. *Event* is defined as a collection of *results* or *outcomes* of an *experiment* we are conducting: it can be the outcome of tossing a coin or whether a particular utterance shows a particular linguistic feature. For example, the event of tossing a coin can have two outcomes: heads or tails. These outcomes are also called *simple events*. So, 'heads' is one simple event – it is one possible outcome. Rolling a die can have 6 outcomes, namely any score between 1 and 6, and an outcome of 4 is one particular simple event.

We can calculate the probability of an event by dividing the number of times a particular outcome occurs by the number of different simple events we *could* obtain. We use P to denote the probability of an event, and A denotes the specific simple event. Accordingly, we can calculate the probability of obtaining 'heads' when tossing a coin as follows: a normal coin has two sides, one heads on tails.

$$P(A) = \frac{\text{number of ways } A \text{ can occur}}{\text{number of different simple events}} = P(\text{heads}) = \frac{1}{2}$$

The probability of 'heads' to be the outcome is hence ½ ('one in two'), or 0.5. Similarly, the probability for the outcome of rolling a standard six-sided die to be 4 is:

$$P(4) = \frac{1}{6}$$

We only have one side that carries a '4' out of 6 sides in total; the probability in hence 1 in 6, or 0.16. The two experiments we have looked at here are special in that respect that all the simple events have the same probability: with a normal die, the probability to roll a 3 is the same as rolling a 6. The probability of a coin landing on heads is as high as landing on tails. These types of experiments are called *Laplace experiments*. We do not have to think too long to realize that real Laplace experiments are rare in linguistics – just consider all the different factors that can influence a particular variable!

Before we go into detail, we shall summarize three of the basic properties of probabilities:

1   The probability of an event always lies between 0 and 1 inclusive.

2   The probability of an event that cannot occur is 0.

3   The probability of an event that must occur is 1.

Properties (2) and (3) deserve a quick explanation: in (2), such an event would be rolling a 7 on a normal die – as a 7 does not exist, we cannot possibly have it as an outcome. Accordingly, for (3), we could imagine a coin with two identical sides, so the outcome will always be heads. These are obviously extreme cases which we are unlikely to come across very often. And if we do, we will not have to calculate the probability anyway (what is the probability of meeting a woman in a room with only women in it?).

A second approach to probabilities is via the relative frequency of an event. We can approximate the probability of a simple event by looking at its relative frequency, that is, how often a particular outcome occurs when the event if repeated multiple times. For example, when we toss a coin multiple times and report the result, the relative frequency of either outcome to occur will gradually approach 0.5 – given that it is an 'ideal' coin without any imbalance. Note that it is important to have a very large number of repetitions: if we toss a coin only 3 times, we will inevitably get 2 heads and 1 tail (or vice versa) but we obviously must not conclude that the probability for heads is $P(\text{head}) = \frac{2}{3}$ (0.66). However, if we toss our coin say 1,000 times, we are likely to get something like 520 heads and 480 tails. P(heads) is then 0.52 – much closer to the actual probability of 0.5.

Approximating the probability of an event via the relative frequency is particularly useful for linguistic applications. As briefly mentioned above, events in linguistics are unlikely to come from Laplace experiments were all events have the same probability to occur (unlike tossing coins or rolling dice). Chambers (2004) for example summarizes a study by Macaulay and Trevelyan (1977) on the use of the glottal stop across three age groups and three socio-economic classes in Glasgow. For 10-year-old middle-class children, the glottal stop was used in around 60% of all possible occurrences. In theory, a glottal stop can either be produced or not, so, theoretically, the probability of either event should be 1 in 2, or 0.5. In practice, however, it is obvious that glottal stop use is not a Laplace experiment, but dependent on a whole collection of other factors which favour either production or non-production. If we now take a large number of 10-year-old middle-class speakers and analyse their glottal stop usage, the relative frequencies will eventually give us a good approximation of the probability for the glottal stop being used or not by this group. Hence, we may interpret a relative frequency of 60% glottal stop use also as a probability, whereby the probability of a (random) 10-year-old middle-class Glaswegian is using the glottal stop is 0.6. As before, the more data we have the better and more accurate our result will be.

We have said that the probability of an event occurring lies between 0 and 1. Based on this, it is easy to calculate the probability of an event *not* occurring: if the probability of rolling a 3 is 1/6, the probability of not rolling a six is:

$$\bar{P} = 1 - 0.16 = 0.83$$

This is called the *complementation rule*. Accordingly, for our Glaswegian 10-year-old, the probability of *not* using the glottal stop is 0.4.

7.2. Probabilities: More than one event

So far we have dealt with simple events, that is, events were we are interested in one particular outcome. However, in reality it is likely that we are interested in the probability of more than one simple event occurring together. In this case we talk about *compound events*. For example, one simple event is whether a respondent in a sample is male or female. Another simple event is whether a person in the sample is a native or a non-native speaker. One possible compound event would be that a particular person is both a woman *and* a non-native speaker.

An example: Table 7.1 shows the distribution of men and women as well as native speakers (NS) and non-native speakers (NNS) in a sample of 100 respondents (N=100).

Task 7.1

Calculate the following probabilities: P(male), P(female), P(NS), P(NNS).

Out of a sample of 100 respondents, 60 are male, so if we randomly selected a respondent from this sample, the probability that this respondents it P(male)=60/100=0.6. Accordingly, P(female)=0.4, P(NS)=0.55 and P(NNS)=0.45.

We are now interested in the probability of selecting *either* a non-native speaker *or* a woman. In technical terms, we talk about a *union of events*. A related concept is the *intersection of events*: our selectee is *both* a woman and a non-native speaker. The two concepts are denoted as follows:

- Union of events: P(A ∪ B)
- Intersection of events: P(A ∩ B)

We calculate P(A ∪ B) by means of the *addition rule*: we add the probabilities of the two simple events, and subtract the probability of the intersected

TABLE 7.1 Absolute frequencies of men/women and native/non-native speakers (N=100)

	NS	NNS	Total
Male	40	20	60
Female	15	25	40
Total	55	45	100

event from the result in order to avoid double counting. Hence, we calculate:

P(female ∪ non-native speaker) = P(female) + P(non-native speaker)
                               – P(female ∩ non-native speaker)

The first event, P(woman) has a probability of 0.4, and P(NNS) is 0.45, as calculated above. However, from Table 7.1 we can also see that there are 25 respondents who are both female *and* non-native speakers. The probability of this is 25/100=0.25. We can hence calculate the probability of our union event as:

P(female ∪ non-native speaker) = 0.4 + 0.45 – 0.25 = 0.6

In plain English, the probability that a randomly selected respondent is *either* a woman *or* a non-native speaker is 0.6.

We shall consider two more cases: *joint* and *conditional probabilities*, and the *multiplication rule*. We have met *joint probabilities* already in the disguise of intersected probabilities, that is, the probability that someone is both female and a non-native speaker. Sometimes, however, we might be interested in whether the probability of a certain simple event, such as being a non-native speaker, depends on another event, such as being male or female. So, we might be interested whether the probability of being a non-native speaker is conditional on being a woman.

In a first step, we calculate the joint probabilities P(male ∩ NS), P(male ∩ NNS), P(female ∩ NS), and P(female ∩ NSS).

Task 7.2

Calculate the joint probabilities for all combinations of male/female and NS/NNS.

Table 7.2 shows the joint probabilities for all combinations of gender and speaker status. 'Marginal' refers to *marginal probabilities* – the sums of each row and column. Note that the marginal probabilities are exactly those we have calculated in task 7.1.

With Table 7.2, we can easily calculate our conditional probabilities. We said at the beginning we were interested in the probability of a person being

TABLE 7.2 Joint probabilities

	NS	NNS	Marginal
Male	0.4	0.2	0.6
Female	0.15	0.25	0.4
Marginal	0.55	0.45	1

a non-native speaker on the condition of being a woman. We denote this as P(NNS|female), and calculate is by dividing the joint probability by the appropriate marginal probability for the female sample *only*:

$$P(NNS|female) = \frac{0.25}{0.4} = 0.625$$

So, given that a respondent is female, there is a 62.5% chance that she is a non-native speaker.

We can also do this the other way round, and calculate the probability for the argument that someone is female on the condition of being a non-native speaker. In this case, we divide the joint probability by the appropriate marginal probability for the non-native sample only.

$$P(female|NNS) = \frac{0.25}{0.45} = 0.625$$

With the marginal probabilities being very similar, so is the result. Here, we would argue that given that a respondent is a non-native speaker there is a 62.5% chance that she is a woman.

Task 7.3

Calculate the following conditional probabilities, and briefly explain them: P(NS|male), P(NNS|male)

Let's briefly use this to compare different groups. We said that P(NNS|female)=0.625 or 62.5%. Hopefully, in task 7.3 you have calculated P(NNS|male)=0.33, that is, given that the respondent is male, there is a 33.3% chance that he is a non-native speaker:

$$P(NNS|male) = \frac{0.2}{0.6} = 0.33$$

If we now compare those two, we will find that men are much less likely to be non-native speakers than women. However, it is crucial to understand that this comparison does *not* imply causality in any way – it merely compares two sets of observations.

Lastly, there may be cases where we are interested in a union event that includes a conditional event. For example, in our fictive sample we know that 45% are non-native speakers, that is, P(NNS)=0.4. Let's assume that a quarter of these non-native speakers speak more than one foreign language, that is, are multilingual. We denote this as (multilingual|NNS)=0.25. What is the joint probability that a non-native speaker is also multilingual? We have to use the *multiplication rule*:

$$P(NNS \cap multilingual) = 0.4 \times 0.25 = 0.1$$

In other words, 10% of our non-native speakers speak more than one foreign language. In yet other words, the probability that a randomly selected person in our sample who is multilingual non-native speaker is 0.1.

Before we leave our short excursion into the world of probability theory, a final example and task – solutions in Chapter Eleven. Henry's (2004) study focused on the variability in syntax, more specifically subject-verb agreement in language between young children and their caregivers in Belfast.

> [I]n Belfast English, there is a process known as 'singular concord' [. . .] under which subject-verb agreement is optional where the subject is a full noun phrase (rather than a pronoun); where there is no agreement, the verb shows up in the default third person singular form. (2004: 278)

This allows for the alternating use of either

The children play in the garden (+agreement), and
The children plays in the garden (–agreement).

Table 7.3 shows the absolute frequencies of +/– agreement for both children and caregivers Henry investigated.

Task 7.4

Calculate the following probabilities:

- P(child); P(caregiver); P(+agr); P(–agr)

- P(child ∪ –agr) – child *or* agreement violation

- P(caregiver ∪ +agr) – caregiver *or* agreement

- P(caregiver | +agr) – agreement on the condition of being uttered by a caregiver

Working with probabilities may seem daunting at first, but once you have come to grips with it, you will realize that it is all about knowing in which

TABLE 7.3 Absolute frequencies for third-person singular agreement

	Child	Caregiver	
+agr	131	218	349
–agr	24	55	79
	155	273	428

cell of a table to look and then to calculate the probability with some basic arithmetic. When using probabilities, especially in situations where you have to approximate probabilities via the relative frequencies, make sure you have a sufficiently large sample, so as to avoid any outlying values skewing your results. And as with all statistical tools, probabilities can be very effective when used at the right time in the right place, but be careful not to randomly drop obscure probabilities into a study – it just shows that you have not fully understood what you are doing.

7.3. The chi-squared test

We leave our discussion of probabilities here, and move on to discuss the relationship between two or more variables. At this point, is may be wise to revise your knowledge of different types of variables and levels of measurement, as discussed in Chapter Two. We start with the *chi-squared test of independence*, named after the Greek letter χ ('chi') on which the calculation is based.

Clark (2003) summarizes a study by Schwartz and Leonhard (1982) on the acquisition of consonant inventories of very young children. In essence, 1-year-olds were presented with two sets of made-up words: IN words, containing consonants used by the children, and OUT words, containing consonants the children did not use. IN and OUT words were presented equally to children for a period of time, before the researchers measured both production and comprehension of both IN and OUT words. Table 7.4 shows the results in absolute frequencies.

Note that here we deal with *categorical data* – the words fall into two categories: IN or OUT, but an individual word cannot be 'a bit an IN word but more an OUT word'. As a comparison, think of a group of people who we have to divide according to obesity status (yes/no) and suffering from diabetes (yes/no). Again, any one person can only fit in *one* category in each dimension, for example, being obese/suffering from diabetes or being obese/

TABLE 7.4 Production and comprehension of IN and OUT words

	IN	OUT	
Produced spontaneously	33	12	45
Understood correctly	54	50	104
	87	62	149

Source: Clark (2003: 114).

not suffering from diabetes (or -obese/+diabetes and -obese/–diabetes) There are no in-betweens: someone cannot be 'a bit obese and a bit diabetic' – you either are or are not.[1]

Table such as 7.4. are also called 2×2 contingency tables. Clark and Schwartz and Leonhard suggest that children 'produce significantly greater number of IN words [. . .] [and] are selective in what they try to say' (Clark 2003: 113). What we are interested in here, in the first instance, is whether the two variable 'type of word' and 'comprehension/production' are related, that is, do word-type and comprehension/production have anything to do with each other; and the chi-square test will give us a quantitative measure for this.

The chi-squared test is essentially based on the comparison of the observed values with the appropriate set of expected values. That is, it compares whether our expectations and our actual data correspond. Accordingly, as a first step we have to calculate a contingency table with *expected values*, based on our actual (or observed) values. The expected values are calculated by multiplying the row and column totals with each other, and dividing the result by the total number in the sample, as shown in Table 7.5.

$$\text{Expected frequency} = \frac{\text{Total of row} \times \text{Total of column}}{\text{Grand total}}$$

This gives us expected values as displayed in Table 7.6.

TABLE 7.5 Calculation of expected values

	IN	OUT	
Produced spontaneously	87*45/149	62*45/149	45
Understood correctly	87*104/149	62*104/149	104
	87	62	149

TABLE 7.6 Expected values

	IN	OUT	
Produced spontaneously	26	19	45
Understood correctly	61	43	104
	87	62	

By comparing Tables 7.4 and 7.6 we can see immediately that observed and expected values differ by approximately seven points throughout. To pick out a few examples, based on the general distribution of values across rows and columns we would *expect* that children would spontaneously produce 26 IN words; in real life however, they produced 33 IN words spontaneously (see Table 7.4), so they produce seven more IN words that we would expect. Similarly, we would expect them to understand 61 words containing sound clusters they know; our observed values however show that in reality they only understood 54 – in this cases, they are seven words below our expectations. It is these differences we are interested in. What we must do now is to quantify this statistically. I assume, as before, that few people actually want to do this by hand, so I will discuss the Excel method first.

Doing statistics using Excel: *The chi-squared test*

To calculate the χ^2 you will need 2 tables: the table with your original, observed values, and a second table with the expected values – that is, tables similar to 7.4 and 7.6. The Excel formula for the χ^2 test is

=chi-test(actual_range; expected_range).

This should be straightforward: actual_range refers to our observed values, expected_range to our expected values. For our example, you should get a result of 0.01492.

If you would like the function wizard to help you, go to Formulas, insert function, and search for 'chi-test'. Follow the instructions.

→See the companion website for an Excel template that calculates the chi-squared test for 2×2 contingency tables automatically.←

Excel (or any other software you might use) has hopefully given you a result of $p=0.01492$. But how to interpret it? As a guideline, the closer the p-value (of significance level – we will discuss this later) is to zero, the less likely our variables are to be independent. Our p-value is smaller than 0.05, which is a very strong indicator that there *is* a relationship between type of words produced and comprehension/production. With our result from the chi-test, we can now confidently say that in this particular study, there is a rather strong link between the type of word and the level of production and comprehension. And while this conclusion is not surprising (well, at least not for those familiar with language acquisition), it is a statistically sound one. Which is far better than anecdotal evidence or guessing.

For the sake of completeness, the formula for the chi-squared test is $\chi = \sum \frac{(O_i - E_i)^2}{E_i}$, whereby O denotes the observed and E the expected frequency.

In real language, we calculate the difference between each observed and its respective expected value, square this difference and divide the result by the expected value. Then add it all up:

$$\chi^2 = \frac{(33-26)^2}{26} + \frac{(54-61)^2}{61} + \frac{12-19^2}{19} + \frac{50-43^2}{43}$$
$$= 1.86 + 0.81 + 2.62 + 1.13 = 6.42$$

Unlike our Excel result, this result as such does not tell us much. What we need are two things: ssa table of *critical values* for the χ^2, which you can find in Chapter Ten, and the *degrees of freedom*. Roughly, critical values are the values we can accept for a particular significance level. For the chi-test we can say that as long as our result (the manual one, not the one Excel gives us) is equal to or exceeds a critical value, a particular significance level has been met. Again, we discuss significance later in this chapter. In our example, Excel has already shown us that p=0.01, so we know that any values equal to or larger than 6.42 will also be significant on this level (or even more significant).

Degrees of freedom (or df) refers to how many values in a table you need to know in order to complete the table. So, in a table such as Table 7.7, with the row and column totals given, you need one value in order to complete the table. That is, you have 1 degree of freedom.

Try it out: we know that 50 OUT words were correctly understood, and we know that the row total must be 104. So, we can calculate the understood IN words as 104–50=54. With these two values and the row/column totals it is now easy to calculate the frequencies for spontaneously produced words. For the χ^2, df are calculated as

$$df = (\text{number of rows} - 1) \times (\text{number of columns} - 1)$$

TABLE 7.7 Calculating *df*

	IN	OUT	
Produced spontaneously	?	?	45
Understood correctly	?	50	104
	87	62	149

So, for a table with 2 rows and 2 columns, we calculate

$$df = (2-1) \times (2-1) = 1$$

With the result of our earlier calculations (6.42) and our df (1) we now go to the table of critical values. Since df=1, we look in the first row (the one below the header row). We can see that our 6.42 falls between 3.841 and 6.635. Looking in the header row, we can see that it hence falls between a significance level of 0.05 and 0.01, so our result is significant on a level of 0.05. If you remember, Excel has given us a p value of 0.014 – not quite 0.01, but very close. As before, with $p<0.05$, we can confidently reject the idea that the variables are independent, but suggest that they are related in some way.

Note: a number of statisticians argue that the chi-squared test only works reliably when the minimum count in each cell is 5, and they provide several sophisticated methods of correcting this. Others suggest that the minimum count does not play a role. In this book, we stick with the latter opinion. Yet, it is worth bearing potential problems in mind when interpreting results – as I have explained so frequently throughout the last few chapters, quantitative methods work best with larger amounts of data anyway.

Task 7.5

Let's go back to Henry's example introduced above in our discussion of probability theory. Is there a relationship between agreement and type of speaker? Solution in Chapter Eleven.

	Child	Caregiver	
+agr	131	218	349
−agr	24	55	79
	155	273	428

QUICK FIX: CHI-SQUARED

Use chi-squared test to check relationship between categorical data. If $p<0.05$, then there is a relationship between the variables.

7.4. Pearson correlation

As illustrated in the previous section, the χ^2 test allows us to investigate relationships between variables that are based on a nominal/categorical scale. But what happens with data that is on a ratio scale? How can we determine the relationship between two ratio-scale variables? A good linguistic example is the influence age of acquisition onset has on eventual second language (L2) proficiency. We will base the discussion primarily on Johnson and Newport (1989) and (1991). I suspect most people will be familiar with the argument that 'the older you are, the harder it is to learn a foreign language'. Quantitative researchers that we are (or would like to become), we will need an appropriate measure to show the relationship between the two variables. And even more, we would like something that also shows us the direction of the relationship as well as its strength – too much to ask for?

Based on a study of the acquisition of subjacency (a particular syntactic rule) in English as a second language with native speakers of Chinese, Johnson and Newport argue that,

> these studies suggest that linguistic universals such as subjacency become less accessible to the language learner with increasing maturation. (1991: 254)

They even provide a quantitative measure for it:

> As can be seen, there is a fairly continuous decline in the observance of subjacency as age of expose to the language increases. This continuous decline is supported by [. . .] a corresponding significant correlation between age of arrival and subjacency score ($r=-0.63$, $p=.001$). (1991: 247–48)

The statistically versed will just look at two pieces of information which tell us everything we need: the *correlation coefficient r* and the *significance value p*. But let's proceed step by step. Table 7.8 shows the age of acquisition onset in years as well as a fictive proficiency score running from 0 to 100, with 0 indicating zero proficiency in the L2 and 100 indicating native-speaker-like competence.

It is usually a good idea to draw a *scatter plot* of our data set. We have met scatter plots in Chapter Five already: they are a type of graph where we plot the values for each individual respondent onto the x- and the y-axis. For example, we plot Amelie's score for age of onset (4 years) at 4 on the x and her proficiency score of 95 at 95 on the y-axis. That is, she will show up as a dot somewhere top-left of our graph. Accordingly, Harry will turn up in the right bottom area, with an onset age of 15 years and a proficiency of 46. Figure 7.1 is the scatter plot for our data set.

TABLE 7.8 A fictive example

	Onset age	Score
Amelie	4	95
Bert	5	82
Charles	7	80
Doreen	8	76
Emily	8	79
Fred	10	70
Gemma	11	68
Harry	15	46

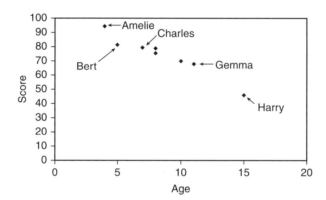

FIGURE 7.1 *Scatter plot for fictive data set.*

Doing statistics using Excel: *Scatter plots*

To create a scatter plot, highlight the two data arrays, that is, the age of
onset scores and the proficiency scores – do NOT highlight the row/column
headings. Click on 'Insert' and select the 'scatter plot' icon and choose
scatter plot.

Looking at our scatter plot, we can immediately see that the two variables
seem to be related in such as way that the higher the age of onset score is (i.e.
the further right we go on the horizontal x-axis), the lower the proficiency

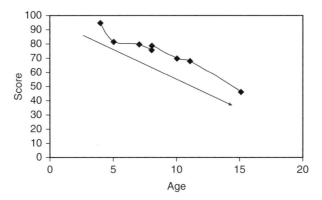

FIGURE 7.2 *Scatter plot with line.*

scores become (i.e. the lower we go on the vertical y-axis). If we draw a line through the individual data points, we can see this even better.

In an 'ideal' world, our variables are related in such a way that we can connect all individual points to a straight line. In this case, we speak of a *perfect correlation* between the two variables. As we can see in Figures 7.1 and 7.2, the world isn't ideal and the line is not quite straight, so the correlation between age of onset and proficiency is not perfect – although it is rather strong! Before we think about calculating the correlation, we shall consider five basic principles about the correlation of variables:

1   the Pearson correlation coefficient r can have any value between (and including) –1 and 1, that is, $-1 \leq r \leq 1$.

2   $r=1$ indicates a *perfect positive correlation*, that is, the two variables increase in a linear fashion, that is, all data points lie is a straight line – just as if they were plotted with the help of a ruler.

3   $r=-1$ indicates a *perfect negative correlation*, that is, while one variable increases, the other decreases, again, linearly.

4   $r=0$ indicates that the two variables to not correlate at all. That is, there is no relationship between them.

5   The Pearson correlation only works for normally distributed (or 'parametric') data (see Chapter Six) which is on a ratio scale (see Chapter Two) – we discuss solutions for non-parametric distributed data in Chapter Nine.

According the these principles, the closer r is to 1 (or –1), the stronger the correlation between the two variables is, the closer r is to 0, the weaker it is – see Figure 7.3.

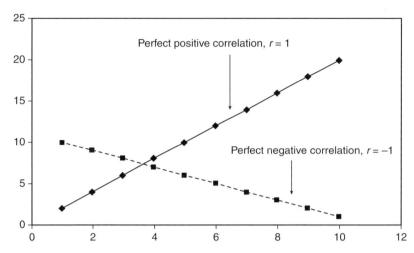

FIGURE 7.3 *Scatter plot showing positive and negative correlation between variables x and y.*

The Pearson coefficient of correlation is based on the variances of the two variables (see Chapter Six). It is calculated as

$$r_{xy} = \frac{\text{Covariance of variable } x \text{ and } y}{(\text{Standard deviation of } x) \times (\text{Standard deviation of } y)}$$

The covariance of A and B is calculated by using the following equation:

$$\text{Covariance}_{xy} = \frac{\text{Sum of } [(\text{mean } x - \text{each } x \text{ score}) \times (\text{mean } y - \text{each } y \text{ score})]}{N - 1}$$

(from Cramer 1998: 139)

As you can imagine, this can be rather painful to calculate by hand, especially for large data sets.

Doing statistics using Excel: *Pearson's r*

The correlation coefficient in easily calculated with Excel. The function is:

=correl(array1, array2), whereby 'array1' is the list of one set of scores (for example, age of onset) and 'array2' is the second set (such as L2 proficiency).

(→See the companion website for a clip on how to calculate the Pearson correlation and create a scatterplot with Excel.←)

Task 7.6

Calculate r for our fictive example in Table 7.9. What does the result tell us?

In our example $r=-0.97$, that is, we have a very strong negative correlation between age of onset and L2 proficiency – the older a learner is, the worse gets his or her competence in the L2. Unfortunately, our result is not quite complete. In Chapter Six, we said that the arithmetic mean can be identical for two completely different sets of data, simply because it is a mathematical construct. In a similar way, our Pearson coefficient may end up as $r=-0.97$ by mere chance: data might be distributed in such a way that the coefficient turns out to have a particular value simply and only because the arithmetic make it to, yet, the result (or 'true meaning') may be useless. As with the chi-squared test, we need to determine the significance level first. And for this, we once again need our degrees of freedom.

Degrees of freedom for a Pearson correlation are calculated as follows:

$df = N - 2$, where N is the number of paired scores

We have 8 participants in our example, hence 8 pairs of scores, so $N=8$. Accordingly,

$$df = N - 2 = 8 - 2 = 6$$

Before we can look up our significance level, we have to decide whether our test is *1-tailed* or *2-tailed*. To cut a long story short, in a 1-tailed test we have a pretty good idea in advance in which direction the relationship between the variables is going (i.e. positive or negative correlation), while in a 2-tailed test we do not predict this direction. In our example, based on previous research, we assume that there is a negative correlation (age influences proficiency negatively, not vice versa), so we go for a 1-tailed test. Note that this does *not* influence the way r is calculated, but only influences the significance level!

We now have to go to our table of critical values for the Pearson coefficient (Chapter Eleven) and look up the significance level: df=6, so we look in the appropriate row. We know that for a given significance level, r must be equal or exceed the critical value of this level. Our $r=-0.97$ – it does not matter whether r is positive or negative, what counts is the absolute value, that is, the 0.97. On the rightmost column of row 6, the critical value for a 0.0005 significance level is 0.9241. Our coefficient is larger than this (we can ignore the minus sign), so we can say our correlation is significant on a level of $p=0.0005$ (in fact, it is even more significant than $p=0.0005$). In plain English, this means that the probability that our correlation coefficient is a fluke is smaller than 0.05% – very good! Note: some statistical software, such as SPSS, will automatically provide both the Pearson correlation coefficient and the significance level in one go. That is, we do not have to look it up in a table.

For the sake of illustration, our fictive example has provided us with some marvellous values. Let's go back to Johnson and Newport's original study. We said above that Johnson and Newport (1991) found that age of acquisition onset and proficiency in L2 subjacency was $r=-0.63$, $p=0.001$. Now, it should not be a problem to interpret this result: with $r=-0.63$ we have a moderately strong, negative correlation, that is, we have an obvious decline in performance with increasing age. With $p=0.001$, the probability that this result is a fluke is a mere 0.1% – again, this is a pretty impressive result!

While the Pearson correlation provides us with a useful tool for investigating the relationship between variables, we should be careful not to accept its results too enthusiastically. For a start, the correlation coefficient as a measure of *association* only tells us that there is a relationship between the two variables, and it also indicates the strength of this relationship on a scare from –1 to 1. It does not, however, tell us anything about *causality*. So, just because there is a strong negative correlation between age of onset and L2 proficiency does not mean that a later onset *causes* limited success in acquiring a second language. In Chapter Two, we have had a thorough look at dependent (DV) and independent variables (IV), and said that the former is influenced by the latter. We have also said that it is not always clear which variable is the independent and which one the dependent variable. Unfortunately, a simple Pearson correlation does not help us here either – we still need to look elsewhere to explain causality.

A second major problem is the influence of latent variables, also discussed in Chapter Two. In my own research (Rasinger 2007) I, too, found a strong negative correlation between age of onset and L2 English proficiency of Bangladeshi migrants in London. Yet, the situation was a bit trickier: especially when talking about second language acquisition in a migration context, the amount actual L2 usage will inevitably influence the development of the second language. And as a general rule, one could assume that the longer someone lives in the target language country (England in this example), the more opportunities they have to practice. In my research, I found that the two potential independent variables (age of onset and length of residence) also strongly and negatively correlated with each other: the older a respondent was at the time they entered the United Kingdom and started to learn English, the fewer years they had spent in the country, and hence the less input/output in the second language they had). This phenomenon, whereby independent variables strongly correlate with each other is known as *collinearity*.

The question now is, which of the two variables does actually influence L2 proficiency? Age of onset or length of exposure? A statistical method called *partial correlation* is the way out. In essence, a partial correlation is calculated between two variables, for example, age and proficiency, while simultaneously controlling for the third variable (e.g. exposure), whereby 'controlling' means to take it into account while doing the maths. The partial correlation gives us a more accurate picture of the 'true' correlation between two variables. Unfortunately, there is no easy way to carry out a partial correlation in Excel. Other software, such as SPSS, provides partial correlations at the click of the mouse button.

QUICK FIX: PEARSON'S CORRELATION

Use a Pearson's correlation to determine the strength of the relationship between to ratio-scale variables. $-1 \leq r \leq 1$, whereby 1=perfect positive, −1=perfect negative correlation, and 0=no correlation at all.

7.6. Partial correlation

A correlation coefficient that is potentially substantially flawed is obviously no good. The last thing we want is our analysis to be sabotaged by something we cannot even account for. The easiest way to carry out a partial correlation is to use software that includes it as a tool for partial correlation analysis. The more tedious way is to do it as a multi-step process using a calculator or Excel, and pen and paper.

Let's assume we have a situation with three variables, labelled A, B and C. We start our discussion at the point where we have already calculated all simple correlation coefficients, that is, r_{AB}, r_{AC} and r_{BC}. For the sake of convenience, let's say our coefficients are

$$r_{AB}=0.8 \quad r_{AC}=0.5 \quad r_{BC}=0.4$$

We have also checked the significance levels, and all our coefficients are statistically significant. *Note*: if in real life one of your coefficients does not turn out to be significant, the need for a partial correlation is less imminent.

We are now interested in the 'true' correlation between A and B, and we want to ensure that the C does not influence our result. That is, we *control* for C. The generic formula for this partial correlation is:

$$r_{AB} = \frac{r_{AB} - (r_{AC} \times r_{BC})}{\sqrt{(1-(r_{AC})^2) \times (1-(r_{BC})^2)}}$$

This looks far scarier than it is. We will go through this equation step by step – have pen and paper ready.

1 multiply $r_{AC}=0.5$ with r_{BC}. Call the result r_{ACBC}.

$$r_{ACBC} = 0.5 \times 0.4 = 0.2$$

2 multiply r_{AC} with itself:

$$(r_{AC})^2 = 0.5 \times 0.5 = 0.25$$

3 multiply r_{BC} with itself: $0.4 \times 0.4 = 0.16$

$$(r_{BC})^2 = 0.4 \times 0.4 = 0.16$$

4 subtract r_{ACBC} from r_{AB}. This gives you the upper half of the equation.

$$0.8 - 0.2 = 0.6$$

5 subtract r_{AC}^2 from 1: $1-0.25=0.75$

$$1 - 0.25 = 0.75$$

6 subtract r_{BC}^2 from 1: $1-0.16=0.84$

$$1 - 0.16 = 0.84$$

7 multiply the results from steps 5 and 6:

$$0.75 \times 0.84 = 0.63$$

8 calculate the square root of the result in step 7: SQRT(0.63)=0.79

$$\sqrt{0.63} = 0.79$$

9 divide the result from step 4 by the result from step 8:

$$r_{AB\_partial} = \frac{0.6}{0.79} = 0.76$$

Here is the equation with all values filled in.

$$r_{AB} = \frac{r_{ab} - (r_{AC} \times r_{BC})}{\sqrt{(1-(r_{AC})^2) \times (1-(r_{BC})^2)}} = \frac{0.8 - (0.5 \times 0.4)}{\sqrt{(1-(0.5)^2) \times (1-(0.4)^2)}}$$

$$= \frac{0.8 - 0.2}{\sqrt{(1-0.25) \times (1-0.16)}} = \frac{0.6}{\sqrt{0.75 \times 0.84}} = \frac{0.6}{\sqrt{0.63}} = \frac{0.6}{0.79} = 0.76$$

That is, the correlation between A and B is r=0.76 when controlled for C – lower than the original value of 0.8, indicating that the C indeed has an impact on the relationship between these variables. This impact is in such a way that is increases the 'true' correlation between A and B, making it appears stronger than it actually is. This should not be too difficult to understand when we consider that C correlates considerable with both A and B, with $r_{AC}=0.5$ and $r_{BC}=0.4$. That is, we have a rather strong collinearity between all variables, and seeing that all correlation coefficients between all our variables are positive, there is a general 'upwards push' for the coefficients. To strengthen this argument, let's calculate r_{AC} and r_{BC}, either by and or using the Excel template below. If everything goes to plan, the correlation between A and C, when controlled for B, is $r_{AC}=0.33$; again, this is lower the original uncontrolled coefficient. And if we calculate r_{BC}, we will be astonished to see that, if controlled for A, the partial coefficient is 0: if controlled for A, there is no detectable relationship between B and C – what we saw before ($r_{BC}=0.4$) was simply the product of a particular constellation of numbers. This is obviously a constructed example for illustration purposes, and in real life it is unlikely that results will be that extreme. Nevertheless, it is important to understand the basic concepts of how variables can influence each other and lead to results which are misleading and potentially seriously flawed.

Doing statistics using Excel: *Partial correlation*

While there is not a direct function in Excel that allows us to calculate partial correlations, I provide here, as a special 'treat' for readers who followed me through the onerous process of calculating it manually, a basic template for a partial correlation with 3 variables. The template works for the partial correlation of A and B, controlling for C. If you are interested in another coefficient and another control variable, you will have to adjust the template manually.

1. Calculate the three 'normal' Pearson correlation coefficients r_{AB}, r_{AC} and r_{BC}.
2. Copy the template into Excel – make sure you copy it in *exactly* the same cells as illustrated in the template, that is, make sure that 'Var A' is in cell B2, etc. You can use this as a template for partial correlations involving three variables.

	A	B	C	D
1		Var A	Var B	Var C
2	Var A			
3	Var B	0.8		
4	Var C	0.5	0.4	
5				
6	r_partial			

3. The coefficients of the example are given – replace them by entering your own coefficients into the template.
4. In cell B6, enter the following function exactly:

   =(B3–(B4*C4))/SQRT((1–(B4*B4))*(1–(C4*C4)))

5. The correlation coefficient between A and B, controlled for C, will be displayed in cell B6. Note: Excel might display ##### instead of a number – in this case, you have to adjust the column width.

(→See the companion website for a simple Excel template for calculating partial correlations.←)

We shall finish our discussion of Pearson and partial correlation with a real example. Figure 7.4 is taken from Rasinger (2007: 96) and graphically represents the performance of 12 speakers with regard to copula and auxiliary verbs as well as a more general Accuracy Index (AI). The higher the score, the better the performance, with the maximum possible value for all three variables being 100. The scatter plot also shows the trend lines for all three variable constellations, which shows us the general trend of the relationship. As we can see, all the variables correlate positively with each other, and the coefficients are as follows: $r_{AI/Aux}=0.41$, $r_{AI/Cop}=0.66$ and $r_{Aux/Cop}=0.53$. I guess it does not take long for you to spot that trouble looms: if we have a strong collinearity with positive correlation throughout, is it not likely that the 'true' results are somewhat different? The obvious answer is yes, and if we carry out a partial correlation, controlling step by step for each of the three variables, we will see that the true coefficients are slightly lower (this is a subtle hint that you should practice your statistical

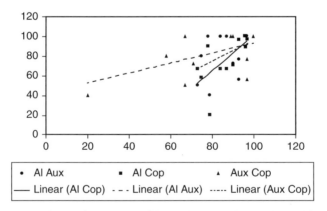

FIGURE 7.4 *Correlation for two variables and 12 speakers (adapted from Rasinger 2007).*

skills . . .), and if we plot the scatter plots, the trendlines' slopes will be less steep.

7.7. Causality

We said above that the correlation coefficient does not tell us anything about causality. However, for reasons whose explanations are beyond the scope of this book, if we square the correlation coefficient, that is, multiply it with itself, the so-called R^2 (R squared) tells us how much the independent variable accounts for the outcome of the dependent variable. In other words, causality can be approximated via R^2 (Field 2000: 90). As reported, Johnson and Newport (1991) found that age of onset and L2 proficiency correlate significantly with $r=-0.63$. In this situation it is clear that *if* there was indeed causality, it would be age influencing L2 proficiency – and not vice versa. Since we are not provided with any further information or data about third variables, we cannot calculate the partial correlation and have to work with $r=-0.63$. If we square r, we get $-0.63 \times -0.63 = 0.3969$. This can be interpreted in such a way that age of onset can account for about 40 per cent of the variability in L2 acquisition.

This is pretty good, but it also shows us that there *must* be something else influencing the acquisition process. So, we can only say that age has a comparatively strong *influence* on proficiency, but we cannot say that is *causes* it. The furthest we could go with R^2 is to argue that if there is causality between age and proficiency, age only causes around 40%; but to be on the safe side, we should omit any reference to causality altogether.

If you think about it carefully, if age was the one and only variable influencing (or indeed causing) L2 acquisition, the correlation between the two variables should be perfect, that is, $r=1$ (or $r=-1$) – otherwise we would never get an R^2 of 1! In fact, Birdsong and Molis (2001) replicated Johnson and Newport's earlier (1989) study and concluded that exogenous factors (such as expose and use of the target language) also influence the syntactic development. And with over 60% of variability unaccounted for, there is plenty of space for those other factors!

Doing statistics using Excel: R^2

Two easy ways to calculate R^2 in Excel:

- Simply multiply the *r* value with itself. So, if *r* is in cell F12, for example, the formula is =F12*F12
- Use the RSQ function in Excel: =rsq(array1, array2)

7.8. A word on significance

Throughout this chapter, I have repeatedly used the concept of *significance*, but I have yet to provide a reasonable explanation for it. Following the general objectives of this book of being accessible and not to scare off readers mathematically less well versed, I will limit my explanation to a 'quick and dirty' definition.

Statistical significance in this context has nothing to do with our results being of particular important – just because Johnson and Newport's correlation coefficient comes with a significance value of 0.001 does not mean it is automatically groundbreaking research. Significance in statistics refers to the probability of our results being a fluke or not; it shows the likelihood that our result is reliable and has not just occurred through the bizarre constellation of individual numbers. And as such it is very important: when reporting measures such as the Pearson's r, we *must* also give the significance value as otherwise our result is meaningless. Imagine an example where we have two variables A and B and three pairs of scores, as below:

A	B
1	3
2	3
3	4

If we calculate the Pearson coefficient, we get $r=0.87$, this is a rather strong positive relationship. However, if you look at our data more closely, how can we make this statement be reliable? We have only three pairs of scores, and for variable B, two of the three scores are identical (viz. 3), with the third score is only marginally higher. True, the correlation coefficient is strong and positive, but can we really argue that the higher A is the higher is B? With three pairs of scores we have 1 degree of freedom, and if we look up the coefficient in the table of critical values for df=1, we can see that our coefficient is not significant, but quite simply a mathematical fluke.

Statistical significance is based on probability theory: how likely is something to happen or not. Statistical significance is denoted with p, with p fluctuating between zero and 1 inclusive, translating into zero to 100 per cent. The smaller p, the less likely our result is to be a fluke.

For example, for a Pearson correlation we may get $r=0.6$ and $p=0.03$. This indicates that the two variables correlate moderately strongly (see above), but it also tells us that the probability of this correlation coefficient occurring by mere chance is only 3%. To turn it round, we can be 97% *confident* that our r is a reliable measure for the association between the two variables. Accordingly, we might get a result of r=0.98 and p=0.48. Again, we have a very strong relationship; however, in this case the probability that the coefficient is a fluke is 48% – not a very reliable indicator! In this case, we cannot speak of a real relationship between the variables, but the coefficient merely appears as a result of a random constellation of numbers. We have seen a similar issue when discussing two entirely different data sets having the same mean. In linguistics, we are usually looking for significance levels of 0.05 or below (i.e. 95% confidence), although we may want to go as high as $p=0.1$ (90% confidence). Anything beyond this should make you seriously worried. In the following chapter, we will come across the concept of significance again when we try and test different hypotheses.

Clegg (1982: 66) points out that 'in stating a certain degree of confidence in your results, you are also admitting the possibility of being wrong.' Naturally, the last thing we would like to be is to be wrong, after all the effort we have put into our data collection and analysis. Yet, admitting to be wrong is far less embarrassing than presenting wrong results – especially if other people find out that you are wrong!

Quantitative research distinguishes between two types of 'being wrong': type I and type II errors. A type I error occurs when we accept a relationship between variables (or difference in variables – see Chapter Eight) when in fact there is none. A type II error refers to the phenomenon of us rejecting a relationship/difference when in fact there is one (see also Cramer 1998: 66, among many others). The significance level relates to a type I error: if we have a significance level of $p=0.05$, the probability that we detected a relationship which in reality does not exist is only 5%. This is why it is so important to pay attention to the significance level of our result: we might have a great result, for example, a near-perfect correlation between two variables, but we may also have a significance level of only 0.4. In this case there is a 40% chance that we have detected a relationship when in fact there is none – a typical type I error.

A type II error – the non-detection of what is actually present – is more complex and often relates to too small a sample size or a wrong methodology altogether. And this would lead us straight back to Chapters Two to Four and the discussion of research designs and methodological approaches.

7.9. Simple regression: Making forecasts

In our discussion of the Pearson correlation under Section 7.4, we have seen that if variables correlate with each other, they form a particular pattern if we plot a scatter graph: the stronger the correlation between the two variables is, the more the individual dots on the graph form a straight line. We also said that in a perfect correlation, all dots will lie on this straight line, but, unfortunately, hardly anything is ever perfect, so we only get this straight line in exceptional circumstances. However, mathematicians and statisticians have figured out a way to calculate a 'virtual' straight line through all our data points. In other words, we can, using various statically tools, project an imaginary straight line into our data. This *regression line* (or *trend line*, which we have already met in the partial correlation example) is an idealized representation of our data, and it is calculated in such a way that is lies in the middle of all data points – independent from how spread out data is. Look at the data in Table 7.9, indicating fictive pairs of scores for two variables: lengths of practice (in years) and score (on a scale from

TABLE 7.9 Fictive pairs of scores for two variables: Lengths of practice (in years) and score (on a scale from 0 to 100)

	Practice	Proficiency
A	4	12
B	5	30
C	7	28
D	8	80
E	8	60
F	10	55
G	11	67
H	15	80

0 to 100). For practice reasons, you may want to calculate a full set of descriptive tools as well as the Pearson correlation coefficient.

All going well, you will have found that $r=0.8$, that is, a rather strong positive correlation between the two variables, significant on a level of $p<0.05$ (2-tailed). Figure 7.5 shows the scatter graph of the data, with 'practice' on the x-axis and 'proficiency' scores on the y-axis. I have inserted the regression/trend line for the data, that is, the straight line which best represents our data overall (as, like the name suggests, a trend).

Doing statistics using Excel: *Trendlines*

To insert a regression line to a scatter plot in Excel, produce the scatter graph as described above. Then, click on one of the data points in the graph, in such a way that all data points are highlighted. You may have to zoom in to hit a point if it is a small graph. Right click. Choose 'Add trendline'. In the menu, select the 'linear' option (often selected as a default anyway). Click ok.

Our regression line, as a general representation of our data, has several properties, all of which tell us something very useful about our data. First and foremost, it has a *gradient* or *slope*. If the data correlates positively, the slope will be from bottom-left to top-right; if the correlation is negative, it slope will be from top-left to bottom-right. The stronger the correlation is, the steeper is the slope; the weaker, the flatter it is. If there is no correlation, there will be no slope and the trendline horizontal. Here, $r=0.8$, which is a fairly strong positive correlation, so we have a rather steep slope, starting bottom-left of the graph moving towards the top left.

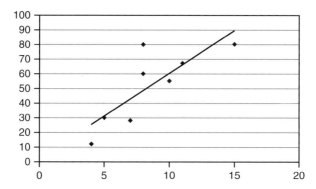

FIGURE 7.5 *Scatter plot with regression/trend line.*

If you take a ruler (or just do this virtually) and extend the regression line to the left, you see that it will eventually hit the (vertical) y-axis. If you actually do this with the graph, you will see that the line will hit the y-axis just above 0. This point where the regression line meets the y-axis is called the *intercept*. Slope and intercept are all we need for a simple further analysis.

We can mathematically describe our regression line with the following equation (you will find different labels in different literature, but they all refer to the same):

$$y = b_1 + b_2 x$$

Here, y stand for a score we are interested in, b_1 stands for the intercept, b_2 stands for the slope, and x for a given x value. You will sometimes find that something else is added to this equation, like '+u' or '+e'. This is called the residual, which is basically a measure to balance out inaccuracies. We shall ignore it here and work with the basic model. With this equation, we can describe any line representing our data, given that we have a *linear* relationship. If the relationship is not linear (but, for example curvilinear, see Chapter Nine), this will not work. And, as with the Pearson correlation, we assume that our data is normally distributed and on a ratio scale of measurement. Below are the instruction for how to calculate the different parts for our regression equation.

Doing statistics using Excel: *Slope* and *intercept*

Based on our data in Table 7.12, we want to develop a model which allows us to describe proficiency in terms of practice – in other words, we want to look at practice and see how proficiency develops. So, proficiency will be the '*y*' in our equation, and practice the '*x*'. Excel has straightforward functions to calculate slope and intercept.

- The function for calculating the slope is =slope(known *y*'s, known *x*'s). 'Known' refers to the data set we have (not one we might predict – see below). So, for our data with *y*=proficiency and *x*=practice, the function is

  =slope(all proficiency scores, all practice scores) or
  =slope(C2:C9,B2:B9)
  For our data, the slope is b_2=5.80.

- The function for the intercept is =intercept(known *y*'s, known *x*'s), so, again, for our data:

  =intercept(all proficiency scores, all practice scores) or
  =intercept(C2:C9,B2:B9)
  The intercept is b_1=2.18.

Now that we have got everything we need, we can create our complete equation for the regression line:

$$y = 2.18 + 5.8x$$

But what exactly does this mean? We have already seen above when we looked at the graph that the line hits the y-axis just above the zero point, and this is concordant to our calculations of the intercept of 2.18 – the regression line hits the y-axis at 2.18. The slope tells us how much y increases with every unit increase of x. We said x represents practice in years and y represents proficiency on a scale from 0 to 100. Our slope coefficient is $b_2 = 5.8$, and this means that with every unit (i.e. year) practice increases, proficiency increases by 5.8 points. And now comes the important bit: our regression line is a model, that is, something that represents reality in a small, simplified and somewhat ideal way. So it also tells us what *ought* to happen mathematically, but if we look at our real data it does not necessarily happen in real life.

It is important that you understand this difference. With the slope coefficient in mind, look again at our original data. You will see that with every year increase proficiency does not necessarily increase by 5.8 points. On the contrary, between four and five years practice, practice increases by one year only, but proficiency increases by 18 points from 12 to 30. Between seven and eight years of practice the difference in proficiency is a staggering 52 points! And, irritatingly, for respondent F, who has ten years of practice, proficiency is a mere 55. So, again, the regression line is only a model, some kind of indicator or simulator of what *ought* to happen, or what happens *on average*. It does not, however, provide an accurate picture of what actually happens in reality.

This may sound very negative: why have something that seems to give wrong results? Here, it is crucial that we understand that a large part of statistics is really about *modelling reality*, that is, it is about developing concepts which go beyond the data they have originated from. And this is where forecasting and predictions come into play. Statistical modelling, predicting and forecasting are complex issues, in fact, they are too complex to even go into peripherally in this book. So, here we limit our discussion to some very basic forecasting/predicting. For this, we have to assume that in our practice/proficiency example there are no other variables involved. That is, practice is the one and only variable that influences proficiency – it does not take long to see that this is rather simplistic. Yet, we will get a good idea what forecasting looks like.

The data in our example starts with 4 years of practice and a proficiency score of 12, and stops with 15 years of practice and a proficiency score of 80. Obviously, in the real world, we inevitably have people who have more than 15 years or less that 4 years practice. So, what will their proficiency score look like? For example, what will the proficiency of someone with

23 years practice be? Before we start, a preliminary warning: when we do forecasts, we have to assume that our sample data is representative for our population (which is something it should always be anyway), as the forecast projects values on the assumption that all other characteristics (or variables) are constant. If our example comprises data from English native speakers learning Spanish, we cannot use the data to make predictions about Hungarian learners learning Chinese, but only to make statements about other English Spanish-learners.

In order to make predictions, we could simply use or scatter plot with its regression line, extend the line and simple read the values of the x and y-axis. This is fair enough as a first visual measure, but we want something a bit more reliable. Let's assume we are interested in the proficiency score of someone with 16 years practice. The proficiency score is what we are interested in, so it is our y, while the 16 years are our known value, so that is our x. In our equation, it looks like this:

$$y = 2.18 + 5.8 \times 16 = 2.18 + 92.8 = 95.02$$

So, based on our regression model, we would predict that a learner with 16 years practice will have a proficiency score of approximately 95 out of 100 points. With comparatively little effort and a small data set we can make interesting forecasts about data that is not even there! Isn't statistics great!

Doing statistics using a Excel: *Forecasts*

You can given get Excel to do this simple calculation for you: the function for the forecast is

=forecast(x, known y's, known x's).

If you have not guessed it, this all come at a cost. For a start, there is the issue of our regression being a model *only*. And, even worse, it is only a summary of several complex mathematical procedures, which our computer is doing for us. However, the model does not know what it is calculating – it still needs a human brain to sort out the issues. Two more examples.

Task 7.7

Based on the example, forecast the proficiency scores for $x=0$ and $x=23$. Interpret the result.

Statistic whizzes that you are by now, this was surely not a problem . . . or was it? You have probably calculated (or had Excel do the calculation for you) that for $x=0$, $y=2.18$, and for $x=23$, $y=135.6$. And here it becomes all too obvious that our model is only a model. If it predicts a proficiency score of 2.18 for someone with zero practice, how do we interpret it? Do all native speakers of English learning Spanish have an inbuilt ability to speaking at least a tiny bit of Spanish? Shouldn't someone with no practice have no proficiency? Is our model flawed? Or is something else wrong? Once again, it is paramount that we interpret our statistical output in the light of our theoretical and methodological framework before we can come to any conclusions – and since this is a fictive example, there aren't any conclusions – a statistic result is only as good as what you make of it, and it has to be embedded into the entire project, and not seen on its own. The result for x=23 is equally irritating, since the model predicts proficiency that is beyond our scale of measurement – can anyone become more than perfect? More likely, we have to cap the result at the potential maximum value of 100. Unless, of course, the proficiency score you have used does indeed have scope for higher levels – again: check it!

There are several ways of checking whether our model makes sense, or to see how reliable it is. One tool we have already met in this chapter when we looked at causality: R^2. We said that is nothing but R^2 is nothing else but the Pearson correlation coefficient multiplied by itself, and that R^2 provides us with information on how much a variable x is accountable for variability in variable y. Since Pearson correlation and regression are closely related – mathematically as well as conceptually – we can use R^2 to assess our regression model, too, and it is interpreted in the same way: how much of the variability in for variable y can be explained by the model?

In our example, $r^2=0.64$: our regression model can explain 64% of variability in proficiency, and 46% of variability are unexplained – unsurprisingly, as there ought to be other factors influencing linguistic development!

Doing statistics using a spreadsheet software: *Regression (full version)*

Apart from calculating all parameters for our regression individually, using the functions described above, we can also ask Excel to calculate the entire set of information simultaneously. Go to 'Data and click on the 'Data Analysis' icon. You might have to install the features first: Clock on the Office Button (the big round button in the top-left corner). Select 'Excel options'. Then select 'Add-ins' and install the AnalysisToolPak (sic!). You might need the CD-Rom for installation, or download it from the internet.

Using the Data Analysis tool:

- Go to 'Data', 'Data Analysis'.
- Choose 'Regression'.

- For 'Input Y range' highlight the scores for the (assumed) dependent variable – in our example, proficiency. For 'Input X range', select the dependent variable scores (practice).
- If you would like Excel to include the labels (i.e. variable names) when displaying the result, tick the 'label' box but do make sure that the variable names ('practice' and 'proficiency') are also selected. If you do not want Excel to display the labels, untick the box and ensure the headings are *not* selected. Otherwise, Excel gets confused and displayed the wrong results.
- Select 'Confidence Level' and enter the confidence level you want. Remember, confidence equals 100 minus the significance level: the default 95% confidence means a significance level of 0.05 – usually the best option.
- Click ok.

($\rightarrow$See the companion website for a clip on how to conduct and interpret a regression analysis in Excel.$\leftarrow$)

The Excel output for our example will look like Table 7.10; note that there is more information that we are covering in this book, so do not despair.

The 'Regression Statistics' table summarizes the results for the variance and the R^2. It also shows us the adjusted R^2, which:

> tells us how much of variance in Y would be accounted for if the model had been derived from the population from which the sample was taken. (Field 2000: 130)

In other words, if our data had been based on the population rather than a sample, practice could account for 58% of the variability in proficiency. Mathematically, it takes the variance into account – we shall ignore the details here. The third table shows us, among a lot of other information, the coefficients: the intercept and the slope (here 'practice'). The middle table shows the results for the ANOVA (for ANalysis Of VARiance), which we will discuss in the next chapter in more detail. However, it gives us a useful bit of information: the 'Significance F' value tells us whether our regression model is statistically significant: remember that we are dealing with a model only, and hence it is useful to know how reliable our model actually is. In other words, can we confidently use our model to make predictions? In our example, $p=0.02$, that is, our model is significant at a 98% confidence level (see Brace et al. 2003: 220, *inter alia*). In other words, we can happily use it to make predictions without having to worry whether our model really works.

TABLE 7.10 Simple regression, full information

SUMMARY OUTPUT	
Regression Statistics	
Multiple R	0.80
R Square	0.64
Adjusted R Square	0.58
Standard Error	16.48
Observations	8

ANOVA					
	df	SS	MS	F	Significance F
Regression	1	2895.36	2895.36	10.67	0.02
Residual	6	1628.64	271.44		
Total	7	4524			

	Coefficients	Standard Error	t Stat	P-value	Lower 95%	Upper 95%
Intercept	2.18	16.19	0.13	0.90	−37.42	41.78
Practice	5.80	1.78	3.27	0.02	1.46	10.15

7.10. Multiple regression

With our simple regression we have a good tool to construct predicting models containing one dependent and one independent variable. However, more likely than not, we will come across the situation where we do not have one but many independent variables, all of which will influence the dependent variable to a certain extent. Using a simple regression as we did above will lead to flawed results. A *multiple regression* analysis, however, allows us to build a model which contains several independent variables ad e are, to a certain extent, able to tell how much each of them influences our dependent variable. We can carry out multiple regressions with Excel (in fact, the steps to do so are almost identical to the simple regression), but the level of detail and sophistication are limited. If you think you require a multiple regression analysis and other more sophisticated statistical forecasting tools, you may want to consider changing to a different software package.

In task 7.8, Table 7.14 (below), you find a set of data taken from a study on linguistic vitality in different migrant communities in The Hague, Netherlands, based on the analysis of four linguistic dimensions: proficiency, choice, dominance and preference (Extra et al. 2004: 127). In this example, we have vitality as the dependent variable, as it is influenced by the four other variables. The question now is, how good a predictor are the independent variables? How well can each of them predict vitality?

Doing statistics using Excel: *Multiple regression*

Warning: multiple regression is a serious statistical method, but Excel is not a serious statistical software – it's a spreadsheet. Even though it allows us to conduct multiple regressions, do proceed with caution. If multiple regression is a vital part of your study, you ought to look for alternative software, such as SPSS or R, as discussed in Chapter Ten.

Carrying out a multiple regression analysis in Excel is analogous to doing a simple regression. The only difference is that for the 'Input X range', we select *all* our independent variables, that is, in our example, 'Input X range' includes proficiency, choice, dominance and preference.

The result for the multiple regression for the linguistic vitality example should look like Table 7.11; Figure 7.6 is a scatter plot showing all constellations of independent and dependent variables.

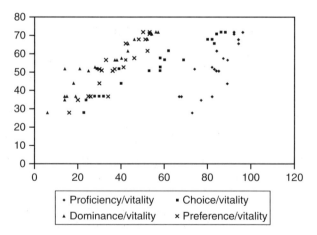

FIGURE 7.6 *Scatter plot for multiple regression example.*

TABLE 7.11 Multiple regression result

SUMMARY OUTPUT	
Regression Statistics	
Multiple R	0.97
R Square	0.95
Adjusted R Square	0.93
Standard Error	3.44
Observations	21.00

ANOVA					
	df	SS	MS	F	Significance F
Regression	4.00	3410.85	852.71	72.02	0.00
Residual	16.00	189.43	11.84		
Total	20.00	3600.29			

	Coefficients	Standard Error	t Stat	P-value	Lower 95%	Upper 95%
Intercept	10.04	11.66	0.86	0.40	−14.67	34.75
Language proficiency	0.08	0.17	0.46	0.65	−0.28	0.44
Language choice	0.31	0.13	2.44	0.03	0.04	0.58
Language dominance	0.01	0.22	0.04	0.97	−0.45	0.47
Language preference	0.52	0.17	3.04	0.01	0.16	0.88

The interpretation of the result is similar to that of a simple regression: in the first table, the Regression Statistics tell us that our four independent variables in the model can account for 95% of the variability of vitality, that is, the four variables together have a massive impact on vitality. This is not surprising, seeing that vitality is a compound index calculated from those very variables. In fact, the result for R^2 should be 100%: with vitality being calculated from the four independent variables, there cannot be any other (latent) variable influencing it! This again reminds us that we are dealing with models – a simplified version of reality. The ANOVA part shows us that the model is highly significant, with $p=0.00$.

The most interesting part of our result is the third table: it shows us the regression coefficients, that is, how much each of our four independent variables influences vitality. It also shows us the p-value, that is, the significance level, for each variable individually. Let's look at this in detail:

- Proficiency: $b_2=0.08$. For every point the index 'proficiency' increases, vitality increases by 0.08 points. This is fairly weak. With $p=0.65$, it is also a highly insignificant predictor in this model.

- Choice: $b_2=0.31$. For every point the index 'choice' increases, vitality increases by 0.31 points. This is much stronger. With $p=0.03$, 'choice' is also a significant predictor in our model.

- Dominance: $b_2=0.01$. This predictor is even weaker than proficiency, with an increase of only 0.01 vitality points per increase of the index 'dominance'. However, with $p=0.04$, it is significant, so we can confidently include it into any forecasts we may wish to make.

- Preference: $b_2=0.52$. Language preference is the strongest predictor, with vitality increasing by more than half a point with every increase of the preference index. With $p=0.01$, preference is also a highly significant predictor.

In summary, although our overall model is highly significant and can predict vitality almost entirely on its own, not all individual variables can do so. If we made the mistake to analyse the data using a simple regression, looking for example at proficiency and vitality only, our results would be fundamentally flawed. The multiple regression model including all independent variables, however, is highly significant and we can use it do make predictions about vitality levels.

7.11. Correlation and reliability

We shall finish this chapter by going right back to an issue raised at the beginning of this book. With the Pearson correlation we have a good tool for measuring the relationship between two variables, and I am convinced that with practice you will realize just how useful it is for the analysis of your data. We can, however, use the Pearson correlation not only for the analysis of our data, but can also use it to test whether our measurement is reliable. In Chapter Two, we introduced the test-retest method as a good way to evaluate a method's reliability. Back then, we said that a reliable measure should give us similar results if applied at two different points in time, even though we have to bear in mind some of the problems that come with working with human beings (such as the ability to learn from experience).

In a test-retest situation, we obtain two sets of data, D_1 and D_2, at two points in time, T_1 and T_2. For our method to be reliable, our respondents should show similar response patterns in both D_1 and D_2; our data should hence look similar to Table 7.12.

If we calculate the Pearson coefficient, we will find that $r=1$ (surprise!), so there is a very strong (and significant) relationship between the data obtained at T_1 and the data obtained at T_2. In other words, individual respondents' data is *stable*: respondents with high scores obtain high scores at both T_1 and T_2, and those with low scores obtain low scores in both test and retest, too. Our measure produces similar data at two points in time – a good (but not sufficient!) indicator that it is reliable.

If there is no correlation between D_1 and D_2, we should start getting some serious doubts about the reliability. For example, in Table 7.13, D_1 and D_2 appear fairly random, and a correlation analysis shows that there is no correlation between them ($r=-0.04$).[2]

TABLE 7.12 Test-retest, same pattern

Respondent	T_1	T_2
A	2	3
B	4	5
C	6	7
D	8	9
E	10	11

TABLE 7.13 Test-retest, no pattern

Respondent	T_1	T_2
A	2	6
B	4	1
C	6	1
D	8	10
E	10	1

If our method delivers such different results in the retest, it means that our respondents' answers are not stable. And this could indicate that our method is unreliable – but it is not necessarily the case.

It is important to understand that using Pearson's r to evaluate a method's reliability only works if other variables are kept constant between T_1 and T_2, and where the data is unlikely to change between T_1 and T_2. Another language proficiency example: we take a group of beginners English language students and measure their knowledge of the third person singular 's' rule for present tense by simply calculating the relative frequency with which they apply the rule correctly (or incorrectly – your choice). This will give us D_1 at T_1. We now administer a brand new and fancy teaching method to the group, and after eight weeks we measure their proficiency again, using the same method, giving us D_2 at T_2. Now the problem starts: there might be a strong correlation between D_1 and D_2. However, what we have done is not a test-retest in the sense of testing reliability. Inevitable, D_1 and D_2 will show differences, and if our method is any good, all students should improve. However, in this case, the retest does not tell us anything about our measure's reliability, but it provides us with information about the stimulus (i.e. the teaching method) we have introduced. Even if D_1 and D_2 do not correlate it is no prove that our measure is flawed – let's face it, counting whether a simple rule is applied or not is pretty easy – but it is likely to indicate that something is awfully wrong with our new teaching style: it could be, for example, that weak students benefit, hence obtaining higher scores at T_2, while good students get so confused that they score worse than before – in this case, improvement and deterioration would balance each other out and skew the correlation coefficient between D_1 and D_2.

In conclusion, while the calculation of the correlation between test and retest data is one way of evaluating our measures reliability, we have to be very careful when we use this in a context where, by the every nature of the context, data is likely to change between T_1 and T_2. Language acquisition related issues are bound to give us problems when we use the test-retest to check reliability, simply because progress is relatively fast. In other areas, such as linguistic change or attitudes, things are usually changing comparatively slowly, so, given that no stimulus is introduced, the test-retest is a good tool.

Task 7.8

Over the last three chapters we have covered a lot of material. Time now to apply all your newly acquired knowledge and skills. But this time, we make it a bit trickier. Below is a set of data taken from a study on linguistic vitality in different migrant communities in The Hague, Netherlands, based on the analysis of 4 linguistic dimensions: proficiency, choice, dominance and preference (Extra et al. 2004: 127). Using as many *applicable* and *reasonable* tools(!) we have discussed so far as you can think of, try a detailed analysis of this data set. Your analysis should be based on a particular line of argument or hypothesis – whatever you find interesting in the data, but do not just compute random statistics! Then, write a short summary reporting your results (no more than 300 words). An example analysis and a detailed step-by-step checklist can be found in Chapter Eleven.

TABLE 7.14 Language vitality index per language group, based on the mean value of four language dimensions (in %)

	Language proficiency	Language choice	Language dominance	Language preference	Language vitality
Akan/Tiwi	89	69	37	33	57
Arabic	89	60	38	42	57
Berber	94	83	43	42	66
Chinese	94	82	52	48	68
English	83	29	21	37	52
Farsi	92	84	54	53	71
French	68	32	19	25	37
German	77	24	14	20	35
Hindi	89	40	18	30	44
Italian	67	30	14	26	37
Javanese	73	23	6	16	28
Kurdish	85	58	31	31	51
Malay	74	39	14	30	52
Papiamentu	87	58	40	46	58
Portuguese	82	58	28	41	53
Serbian/Croatian	84	62	43	52	62
Somali	92	88	57	53	72
Spanish	84	53	25	36	51
Sranan Tongo	82	28	15	34	37
Turkish	96	86	56	50	72
Urdu	94	80	46	51	68

Source: Extra et al. (2004: 127).

CHAPTER EIGHT

Testing hypotheses

Key words: causality – dependent *t*-test – *F*-test – hypothesis testing – hypothesis testing using χ^2 – independent *t*-test – tails– testing experimental and non-experimental data – ANOVAs

8.1. Hypotheses, causality and tails

Without explicitly mentioning it, to a certain extent we have already touched on hypothesis testing in Chapter Seven when we discussed the chi-squared test and correlation. In Chapter Two, we defined hypotheses as statements about the potential and/or suggested relationship between at least two variables and said that a hypothesis *must* be phrased in such as way that they can be proven right or wrong – tautological hypotheses are not permissible. Now it is about time that we specify this definition a bit more. In the previous chapter, we have seen that correlation only indicates the strength of *association* between two variables, not *causality*. Indeed, frequently when we carry out a correlation analysis between variables in our data, we will find that several of them correlate, that is, their scores occur in a particular pattern with each other. Using (multiple) regression analysis, we are able to make predictions or forecasts about what may happen given the current pattern of our data, but again, regression does not give us any empirical evidence about causality.

In the example from my own research, we have seen that age of onset and length of exposure correlate; yet, we cannot say that age of onset *causes* length of exposure. Rather, the two variables occur in a distinct pattern. In a fictive example, we may find that there is a positive correlation between the number of children a linguist has and number of pages their books have (the more children, the longer the books), but we would have to go a long way to argue that there is a causal relationship, that is, that the children are *causing* them to write longer books.

In a typical hypothesis, on the other hand, we do want exactly this: we want a clear constellation of one (or more) independent variables and a dependent variable. In other words, our hypothesis should contain a constellation where there is at least a thorough theoretical basis for assuming causality between the independent and the dependent variable, with the former causing the latter. In an experimental setup, where the researcher has full control over the independent variable(s), any change in the independent variable(s) would cause a change in the dependent variable, given that there is a causal relationship. If there is no relationship, we will not see a change in the dependent variable. We have outlined the three criteria for causality in Section 2.5.

A clear definition of the independent and the dependent variable is also important for the choice of statistical test and their significance level. If we predict causality between variables A and B in such as way that A influences B, we speak of a *1-tailed hypothesis*, and we will eventually use a significance level that reflects this. If you have a look at the tables of critical values in Chapter Ten, you will see that the significance levels for 1-tailed hypothesis are exactly 1/2 of that of 2-tailed tests: since we only consider causality in one direction, we have to ensure that we account for significance in only one direction, that is, we want to be confident that A influences B only, not the other way round. If our hypothesis is *2-tailed*, where *either* A influences B *or* B influences A, we have to check for significance in *both* directions.

Strangely enough, quantitative research has traditionally always assumed that there is no relationship between two variables, and statistical tests are based on this assumption. This is reflected in the way we phrase hypotheses: we generally phrase our hypotheses in such as way that they imply no relationship between A and B. This is also known as the *null hypothesis*, or H_0:

> H_0: There is no relationship between social class and use of non-standard forms.

The task of our statistical test, and indeed our entire research, is to prove or disprove H_0. Paradoxically, in reality most of the time we are interested in disproving H_0, that is, to show that in fact there *is* a difference in the use of non-standard forms between socio-economic classes. This is called the *alternative hypothesis* H_1 or H_A. Hence:

> H_0: There is no relationship between social class and use of non-standard forms.
>
> H_A: There is a relationship between social class and use of non-standard forms.

The tools discussed in Chapter Seven are all measures of association, that is, they tell us to what extent two variables co-occur. By its very nature, especially the Pearson correlation requires a comparatively large amount of different scores for each variable in order to detect a relationship: we need, for example, several different age of onset scores and several different proficiency scores if we would like to show a relationship between these variables. In other words, we need a variety of scores for the independent variables (here probably age).

However, sometimes this is either not possible, or we deliberately want to avoid this. Traditionally, real experiments are set up in such a way that only one independent variable is deliberately manipulated (with other variables being held constant) and the effect on the dependent variable is measured – see Chapter Three. A typical example is that of a study on the influence of background knowledge on learners' listening comprehension:

> The experimental group received some treatment in the form of topic familiarity, and their background knowledge was activated. Then a 50-item TOEFL test of listening comprehension was administered to both experimental and control groups. A statistical analysis of the results provides some evidence in support of the effect of background knowledge on listening comprehension. (Sadighi and Zare 2006: 110)

In terms of research design, Sadighi and Zare's study is a typical experimental study. The experimental group receives the 'knowledge activation' stimulus; the control group receives just 'normal' input.

	Step 1	Step 2	Step 3	Step 4
Experimental group	Obtain pre-test score A	Stimulus: 'knowledge activation'	Obtain post-test score X	Statistical Analysis
Control group	Obtain pre-test score B	No stimulus	Obtain post-test score Y	

Step 4 leaves us with four options for analysis:

1 Compare A with B; that is, compare the two pre-test scores.
2 Compare X with Y; that is, compare the two post-test scores.
3 Compare A with X; that is, compare pre- and post-scores for experimental group.
4 Compare B with Y; that is, compare pre- and post-scores for control group.

We will discuss each step in the course of this chapter. We can obtain a rough idea about the relationship between pre- and post-scores by running a simple Pearson correlation: ignoring the questions of causality and whether pre- and post-test scores a significantly different, the Pearson correlation will tell as whether there is a relationship between the two scores, which direction is takes, and how strong it is. For the experimental group, we would expect to see a positive correlation, as we assume that the stimulus improves respondents' post-test scores, so there should be a pattern whereby post-test scores are higher than pre-test scores. If the stimulus does not have any effect, there should not be a difference in pre- and post-test scores, and the correlation coefficient will be small, indicating a weak relationship. For the control group, we would expect exactly that: there is no stimulus, so improvement should be less pronounced, indicated by a small correlation coefficient.

The question is, how exactly can we compare pre- and post-test scores statistically? How can we show that the post-test scores are statistically significantly higher than the pre-test scores? That is where the *t*-test can help us.

8.2. The *t*-test: Preliminaries

The *t-test* (sometimes also known as the *Student's t-test*) allows us to compare the scores, or more precisely the arithmetic means of either two groups of respondents or two sets of data from the same sample. We will discuss both issues here subsequently. First, let's have a look at some basic underlying issues.

In our discussion of the arithmetic mean in Chapter Six we have said – and shown – that two sets of data can have the same arithmetic mean, even if they are substantially different. Roughly speaking, the t-test is a statistical procedure that compares the arithmetic means of two groups of data while taking their variability (i.e. their standard deviation or variance) into account. Hence, it allows us to draw conclusions whether or not there is a real difference between two groups. To illustrate this problem, Table 8.1 shows two sets of (fictive) scores for ten people as well as the mean score for each set of scores. If we only look at the mean, or if in an article there was only the mean reported, we could assume that the two sets of scores are different: the mean for score B is 3.3 points higher than the mean score for A, so we could easily argue that B scores are higher than A scores. Yet, if we have a closer look at the actual data, we can see that A and B only differ by a single pair of scores: only R10 has a higher B than A score; for all other respondents the two scores are identical. So, the difference in means for the two sets is based on only one differing score in a set of 20 scores overall. One score for one person makes all the difference. Imagine this table were

TABLE 8.1 Fictive example

	Score A	Score B
R1	2	2
R2	3	3
R3	4	4
R4	6	6
R5	7	7
R6	8	8
R7	12	12
R8	13	13
R9	16	16
R10	17	50
Mean	8.8	12.1

the results for Sadighi and Zare's experimental group: would it not be odd to argue that the post-test scores (score B) are higher than the pre-test ones, hence the stimulus must have some impact? The answer is, yes, it would be pretty odd. How can we validly argue that the post-test scores are different from the pre-test scores only based on the arithmetic means, when we can see that in fact there is next to no difference, and that the mean by its very nature is notoriously sensitive to any changes in the values that it is based on? We obviously need a solution for this – the t-test.

Note that as a parametric test, the t-test can only be applied to normally distributed data, and should ideally only be applied if we have at least ten items (respondents, scores, etc.) per group; as you can see, sample size and amount of data is a recurring pattern. t-tests come in two main shapes: t-test for independent samples, and t-test for dependent sample. We will discuss independent and dependent t-tests subsequently. But before we go over to the t-test, we need to look at something else.

8.3. *F*-Test

I have mentioned above that the t-test is a statistical method that compares the means of two groups or two sets of scores while also taking their variance into account. If we carry out an independent t-test in Excel, we need to let Excel know whether the variances of the two sets of data are equal or unequal; as before, other software packages do this automatically, or simply do both and give us both results. The *F*-test is based on dividing the larger variance by the smaller variance and looking up the critical values and significance levels in a table, as we did for the chi-squared test and the correlation coefficients. Since for our purposes the *F*-test is only a means to an end (namely to know which *t*-test to use), we shall go for the easy option and just look at how to calculate it with Excel.

Doing statistics using Excel: *F-test*

There are two ways of doing *F*-tests with Excel: a 'long' and a 'short' version. For the former, go to 'Data, 'Data Analysis'. As with the regression analysis, you might need to install the features first: Click on the Office button, go to 'Excel options, 'Add-ins' and select 'Analysis Tool Pak'. You might need the CD-Rom for installation or download it from the Microsoft website.

1. Using the Data Analysis tool:

   - Calculate the variance for both samples (reminder: in Excel, the function is =var(DATA))
   - Go to 'Data, then 'Data Analysis'.
   - Choose 'F-test: Two-sample for Variances'.
   - For 'Variable 1 range' highlight the scores for the group with the higher variance – see Chapter Six on how to calculate it. For 'Variable 2 range' highlight the scores for the group with the lower variance. There is a debate whether this distinction is necessary, but to be on the safe side it is advisable – there are some flaws with the way Excel calculates the *F*-test.
   - We want a sound significance level: choose Alpha 0.05 for a 95 per cent confidence level. If we need to be less strict, we can adjust it to 0.1 (90% confidence) – but we really should not go any lower.
   - Click ok.

2. Directly enter the equation:
   The function for the *F*-test is:

   =ftest(array1,array2), whereby 'array1' refers to the data of the set with the higher variance and 'array2' to the data with the lower variance. The result displayed in Excel is the significance level.

Let's have a look at the *F*-test on a real example. Table 8.2 summarizes Sadighi and Zare's results for the post-test scores, that is, scores that were measured after the experimental stimulus ('knowledge activation') was

TABLE 8.2 EG/CG post-test comparison

	EG	CG
	40	27.5
	40	30
	40	30
	40	30
	42	32.5
	42	35
	44	35
	44	35
	46	37.5
	48	37.5
	48	40
	50	42.5
Mean	43.67	34.38
SD	3.60	4.54
Var.	12	20.6

Source: Adapted from Sadighi and Zare (2006).

implemented. As we can see, the post-test scores for the EG group are higher by almost ten points than the scores of the control group. We can also see that the variances are difference with the variance for the EG $\sigma^2=12$ and the variance for CG $\sigma^2=20.6$. The *F*-test will check whether this difference is statistically significant.

Task 8.1

Carry out the F-test, using the 'long' version via the Data Analysis tool. Bear in mind that the variance for control group (CG) is the higher one!

If everything went to plan, you should get a table of result which looks like Table 8.3: it shows us the means for both variables, the variance and the number of observations. It also gives us the degrees of freedom. The

TABLE 8.3 Result of *F*-statistic

F-test two-sample for variances		
	Variable 1	Variable 2
Mean	34.38	43.67
Variance	20.60	12.97
Observations	12	12
df	11	11
F	1.59	
P(F≤f) one-tail	0.23	
F Critical one-tail	2.82	

F shows us our actual F-statistic; it is based on dividing the higher by the lower variance, that is:

$$F = \frac{20.6}{12.97} = 1.59$$

The most important part for us is the '*P*(*F*≤f) one-tail' row: it tells us the significance level. Here p=0.23. This tells us that the variances of our two groups are not statistically significantly different; in other words, even though the variance for CG is nominally higher, we can disregard this and assume that the variances are equal. This is important for our choice of t-test.

8.4. *T*-test for independent samples

As should be obvious from the name, the *independent samples t-test* (sometimes also called *unrelated t-test*) is used to compare the means of two different *groups*. In Sadighi and Zare's study, we have two groups, experimental (EG) and control group (CG), each one with its own set of results for both pre- and post-test. Respondents belong to either EG of CG, so there is no overlap of respondents and/or scores; hence, they are independent from each other and one group cannot influence the scores of the other.

As for hypotheses, we can assume that:

H_0: There is no difference between EG and CG scores after stimulus was introduced.

H_A: There is a difference between EG and CG after the stimulus was introduced.

Note that the H_0 assumes no change; yet, it is change that we are really interested in. We assume that the stimulus influences respondents' test performance in such a way that ultimately the EG scores are higher than the CG scores, so we can use a 1-tailed hypothesis. If we do not want to make any prediction, we use a 2-tailed test (as, in fact, Sadighi and Zare did). Some people use a 2-tailed test by default for everything. This is not wrong but will have an impact on the significance level applicable to interpret our data, so it might make a difference. If in doubt, you may want to run both a 1-tailed and a 2-tailed test – after all, it is fairly easily done with the appropriate software.

Two aspects should strike us straightaway: the EG scores are higher than the CG scores by 9.29 points, so at a first glance, there seems to be a difference and we could reject H_0. However, we also see that CG scores are slightly more dispersed. The t-test will account for exactly this. The *t*-test is rather tedious to calculate, so will restrict our discussion here to how to calculate it with Excel. The programme will ask you about equal and unequal variances. Our calculations of the *F*-test have just shown that the variances between EG and CG are not significantly different, so we can use the 'equal variances' version of the test. As before, if you use SPSS, the software will make the decision for you (in fact, it provides you with results for both). Note that some people will by default run both versions of the test, to be on the save side, mainly because there are reliability issues with the *F*-test calculated by Excel. While there is nothing wrong with being cautious, bear in mind that contradictory results from the equal variances and unequal variances test may be difficult to interpret. Seeing that this is an introductory textbook which cannot cover the intricacies of the various statistical tools, we trust our *F*-test result.

Doing statistics using Excel: *Independent t-test* (detailed display)

As with the *F*-test, there are two ways of doing *t*-tests with Excel. The former is the preferable.

1. Using the Data Analysis Tool:

   • Go to 'Tools', 'Data Analysis'.

- Choose 'T-test: Two-sample assuming Equal Variances'. Obviously, if you have data where the F-test shows significantly different variances, you choose the 'Unequal variances' version of the test.
- For 'Variable 1 range' highlight the scores for the EG, and for 'Variable 2 range' the scores for CG.
- Leave the 'hypothesised mean difference' box empty.
- We are being picky today and want to make sure we have a sound significance level: choose Alpha 0.05 for a 95% confidence level. If we need to be less strict, we can adjust it to 0.1 (90% confidence) – but we really should not go any lower.
- Click ok.

(→See companion website for a clip on how to conduct a t-test in Excel.←)

You should get the following table (Table 8.4).

The first three lines give us the arithmetic means, variances and number of observations for each group. 'Pooled variance' is the combined variance of EG and CG, which is used to calculate the t-statistic – we ignore it here, and we also ignore the 'Hypothesized Mean Difference'. Df gives us the degrees of freedom, which for the independent t-test is the sum of observations of both samples minus 2 (i.e. 12+12−2=22). The 't Stat' row gives us the

TABLE 8.4 *T*-test between EG and CG. Excel output

	EG	CG
Mean	43.67	34.38
Variance	12.97	20.60
Observations	12.00	12.00
Pooled Variance	16.78	
Hypothesized Mean Difference	0.00	
df	22.00	
t Stat	5.56	
P(T≤t) one-tail	0.00	
t Critical one-tail	1.72	
P(T≤t) two-tail	0.00	
t Critical two-tail	2.07	

result of the actual t-test. Here t=5.56. The most important rows, though, are P(T≤t) one-tail and P(T≤t) two-tail, as these give us the significance levels. We said at the beginning that we predict that the scores for the EG are higher than those of the CG after the stimulus, and we decided to use a 1-tailed test. We see that for the 1-tailed test, $p=0.00$, which is smaller than 0.05. This means that the difference in means between EG and CG is statistically highly significant. In other words, the stimulus seems to have made a real difference in performance between EG and CG. Had we not predicted which group would score higher, the 2-tailed test, too, is highly significant, again with $p=0.00$. In a research paper, we report the result somewhere along the lines of 'after the introduction of the stimulus, respondents in the EG group performed statistically significantly higher than those in the CG, with $t(22)=5.56$, $p=0.00$.'

We can also get a visual representation for this.

Doing statistics using Excel: *Bar chart with error bars*

Create a bar chart as usual, based on the means for both groups. Left-double-click on one of the bars. Choose the 'Y error bars' tab. Choose the error bar you want to display. Choose 'percentage' and enter the error you are prepared to accept. 5% indicates a significance level of p=0.05, that is 95% confidence, so the default is ok. Modify according to your needs. Bear in mind that 10% means only 90% confidence – you do not want to go much lower than this! Click ok.

(→See companion website for a clip on how to create error bars in Excel.←)

If you used the Sadighi and Zare's (2006) data for the graph, you should get a graph similar to Figure 8.1. We can see that the means for EG and CG are different, as the bars are of unequal height. We also see that the two error bars – the vertical lines in the middle of each bar – do not overlap. This indicates that the means are statistically significantly different. In fact, the ends of both error bars are quite far apart, which strengthens the argument even further. Error bars that overlap indicate that the two means are potentially not significantly different; and the more the overlap of the error bars, the less likely a significant difference is. Note, though, that in any report, a bar chart with error bars alone will not do the job – you need to provide the numerical values, too!

Is this really sufficient information to argue that the stimulus 'knowledge activation' results in better performance? If you spend a minute or so thinking about it, you will realise that we have only compared the two post-test scores. It does not actually tell us how the stimulus influenced the result. Sadighi and Zare have also compared the pre-test scores of both

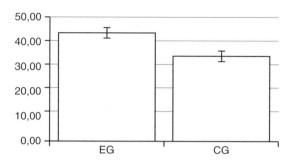

FIGURE 8.1 *EG CG bar chart.*

groups and found no significant difference. That is, both groups were at the same proficiency level before the stimulus was introduced. Yet, we still need a decent measure that tells us the actual change that occurs between EG and CG, o rather: within EG and CG. And this is where the *dependent t-test* comes into play.

8.5. Dependent *t-test*

The dependent *t-test* is also known as *paired t-test, related sample t-test* or *related measures t-test*. I am sure I could find even more terms if I kept trawling through literature. They all refer to the same test though. The main difference between the independent t-test discussed above and the dependent t-test is that in the latter, we compare two sets of data from the *same group* (or sample). In other words, rather than comparing two groups we compare scores from one group under two conditions.

Earlier on in this chapter, we have identified four options with regard to analysing Sadighi and Zare's data. With the independent t-test, we have chosen option two:

2. Compare X with Y; that is, compare the two post-test scores.

We have shown, and indeed Sadighi and Zare have shown that there is a significant different in performance between the two groups in the post-test, and we have seen that the pre-test scores were similar. Now, we need to compare the pre- and post-test scores for each group. Unfortunately, Sadighi and Zare do not give us the pre-test results, so we have to make them up (Table 8.5).

Task 8.2

Run a *t-test* for all *independent* constellations of the data in Table 8.5.

For the dependent t-test, we are interested in the differences between the scores *within* each group, that is, the differences between EG_pre and

TABLE 8.5 Pre- and post-test results

Respondent	EG_pre	CG_pre	EG_post	CG_post
A	22	22	40	27.5
B	24	24	40	30
C	24	25	40	30
D	26	26	40	30
E	27	27	42	32.5
F	30	31	42	35
G	32	32	44	35
H	34	34	44	35
I	35	34	46	37.5
J	35	35	48	37.5
K	36	37	48	40
L	37	37	50	42.5
Mean	30.17	30.33	43.67	34.38
STD	5.36	5.30	3.6	4.54

Source: Adapted from Sadighi and Zare (2006). Fictive values for EG_pre and CG_pre

EG_post, and CG_pre and CG_post, respectively. As both data sets for the dependent *t*-test come from the sample, we do not need to worry about variances and hence, we do not need to conduct an *F-test* first.

Task 8.3

Create a bar chart with error bars for the dependent t-tests EG_pre/post and CG_pre/post. Interpret the result.

Doing statistics using Excel: *Dependent t-test*

As with the independent *t*-test, go to 'Tools', 'Data Analysis'. This time, we choose '*t*-test: Paired Two Sample for Means'. For the dependent *t*-test, variable range 1 and 2 refer to the EG_pre and EG_post scores, respectively. Leave Alpha at the default of 0.05 for 95% confidence. Click ok.

You results for EG pre/post should look like Table 8.6.

TABLE 8.6 Dependent *t*-test for experimental group

	EG_pre	EG_post
Mean	30.17	43.67
Variance	28.70	12.97
Observations	12	12
Pearson correlation	0.94	
Hypothesized mean difference	0	
df	11	
t Stat	−19.86	
$P(T \leq t)$ one-tail	2.88E−10	
t Critical one-tail	1.80	
$P(T \leq t)$ two-tail	5.77E−10	
t Critical two-tail	2.20	

The interpretation of the results are almost identical to the interpretation of the independent samples test. Instead of a pooled variance, we now find the Pearson correlation coefficient, which indicates a strong positive correlation between the pre- and the post-scores for the experimental group: the higher respondents scored in the pre-test, the higher they scored in the post-test. You may want to plot a scatter graph to get visual evidence.

In the bottom four rows, we see that the difference between the two means is statistically significant, with $p<0.05$ in both 1- and 2-tailed test. That is, respondents in the experimental group scored significantly higher after the stimulus had been introduced. To complete our discussion, answer task 8.4.

Task 8.4

Run a *t*-test for the control group.

I am sure you have found in task 8.4 that the difference in means between the pre- and the post-test for the control group is statistically significant for both 1- and 2-tailed test with $p=0.000$ and $p=0.000$, respectively. It might be a small improvement, but a significant one. As before, if you draw a bar chart with error bars, you get some visual information in this, too.

Time to summarize all our results for the Sadighi and Zare (2006) study – including the fictive data. We have found that:

● There was no significant difference in performance between the two groups at the beginning of the experiment
● Performance for the experimental group increased significantly by 13.5 points after the stimulus was introduced.

- Performance for the control group increased significantly by four points when no stimulus was introduced.
- Performance of the EG is significantly higher than that of CG in the post-test, that is, after introduction of the stimulus in EG.

If we assume that all other factors were constant, we now have very strong evidence that the stimulus, that it, 'knowledge activation' significantly improves respondents' performance. Even though the control group's performance also increased, this increase was only marginal and can probably be explained as normal development. As regards causality, we shall refer back to our three criteria in Chapter Two:

a X and Y must correlate. We have seen above that EG_pre and EG_post scores correlate strongly and positively. So, this criterion is met.

b There must be a temporal relationship between X and Y. The post-scores, by their very nature, occur after the pre-scores, hence this criterion is met.

c The relationship between X and Y must not disappear when controlled for latent variables. This is the most difficult one to prove. We can only hope that external circumstances do not change over the period of the experiment. However, we have no reliable evidence that this is the case.

As such, with two out of three criteria met, we have a fairly good indicator that performance and stimulus are causally related; yet, the evidence is not conclusive.

Doing statistics using Excel: *t-test (significance only)*

Sometimes we may only want to quickly check whether differences between two groups are statistically significant or not. For this, we can use the =t-test function. As usual, either type it in directly, or use the function wizard.

=t-test(array1, array2, tails, type). array1/2 refers to the data of each group, tails to the number of tails (1 or 2). There are three types:

- Paired (=dependent sample) – 1
- 2-sample equal variance – 2
- 2-sample unequal variance – 3

For the calculation of the *t*-test in Section 8.2 – the independent sample – the function is:

=t-test(dataEG, dataCG, 1, 2)

The result we obtain only gives us the significance level.
(→See the companion website for an Excel template for t-tests.←)

8.6. Hypothesis testing, *t*-tests and non-experimental data

The Sadighi and Zare (2006) study is a convenient example to illustrate hypothesis testing with the help of the t-test: in a nicely controlled environment we manipulate one particular variable and measure the outcome. However, in linguistics we are frequently confronted with non-experimental data. And where there is non-experimental data, there is always plenty of scope for latent variables to influence any result. Trouble looms!

Another example from my own work: in my research, I looked at target-likeness in spoken English as a second language among Bangladeshi migrants in London. Data was collected by means of interviews and the elicitation of personal narratives – in other words, we have spontaneous speech in an uncontrolled setting. Table 8.7 summarizes the results for 12 respondents, including age of onset, length of residence in England ('residency') and the performance score GPI – the higher the score, the more target like the language is (see Table 8.7).

TABLE 8.7 Performance of 12 speakers

Respondent	Sex	Age of onset	Residency in years	GPI
HF	male	6	24	26.35
SA	male	8	22	23.28
NA	male	26	3	20.49
MA	male	15	12	17.35
MMA	male	30	4	16.46
MFA	male	23	2	15.47
MT	male	26	1.5	15.37
SNF	female	23	9	23.17
SB	female	20	5	22.27
HB	female	13	12	21.67
AZ	female	15	15	20.7
FB	female	19	3	19.34

Source: Rasinger 2007.

Task 8.5

Using a *t*-test assuming *unequal* (!) variance, analyse the difference between male and female performance. Is the answer as straightforward as it seems? What are potential pitfalls?

The full table for the *t*-test is in Chapter Eleven. If you have not made any mistakes – and I guess you have not – then you will have probably found that the mean performance of men is slightly lower than that of women, with $\bar{x} = 19.25$ and $\bar{x} = 21.43$, respectively. However, when we look at the significance values, we see that $p = 0.25$ for the 2-tailed test. We have no predictions as to who scores better, men or women, so the 2-tailed test is the one to choose. That is, the difference is statistically not significant: there is a 25% chance that the difference in means is just a fluke. If you look closely at Table 8.7, you will see that the two male respondents HF and SA are quite different from the rest of the sample, as they have a much lower age of acquisition onset and have lived in England for much longer. From what we know about age of onset in second language acquisition, this should immediately ring alarm bells: if we have two data points which are that far off the rest of the sample, and also cross a theoretical 'magic line', then we should carefully reconsider our result.

Task 8.6

Remove HF and SA from the sample and re-calculate the *t*-statistic, this time assuming equal variance (as we have an equal number of men and women). Interpret the result with reference to your results from task 8.5.

If we remove HF and SA from the sample, the mean for male respondents decreases slightly to 17 points. More importantly, now $p = 0.005$ (2-tailed), that is, the difference is statistically significant. It is almost impossible to say which of the two results is 'correct' – it all depends on your methodological and theoretical viewpoint and line of argument. Outlying values are always potentially problematic. But then, you may find ways to argue around them.

Furthermore, neither result tells us anything about causality: even though women score significantly better in the second test (without HF and SA), there is a myriad of variables we cannot account for and hence cannot control. In fact, when probing a bit further, it became obvious that it was in particular women who had school-aged children *and* had certain interaction patterns who spoke more target like than men without children. And to make it more complex, women with school-aged children do better than those without. So, in a nutshell, even the most sophisticated statistical method with even the fanciest of figures and scores should not ever be accepted unconditionally. Statistics on their own are usually not the answer – always use your critical judgement.

QUICK FIX: *T*-TEST

- Use the independent *t-test* to compare two sets of data from two different groups
- Use the dependent *t-test* to compare two sets of data from the same group
- Excel: =t-test(array1, array2, tails, type) whereby for type

    1: Paired (=dependent sample)
    2: 2-sample equal variance
    3: 2-sample unequal variance

8.7. Hypotheses testing with the chi-squared test

Although the t-test is a very useful and frequently applied tool for testing differences between two sets of data or two groups, we can only apply it when our data is normally distributed and on a ratio scale. But what if our data is neither? How can we analyse categorical data for differences? We have already met the chi-squared test as a measure of association for categorical variables in Chapter Seven. There, we have said that the test is based on the comparison between observed and expected values. Luckily, we can also use the chi-squared test to check differences in means. Spend a moment thinking about this: if you use the comparison of observed and expected values for categorical data to show association, how can we show association if there is no difference?

Let's go right back to Chapter Five and Labov's (1972) example of the use of standard features by two men of different ethnic origin. You can find the entire data set in Table 5.1. What we are interested here is whether there is a significant difference in the use of simplified consonant clusters between the two speakers BF (Afro-American) and AO (white) (see Table 8.8).

From Table 8.8 we can see that BF uses more simplified clusters that AO. But is this a real difference? Our null hypothesis is:

H_0:   There is no significant difference in the use of simplified consonant clusters between the two speakers.

TABLE 8.8 Absolute frequencies of simplified consonant clusters

BF simplified	AO simplified	Total
71	46	117

In a first step, we once again need our expected frequencies. Based on H_0, we would expect both speakers to perform equally, that is, there should be the same number of simplified clusters for both BF and AO. Since we have a total number of simplified clusters of 117 and two speakers (or 'categories'), we would expect each speaker to produce

$$\frac{117}{2} = 58.5 \, \text{simplified clusters}$$

If you are not entirely sure about this step, bear in mind that this is nothing more than probability theory: if you have one red and one blue ball in a box, and both are of identical size and texture, you are as likely to draw the red ball as you are the blue ball (given that you cannot see them, obviously). So, the probability that you draw the red ball is 50%, as is that for the blue ball. If there is a difference between the balls, or indeed you can see them, one is more likely to be drawn, depending on your personal preferences. In our H_0 we assume that BF and AO are equal, so the probability for them to produce a non-standard form is 0.5 for each one (see Table 8.9).

From Table 8.9, we calculate our chi-squared statistics using Excel as discussed in Chapter Seven.

Task 8.7

Calculate the chi-squared statistics.

You will find that $p=2.9E–10$, with is much smaller than 0.05. So, the difference between AO and BF is statistically significant, with BF using significantly more simplified clusters than BF.

Similarly, for Clark's (2003) vocabulary acquisition experiment we have shown in Chapter 7, Section 7.3, using the χ^2 test that word-type and production type are related. Now we want to see whether children (a) produce more correct IN that OUT words, and (b) whether there is a difference between production and comprehension. For convenience, the table is replicated here (see Table 8.10).

TABLE 8.9 Observed and expected values

	BF simplified	AO simplified	Total
Observed	71	46	117
Expected	58.5	58.5	117

TABLE 8.10 Absolute frequencies of IN and OUT words

	IN	OUT	
Produced spontaneously	33	12	45
Understood correctly	54	50	104
	87	62	149

Source: Clark (2003).

Task 8.8

Carry out χ^2 tests for scenarios (a) and (b) above.

For (a), we assume that H_0: There is no difference between IN and OUT words. Accordingly, we set up Table 8.11 with observed and expected frequencies. As before, if we assume no difference, we should find as many IN words as OUT words, so the expected frequency for both is just ½ of the overall number of words:

$$f_{exp}(\text{IN})\frac{149}{2} = 74.5 \text{ and } f_{exp}(\text{OUT})\frac{149}{2} = 74.5$$

The χ^2 shows that $p=0.04$, that is, in general, the children have a statistically significant preference for IN words. Note that this result covers both the comprehension and production domain.

For (b), the assumption is that H_0: There is no difference between the two domains production/comprehension. Accordingly, Table 8.12 shows us the observed and expected frequencies.

For (b), the result of the chi-squared test is $p=1.34E-06$, with is much smaller than $p=0.05$; hence, the number of produced words is significantly lower than the number of understood words.

Task 8.9

Using a chi-squared test and the data on children's vocabulary acquisition, show that:

a the children *produce* significantly more IN than OUT words,

b there is no difference between the two word types in the domain of comprehension.

Task 8.10

The Table summarizes of lifestyle choices across genders in Edwards' study on 'Black English' (Edwards 1986: 62). Test the following null hypotheses.

1 H_0: There is no association between gender and religious practices.

TABLE 8.11 Observed and expected frequencies for two-word types

	IN	OUT	
Observed	87	62	149
Expected	74.5	74.5	149

TABLE 8.12 Observed and expected frequencies for two domains

	Production	Comprehension	
Observed	45	104	149
Expected	74.5	74.5	149

	Males	Females
Christians	6	6
Churchgoers	6	4
Rastafarians	5	1
No religious affiliation	9	8

2 H_0: There is no difference between those with a religious affiliation and those without.

3 H_0: There is an equal number of male and female Rastafarians in the sample.

8.8. Three's a crowd: ANOVA

The analytic tools we have discussed so far essentially allow us to statistically compare pairs of things: two groups, or two sets of data. Yet, unsurprisingly, in real life there are often more than two things that we are interested in. Earlier in the chapter, when discussing the *t*-test, we said that the *t*-test is a statistical procedure that compares the arithmetic means of two groups of data while taking their variability (i.e. their standard deviation or variance) into account. The Analysis of Variance (or ANOVA) does the same, but involving more than just two sets of data. Like the *t*-test, ANOVA is a parametric test, so the key assumption is that our data is normally distributed.

8.8.1. One-way/single factor ANOVAs

Since we are already familiar with it from our discussions of t-test, we will recycle Sadighi and Zade's 2006 study here. Remember that Sadighi and Zade set up their study in such a way that they had an experimental group (EC), which received some sort of treatment, and a control group (CG), which did not, and we compared EC with CG results after the treatment (or lack thereof in the case of CG) to see whether there is a statistically significant difference. In other words, we had two independent variables (treatment/no treatment) and one dependent variable (TOEFL test). ANOVAs, however, can be used to analyse situations where there are more than just 2 IVs. The following fictitious example will illustrate this. Let's assume we are interested in whether different types of treatment facilitate vocabulary acquisition. We base our experiment of the acquisition of 20 new items of vocabulary and set it up in such a way that we have three groups:

- The CG is exposed to a standard 60-minute lesson in which the new vocabulary pops up, but students do not get any specific treatment.

- EC-1 gets 45 minutes standard input plus 15 minutes dedicated to traditional rote learning of the 20 vocabulary items (treatment 1).

- EC-2 gets 45 minutes standard input plus 15 minutes where the vocabulary items are used through the medium of song (treatment 2).

After the lesson, a standardized test measures how many of the items have been retained. The result is displayed in Table 8.13 – note that there are 15 students in each class. I have also calculated the mean, variance and standard deviations, although by now, you can probably do this yourself.

It is pretty obvious that there are differences between the groups: EC1 performs best with an average of 12.87 new vocabulary items retained, closely followed by EC2 with 11.20 items retained on average. The CG, which received no extra treatment, perform worst (9.4 items). Looking at the standard deviation, we can see that the spread of results is similar across all groups. The question is, are these differences statistically significant? On the surface, the easiest way is to conduct a series of t-tests, as discussed earlier in this chapter: we could use a t-test to compare EC1 with EC2, a t-test to compare EC1 with CG and a t-test to compare EC2 with CG. There are, however, problems with it. For a start, with each new independent variable, the number of t-tests increases: in the case of four conditions (EC1, EC2, EC3 and CG), the number of t-tests required are already six (EC1/EC2, EC1/EC3, EC1/CG, EC2/EC3, EC2/CG, EC3/CG). A more problematic issue is that with every t-test we conduct, the probability of making a type 1 error (assuming a relationship when there isn't one – see Chapter 7, Section 7.7) goes up, something we really want to avoid. ANOVAs avoid this problem.

TABLE 8.13 Two treatment and one control group

	EC-1 (rote learning)	EC-2 (singing)	CG (no treatment)
	11	6	5
	13	8	9
	15	7	7
	20	17	11
	20	16	19
	18	11	18
	17	10	3
	13	3	7
	9	2	16
	11	8	15
	16	17	14
	6	20	1
	14	20	8
	3	13	6
	7	10	2
Mean	12.87	11.20	9.40
Variance	25.84	33.46	33.97
SD	5.08	5.78	5.83

In this example, we will use what is known as a one-way ANOVA, sometimes also known as single-factor ANOVA (as there is only one factor in our experiment: type of treatment). It should be said at the start that ANOVAs *only* tell us whether there are significant differences between groups, not what these differences are (i.e. not which treatment is better/ worse than another). In other words, it allows us to make statements as to whether or not there is a significant effect, but not what the effect is. As with the *t*-test, the assumption of the ANOVA, that is, its null hypothesis, is that there is no difference between treatments, with the alternative hypothesis that at least one group is different:

H_0: There is no difference between groups.

H_A: At least one group is significantly different.

Like a *t*-test, ANOVAs take the variance into account (the term Analysis of Variance is a bit of a giveaway). Before you continue, make sure you go back to our discussion of the *F*-test earlier in this chapter. You will need this for interpreting ANOVAs. Also, if you have not done so, please install Excel's Data Analysis tool.

Doing statistics in Excel: ANOVAs

Copy the example in Table 8.13 into a new worksheet, or download it from the companion website. In the Data menu, select 'Data Analysis'. Select the 'ANOVA: Single factor' function. For the 'Input range' select the data for the four groups, EXCLUDING the mean, variance and standard deviation values (they are already the results of an analysis, so not data). Set Alpha to 0.05 if this is not provided by default; this will give us a 95% confidence level. Select where you want the results to go – I suggest you select 'new worksheet'. Click ok.

(→See companion website for how to conduct an ANOVA in Excel.←)

You should receive a table that looks like this:

ANOVA: Single factor

Summary

Groups	Count	Sum	Average	Variance
EC-1	15	193	12.87	25.84
EC-2	15	168	11.2	33.46
CG	15	141	9.4	33.97

ANOVA

Source of Variation	SS	df	MS	F	P-value	F crit
Between groups	90.17778	2	45.08889	1.450322	0.245998	3.219942
Within groups	1305.733	42	31.08889			
Total	1395.911	44				

The summary gives you some of the key information, such as the sample size for each group (count), the sum you get if you add up all values of a group, as well as the arithmetic mean (average) and the variance. It does not provide you with the standard deviation, as it is not relevant for an ANOVA, but if you use the Data Analysis tool and have not calculated the SD separately, remember that the SD is simply the square root of the variance.

The really interesting table is the second one, especially the three rightmost columns labelled F, P-value and F_{crit}. We see straightaway that the p-value of $p=0.25$ is larger than $p=0.05$, our required significance level. Like the interpretation of the t-test, we use this to conclude that there is no significant difference in means between the treatment groups. The means may *look* different, but statistically, they are not. In yet other words, the different type of treatment our students receive does not result in different performance.

The F and $Fcrit$ values provide us with the same information: what the ANOVA does is to compare the variance within groups with the variance between groups. As a guideline, if the F value is greater than the critical value $Fcrit$, then the differences between the groups are not due to chance but due to some real underlying differences – in other words, the difference is statistically significant.

In our example $F=1.45$ and hence is smaller than $Fcrit$, so the variation is due to chance. So, as a quick and dirty rule: for a single factor ANOVA, there is a meaningful effect between groups if:

- $p < 0.05$ (or any other alpha value you set, but it really should not be higher than 0.10 for a 90% confidence level)

- $F > Fcrit$

In our example, neither applies, so despite superficially different means, there is no statistically significant effect between groups – different types of treatment do not influence vocabulary retention.

8.8.2. Two-way ANOVAs

In a paper published in 1986, Doughty and Pica discuss the effect that both task type and participation patterns have on interaction in an ESL (English as a Second Language) classroom. The study was based on two hypotheses:

Our first hypothesis was that activities which required an information exchange for their completion would generate substantially more modified interaction than those in which such exchange was optional.

Thus, there would be more comprehension and confirmation checks, more clarification requests, and more repetitions in the former than in the latter activity. Furthermore, we predicted that the number of interlocutors and the presence or absence of the teacher would influence the amount of modified interaction in the activity. (Doughty and Pica 1986: 309)

In this example, then, we have not only one independent variable, as we had in the example for one-way ANOVAs, but two, so what we need is a statistical tool that shows whether either factor has an effect on the dependent variable. Table 8.14, adapted from Doughty and Pica (1986), presents the data split by type of interaction (teacher-fronted versus group; IV-1) and type of task (optional exchange versus required exchange; IV-2).

Unfortunately, Excel cannot conduct an ANOVA if, as in Table 8.14, the numerical values are disrupted by text, we need to modify it accordingly (Table 8.15)

TABLE 8.14 Interaction/task type

	Type		
Class	Teacher-fronted	Group	Total
	Optional exchange task		
1	52.4	47.5	
2	50.7	36.7	
3	41.4	36.1	
Total	144.5	120.3	264.8
	Required exchange task		
4	50.4	76.5	
5	47.1	56.3	
6	38.3	58.2	
Total	135.8	191	326.8
TOTAL	280.3	311.3	591.6

Source: Adapted from Doughty and Pica (1986).

TABLE 8.15 Excel-ready format of Doughty and Pica's (1986) data

	Teacher-fronted	Group
Optional exchange task	52.4	47.5
Optional exchange task	50.7	36.7
Optional exchange task	41.4	36.1
Required exchange task	50.4	76.5
Required exchange task	47.1	56.3
Required exchange task	38.3	58.2

Doing statistics in Excel: Two-way ANOVAs

Copy the example in table 8.14 into a new worksheet, or download it from the companion website. In the Data menu, select 'Data Analysis'. Select the 'ANOVA: Two factor with replication' function. It is called 'with replication' because we are looking at several cases (namely 6 different classes), so to some extent it is a bit like replicating the same thing six times. For the 'Input range' select the data range. In the 'Rows per sample' box, input 3, as we have 3 different cases for each 'sample' (i.e. for the type of task). Excel terminology is getting rather confusing here. Set Alpha to 0.05 if this is not provided by default; this will give us a 95 per cent confidence level. Select where you want the results to go – I suggest you select 'new worksheet'. Click ok.

You will obtain a table that looks like table 8.16 (I have cut down the number of decimal places).

Task 8.10

Have a go: based on what we have said about one-way ANOVAs, how would you interpret the results in Table 8.16? Solution discussed below.

The first three tables provide you with a summary for each task/input combination, just like we have seen for one-way ANOVAs. As before, the interesting information is located in the bottom table. 'Sample', somewhat confusingly, refers to our different task types (in other words, the rows in Table 8.16; 'columns' refers to the two different groups; 'interaction' we

TABLE 8.16 Excel ANOVA results

Anova: Two-factor with replication			
Summary			
Optional exchange task	**Teacher-fronted**	**Group**	**Total**
Count	3	3	6
Sum	144.5	120.3	264.8
Average	48.17	40.1	44.13
Variance	35.06	41.16	50.01
Required exchange task			
Count	3	3	6
Sum	135.8	191	326.8
Average	45.27	63.67	54.47
Variance	39.12	124.42	166.99
Total			
Count	6	6	
Sum	280.3	311.3	
Average	46.72	51.88	
Variance	32.20	232.85	

ANOVA						
Source of variation	**SS**	**df**	**MS**	**F**	**P-value**	**F crit**
Sample	320.33	1	320.33	5.34401	0.049557	5.317655
Columns	80.08	1	80.08	1.336003	0.281091	5.317655
Interaction	525.36	1	525.36	8.764455	0.018133	5.317655
Within	479.54	8	59.94			
Total	1405.32	11				

will discuss in a moment. For 'sample', we see that $F=5.344$, the critical F value $Fcrit=5.32$, and $p=0.05$. Above we said that for a significant effect, we would like a result of $F > Fcrit$ and $p<0.05$. Both criteria are met here: $F(5.344) > Fcrit(5.32)$, and our p value is smaller (just!) than 0.05. This means that task type has a meaningful effect. Please note: as discussed earlier in this chapter, there are some problems related to how Excel calculates certain values; for this reason, the values in Table 8.16 vary slightly from Doughty and Pica's original.

For 'columns' – type of interaction – we see that $F(1.34)$ does not exceed the critical F value of 5.32, and with $p=0.28$, we can say that interaction type does not have a meaningful effect. So, while task type just by itself does have significant effect, type of interaction as a variable just by itself does not. Our interpretation here is in line with Doughty and Pica (phew!):

> A two-way analysis of variance (ANOVA) revealed that the main effect for task was statistically significant, thus confirming the first hypothesis of this study [. . .]. The ANOVA also showed that while the main effect for participation pattern was nonsignificant, there was a significant interaction of the two variables of task and participation pattern. (Doughty and Pica 1986: 314–15)

The above quote leads us to the final piece of information: for 'interaction', $F(8.76)$ exceeds the critical value of 5.32, and p=0.02. This means that task type and interaction type *together* do also have a significant effect on the outcome. Please note that 'interaction' here refers to the interaction between the two variables, of which one is unfortunately also called 'interaction'. As per quote above, our interpretation is the same as Doughty and Pica's.

The interaction value in a two-way ANOVA can be quite revealing for another reason. Let's imagine an experiment identical to the one we have discussed so far, but instead of the results we and the original authors have calculated, we get the following results:

Source of variation	F	P-value	F crit
Sample	2.413654	0.349557	5.317655
Columns	1.336003	0.281091	5.317655
Interaction	8.764455	0.018133	5.317655

In this fictive example, neither task type nor interaction type have a significant effect as variables on their own; however, taken *together*, they *do* have a meaningful effect. That means that the combined effect of the two variables is a lot more effective that the individual variables alone.

QUICK FIX: ANOVA

Use a *one-way ANOVA* to check for differences between more than two groups in one independent variable, for example, two experimental and one control group.

Use a two-way ANOVA if you have two independent variables to check whether either IV has an effect on the DV.

For both, the effect is statistically significant if:

- <0.05 (or any other alpha value you set, but it really should not be higher than 0.10 for a 90% confidence level)
- *F>Fcrit*

CHAPTER NINE

Analysing non-parametric data: When things are not quite normal

Key words: Kendall's tau – Kurtosis measure – Mann–Whitney U test – non-parametric data – rank and tied ranks – Spearman Rank correlation – Wilcoxon Signed Rank test

In the previous two chapters, we have – rather naively – assumed that our data is normally distributed, and the analytic tools we discussed there reflected this: so-called *parametric tools* such as the Pearson correlation, the t-test and ANOVAs only work with normally distributed data and data that is on a ratio scale. However, things in life are not always normal, and unfortunately, neither is data. In this final chapter, we will have a look at a few *non-parametric tests*, that is, test we can use to analyse non-normal, non-parametric data.

This chapter introduces readers to three statistical tests which can be used with non-normal, non-parametric data:

- The Spearman Rank correlation as the non-parametric equivalent to the Pearson correlation. We will also briefly look at Kendall's Tau, another non-parametric test of correlation.

- The Mann–Whitney test and the Wilcoxon Signed Rank test as non-parametric equivalents to the t-test.

The discussion of the non-parametric tools of statistical analysis also brings us to the limits of what we can reasonably do with Excel. I have included some guidelines on how to perform the analyses we discuss in the chapter using Excel, however, some of the calculations can be rather cumbersome as we have to carry them out semi-automatically. If you intend to use them frequently, you may want to consider changing to software that can deliver the results at the click of a button – see Chapter Ten for an overview.

In Chapter Six, I have introduced the normal distribution and have said that, as a guideline, in a normal distribution the arithmetic mean and the median are (near) identical, with the skewness value being zero or very close to zero. As a result, our distribution is symmetrical. The more different the mean and median are, and the higher the skewness value, the less symmetrical our distribution becomes, and this creates some serious problems for a lot of the parametric tools.

A second quick easy test to check for normality is the *Kurtosis measure*: it tells us how peaked or flat our distribution is, relative to the normal distribution. A positive Kurtosis indicates that we have a tall distribution, that is, its peak is a lot higher than we would expect from a normal distribution; a negative Kurtosis suggests a flat distribution – its peak is a lot lower than that of a normal distribution would be.

Doing statistics using Excel: Kurtosis

The formula for the Kurtosis is =kurt(data)

Positive Kurtosis: tall, peaked distribution (relative to normal distribution)

Negative Kurtosis: flat distribution (relative to normal distribution)

To make things more complicated, even if your data appears to be skewed and/or tall/flat, it does not necessarily mean that it is non-normal. Two common reasons why data appears non-normal are outlying values, and a small sample size. There are several sophisticated tests to check whether data is significantly non-normal, but none of them can easily be done in Excel (at least not with the standard version – there are optional add-ons, which often need to be purchased separately. In this case I suggest you move to a different software altogether). So, as a rough guide, if you suspect your data is not normal because

● the mean and median are substantially different,

● the data is skewed (skewness),

● the data peaked/flat (Kurtosis).

then you should consider using a non-parametric test.

9.1. The Spearman Rank correlation test

In Chapter Seven, we said that the Pearson correlation can only really be applied to data that is normally distributed, and where the relationship between the variables in comparatively linear. However, sometimes variables do not correlate in a linear fashion, but, when plotted in a scatter diagram, form a curve of some sort (which is why the graph is called *curvilinear*). In Figure 9.1 we can see that scores of the y-axis increase moderately up to score 8 on the x-axis; after that, there is a dramatic increase in y-scores. In a situation like this, a Pearson correlation will provide us with a potentially inaccurate coefficient, simply because it cannot take this curve into account. And, for the record, with data such as the one in Figure 9.1, we would also run into trouble with our regression models as discussed in Chapter Seven, for the very same reason.

Similarly, some statisticians suggest that for a Pearson correlation to work properly, the sample size should exceed 15 or even 20. This can be difficult to achieve, especially with small-scale projects.

For these situations, the Spearman Rank correlation is the way forward. In terms of arithmetic, it works identically to the Pearson correlation. However, instead of working with the actual scores, the Spearman Rank correlation works – as the term implies – with *ranks*. In simple words, we assign ranks to our data from the highest to the lowest score (or vice versa) and carry out a 'normal' Pearson correlation – but this time with the ranks instead of with the original scores. Hence, we can apply the Spearman test to non-parametric data, too. However, our data still has to be of at least interval scale!

Example: Table 9.1 shows the relationship between years of practice and language proficiency (on a scale from 0 to 100) for 12 language learners.

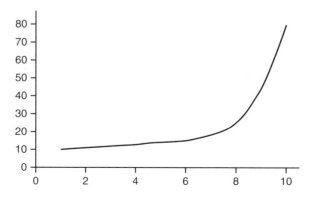

FIGURE 9.1 *Curvilinear graph.*

TABLE 9.1 Practice in years and proficiency scores for 12 speakers

	Practice	Proficiency
A	1	2
B	2	4
C	3	6
D	4	8
E	5	10
F	6	12
G	7	14
H	8	16
I	9	25
J	10	35
K	11	45
L	12	55

Task 9.1

1 Calculate the Pearson's *r* for the relationship between practice and proficiency. Assume that increased practice facilitates proficiency (i.e. use a 1-tailed test). Explain your result.

2 Draw a scatter plot for the data. Do you still agree with your result?

I take it that, without any problems, you found that $r=0.93$, and $P<0.0005$ for a 1-tailed test with 10 df (if you have not, you should have another thorough look at Chapter Seven). So, we have a very strong and highly significant positive correlation. However, once you have drawn you scatter plot (which should approximately look like the one in Figure 9.1.) you will have seen that there is a distinctively sharp bend in the line between 8 and 9 years of practice, whereby proficiency increases dramatically from 9 and more years of practice. And now our Pearson coefficient becomes dubious, as it cannot account for this.

As always, there is a way out – this time in the form of the Spearman Rank coefficient, also known as *Spearman's rho*. In a first step, we have to

TABLE 9.2 Ranks for proficiency and practice scores

	Rank_prac	Rank_prof
A	12	12
B	11	11
C	10	10
D	9	9
E	8	8
F	7	7
G	6	6
H	5	5
I	4	4
J	3	3
K	2	2
L	1	1

assign ranks to both set of scores, with the lowest score obtaining rank 12, and the highest score obtaining rank 1. Your table should then look like Table 9.2.

Doing statistics using Excel: *Ranks*

Especially with large data set, it can be onerous to rank data by hand. The appropriate Excel function is

=rank(number,ref,[order]), whereby 'number' refers to the score you want to rank, and 'ref' refers to the list this score comes from. The 'order' parameter is optional – hence in squared brackets – and the values are 0 (or omission) for a descending order (as we have in Table 9.2.) or any other value for an ascending order.

For example, to obtain the rank for A's practice score, the formula is:

=rank(B2, B2:B13, 0) – as before, we assume that you start your table in the top-left corner in cell A1.

As usual, our example data is idealized for the purpose of explanation, and here each rank is being assigned exactly one score. In reality, though, we will often encounter data sets were several respondents achieve the same score (e.g. several people have 6 years practice). We have what is called a *tied rank*. For example, assume A and B have *both* 2 years practice – in this case we cannot assign rank 1 to A and rank 2 to B. Rather, we have to use the mean rank between the 2. The 'mean rank' between rank 1 and 2 is – well – 1.5. So, both A and B come on rank 1.5 in practice.

Doing statistics using Excel: *Tied ranks*

The RANK function in Excel does not work for tied ranks – we have to use a *correction factor*.

1. Let Excel assign ranks using the =rank function (see above).
2. In a new column, calculate the adjusted/tied ranks:

   =R+((countif(range;R)–1)/2, where 'R' is the original rank, and 'range' is the list of original ranks.

Once we have ranked our data, we calculate the correlation coefficient, this time using the ranks. If you use Excel, the function is, as for the Pearson coefficient, =correl(array1; array2). You will find that rho=1. As with the Pearson coefficient,

- rho can have any value from –1 to 1 inclusive
- rho=1 indicates a perfect positive, rho=–1 a perfect negative relationship
- rho=0 indicates that the variables are not related

As before, we have to look up the critical value and significance level, but this time we have to use the appropriate table for Spearman's rho – looking it up in the Pearson's table will give you the wrong result! The table is in Chapter Eleven. For N=12, our rho=1 is highly significant, with $p<0.005$ (1-tailed).

The Spearman's rho for our example indicates that there is a perfect (and highly significant) relationship between practice and proficiency – what more could we want! Plot a scatter graph and you will see that we get a straight line. However, we have to bear in mind that the Spearman correlation works with ranks, not actual values. And us such, it ignores the sharp increase in our data after 9 years of practice (if you have not already done so, draw two scatter plots, once using the original data and one using the ranks – see the difference). This is both an advantage, as the coefficient is more reliable, but also a disadvantage as we lose a degree of detail. Yet, since the Spearman's rho is the mathematically more sound measure in this situation, it would be the preferable measure. When writing up your results in a report, you *must* make it absolutely clear whether you used a Pearson or a Spearman Rank correlation!

Task 9.2

Calculate the Spearman Rank coefficient for some of the examples we have used for the Pearson correlation. Compare the results. What can you observe?

QUICK FIX: SPEARMAN RANK CORRELATION

Use the Spearman Rank correlation instead of the Pearson correlation if there are signs that your data is not normal, or you have a small sample size. As with the Pearson correlation, $-1 < rho < 1$, whereby -1 indicates a perfect negative correlation and 1 a perfect positive correlation.

9.2. Kendall's Tau

Kendall's tau is the last in our collection of tools for analysing the correlation between two variables. Like the Spearman's rho, tau is a coefficient used to describing relationships in non-parametric/non-normal data, and it uses ranks rather than actual values. It is particularly sensitive to very small sample sizes, or to situations where you have a lot of tied ranks. For example, let's assume we have test scores for both listening and reading comprehension from five students, and score for each student is ranked from 1 (highest) to 5 (lowest):

Student	Listening rank	Reading rank
Annabelle	1	1
Harry	2	3
Tom	3	2
Sue	4	4
Emma	5	5

In the above example, the markers' ranking is identical in all but 2 (Tom and Harry) cases. A Pearson correlation coefficient gives us an $r=0.9$, but the data set is also very small so we ought to proceed with caution. There is no simple way of calculating it in Excel (it starts to look rather unattractive now, doesn't it), and to make matters worse, there are different types of Kendall's tau around (somewhat cryptically called 'a', 'b' and 'c'). We, too, will skip this here and refer to its basic properties, which help you to interpret it if you ever come across it:

● −1≤tau≤1

● tau=1 indicates a perfect positive, tau=−1 a perfect negative relationship

● tau=0 indicates that the variables are not related

In other words, it works just like the Pearson and Spearman correlation. Note that Kendall's tau must also be significant, just like the other coefficients.

9.3. Wilcoxon Signed Rank test

The *Wilcoxon Signed Rank* test is the non-parametric equivalent to the one-sample (dependent/related) t-test discussed in Chapter Eight. You have probably guessed it from the name: similar to the Spearman Rank correlation, the Wilcoxon Signed Rank test works with ranks rather than actual scores. Note that the data must be of at least ordinal level of measurement; if you have categorical/nominal data, you will have to use the chi-squared test.

There is no direct way to calculate the Wilcoxon test in Excel; however, Clegg (1982) provides a set of simple step-by-step instructions to calculate it manually. I provide here a 'semi-automatic' way calculating it using Excel. For convenience and layout purposes, I include the Excel commands in the explanation.

Keim (1984) in her work on the acquisition of German by Turkish migrants discusses, among many other issues, the use of simple and complex verbal phrases by her respondents. Looking at Table 9.3, it seems that respondents in the sample use simple verb phrases more frequently than complex ones. Those of you I have managed to convert into statistics fans will have probably also spotted that there is a significant and perfect correlation between the two scores with r=−1. We could use a related sample *t*-test as discussed in Chapter Eight, but something (mainly the small sample size) tells us that we should be careful and use a non-parametric test instead.

TABLE 9.3 Simple and complex verb phrases in percentage

Resp.	Simple %	Complex %
SA	45.50	54.50
FA	62.10	37.90
R	65.50	34.50
AS	74.60	25.40
H	84.70	15.30
HO	85.10	14.90
K	89.00	11.00
HK	90.10	9.90
O	94.70	5.30
M	95.80	4.20
A	96.60	3.40
C	100.00	0.00

Source: Adapted from Keim (1984: 191).

Since the Wilcoxon test is based on the comparison of *ranked differences* between the two samples, we, first, need to calculate the difference between each pair of scores and then rank the difference. So, we subtract the 'complex' from the 'simple' score for each respondent. If you are following my explanation with your own spreadsheet, make sure you start in the top-left corner with 'Resp' in cell A1.

1 Calculate the difference between complex and simple verb phrases in column D:

Excel: =B2–C2; =B3–C3 and so forth.

2 You will find that you have 11 positive and 1 negative differences. To convert all values into positive (or absolute) scores, use the =abs(number) function in column E:

=abs(D2); =abs(D3) etc.

You should now have a Table like 9.4.

TABLE 9.4 Relative frequencies, difference (d) and absolute difference d(abs)

Resp.	Simple %	Complex %	d	d(abs)
SA	45.5	54.5	−9	9
FA	62.1	37.9	24.2	24.2
R	65.5	34.5	31	31
AS	74.6	25.4	49.2	49.2
H	84.7	15.3	69.4	69.4
HO	85.1	14.9	70.2	70.2
K	89	11	78	78
HK	90.1	9.9	80.2	80.2
O	94.7	5.3	89.4	89.4
M	95.8	4.2	91.6	91.6
A	96.6	3.4	93.2	93.2
C	100	0	100	100

3 We now have to rank our d(abs) scores in *ascending* order. However, we must not assign a rank to any differences that are zero. If you come across data where the difference in a pair of scores is zero, delete this pair from your table. Make a note of how many pairs you have deleted – you need this information later. Here, we simply rank the d(abs) scores in ascending order, that is, the smallest value gets rank 1. If you have tied ranks (which we do not have in this example), use the correction factor as explained in 9.1. You table should be identical to 9.5.

4 Calculate the *sum of all ranks* with a positive difference, then calculate the sum of all ranks with a negative difference:

Sum of ranks of positive difference:
2+3+4+5+6+7+8+7+10+11+12=77

Sum of ranks of negative difference: 1 (there is only 1 negative difference, for SA, with d=−9 on rank 1).

TABLE 9.5 Ranked differences

Resp.	Simple %	Complex %	d	dabs	Rank
SA	45,5	54,5	−9	9	1
FA	62,1	37,9	24	24	2
R	65,5	34,5	31	31	3
AS	74,6	25,4	49	49	4
H	84,7	15,3	69	69	5
HO	85,1	14,9	70	70	6
K	89	11	78	78	7
HK	90,1	9,9	80	80	8
O	94,7	5,3	89	89	9
M	95,8	4,2	92	91	10
A	96,6	3,4	93	93	11
C	100	0	100	100	12

In Excel, use the following function; if your data has any zero difference pairs, use this on the table with the zero difference pairs deleted:

● Positive ranks: =SUMIF(D2:D13,">0",F2:F13)

This checks whether any d-value is *greater* than 0. If it is, it sums up the respective ranks in column F.

● Negative ranks: =SUMIF(D2:D13,"<0",F2:F13)

This checks whether a d-value is *smaller* than 0. If it is, it sums up the respective ranks.

● Optionally, you can ask Excel to check whether there are really no zero differences left (just to be on the safe side with large data sets). The following function will count all zero values and display how many zero values there are in the data set (on this example, it should display '0').

=countif(D2:D13,"=0",F2:F13)

You will find that the Excel functions give you the same results: 77 and 1. We are interested in the smaller value: 1. This is our *T value*. As before, we have to go to the appropriate table in Chapter Ten to find the significance level. N refers to the number of paired scores *whose difference is not zero*. In our example, N=12, as none of our differences are zero. In data with zero difference pairs, adjust accordingly by subtracting the number of zero difference pairs from the overall sample size (this is why it is important to make a note of how many you delete). In the table in Chapter Ten we look in the N=12 row and look for a value that is equal or just about larger than out T value. We have no predictions, so choose a 2-tailed test. Our T=1 is much smaller than the smallest critical value given for N=12 – 7 – so the difference is statistically significant on a level of *p*=0.01 (or even *p*<0.01). Bear in mind that, similar to the Spearman correlation, we lose a degree of accuracy when working with ranks as suppose to actual scores. Try and run a t-test with the same data – you should find that again the difference in scores is statistically significant.

9.4. Mann–Whitney *U* test

Where there is a non-parametric test for a 1-sample *t*-test, the equivalent for the 2-sample *t*-test cannot be far. The *Mann–Whitney U* test allows us to calculate whether the difference between data from two groups of people is statistically significant. As we are already familiar with it, we will reuse Sadighi and Zare's (2006) study from Chapter Eight. The Mann-Whitney test is calculated with the following formula; we will go through it step by step with the appropriate Excel commands.

$$U_1 = (n_1 \times n_2) + \frac{n_1 \times (n_1+1)}{2} - \text{summed ranks of } n_1$$

$$U_2 = (n_1 \times n_2) + \frac{n_2 \times (n_2+1)}{2} - \text{summed ranks of } n_2$$

1 Rank the scores of both groups from Sadighi and Zare's study (see Chapter Eight) in ascending order. However, rank the scores *across both groups*, that is, take the scores of both CG and EG into account when ranking an individual value. Note that we have several tied ranks, so you have adjust the ranking accordingly (see Section 9.1).

2 Calculate the sum of the ranks for each group individually. Your table should look like Table 9.6.

TABLE 9.6 Ranked scores for Sadighi and Zare (2006)

Resp	EG	CG	Rank	Rank
A	40	27.5	13	1
B	40	30	13	3
C	40	30	13	3
D	40	30	13	3
E	42	32.5	16.5	5
F	42	35	16.5	7
G	44	35	19.5	7
H	44	35	19.5	7
I	46	37.5	21	9.5
J	48	37.5	22.5	9.5
K	48	40	22.5	13
L	50	42.5	24	18
		Sum	214	86

3 Count the numbers of scores for each group. We have 12 scores for in both EG and CG, so N_1=12 and N_2=12. Note: if one sample is smaller, call the smaller one N_1 and the larger one N_2.

4 Calculate the U statistics for both groups using the following equation. You can enter the equation straight away into Excel:

For EG: $U_1 = (n_1 \times n_2) + 0.5 \times n_1 \times (n_1 + 1) - \text{summed ranks of } n_1$
$$= (12 \times 12) + 0.5 \times 12 \times (12 + 1) - 214 = 8$$

For CG: $U_2 = (n_1 \times n_2) + 0.5 \times n_2 \times (n_2 + 1) - \text{summed ranks of } n_2$
$$= (12 \times 12) + 0.5 \times 12 \times (12 + 1) - 86 = 136$$

5 We are interested in the lower of the U values: 8. We call this U and the larger value U': $U=8$, $U'=136$.

As usual we now have to look up our U value (not U') in the table of critical values in Chapter Ten. You will see that it is organised in a slightly different way, as we need both N_1 and N_2 (i.e. the sample size of both groups). To read the critical value, go to the point where the N_1 row and the N_2 column intersect, and read the value.

For $N_1=12/N_2=12$, the critical value is 27 for a $p=0.01$ 2-tailed test. Since $U=8$, it is smaller than the critical value, hence the difference between the two groups is statistically significant on a 99% confidence level. So, there's only a 1% probability that the difference has occurred by mere chance.

Independent from whether Sadighi and Zare's (2006) data is normally distributed or not, we can confidently say that the experimental group EG has scored significantly higher than the control group; the probability that our result is a fluke is only around 1%.

PART TWO

Further reading

There are now several books introducing statistics in linguistics. Of those, several deal specifically with statistical software: Gries (2009), Johnson (2008), Baayen (2008) for R, Larson-Hall (2010) for SPSS. I provide a brief description of those at the end of Chapter Ten. To an extent, it makes sense to acquire skills on how to use a statistical software while acquiring statistical skills – unless you would like to do complex mathematical operations manually.

Woods, Anthony, Paul Fletcher and Arthur Hughes (1986), *Statistics in Language Studies*. Cambridge: Cambridge University Press.
> One of the oldest books on the market, this book is one of the Cambridge University Press's 'red textbook' series. So it is thorough and detailed. It is from the mid-1980s, so do not expect an intro to any software packages.

Lowie, Wander and Bregtje Seton (2012), *Essential Statistics for Applied Linguistics*. London: Palgrave.
> One of the newest intros to statistics for linguists, this provides a good overview of the key methods used in applied linguistics. The (basic) companion website contains datasets for both SPSS and Excel.

Oakes, Michael (1998), *Statistics for Corpus Linguistics*. Edinburgh: Edinburgh University Press.
> As the title implies, the focus is very much on tools for corpus linguists, but still, this is a good general intro to the topic.

Rowntree, Derek (2000), *Statistics without Tears: An Introduction for Non-Mathematicians*. London: Penguin.
> Accessibly written, Rowntree provides a good introduction, but, as the lack of 'linguistics' in the title implies, examples are drawn from all over the place, so you need to transfer your skills onto linguistics.

Boslaugh, Sarah and Paul A. Watters (2008), *Statistics in a Nutshell: A Desktop Quick Reference*. Sebastopol: o'Reilly Media.
    Really a reference more than an introductory textbook, this includes examples from the educational and psychology fields, and, to make it more intriguing/ scary, medicine, too.

PART THREE

CHAPTER TEN

Beyond the basics: Other methods, other tools

Chapters One to Nine have focused on how to design a quantitative project, how to collect data and how to analyse it using a variety of tools. At this point, you should hopefully have a general idea of the main statistical methods and be able to use them yourself – or at least interpret them confidently when you encounter them in a piece of research you read. In this final chapter, we will explore some more advanced methods: the first section will provide a discussion of how to interpret MANOVAs (a step beyond the ANOVAs you have already met in Chapter Eight). This is followed by an introduction to the concept of meta-analysis – a neat way or recycling already existing data. And lastly, we will have a brief look at what software packages other than Excel can offer us.

10.1. Interpreting MANOVAs: A quick guide

In Chapter Eight, we have looked at how we can use the *t*-test to compare differences in means when there is only one independent variable involved, and how ANOVAs can tell us whether there are differences in means when there is more than one independent variable. What both *t*-test and ANOVA have in common is that they both deal with only one dependent variable. In the examples we used for *t*-tests and ANOVA both focused on only one dependent variable: test result (of some sort). We can illustrate *t*-tests and ANOVAs like this (Figures 10.1 and 10.2):

FIGURE 10.1 T-*test – 1 IV, 1 DV.*

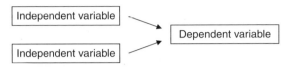

FIGURE 10.2 *ANOVA – 2 IVs, 1 DV.*

There is, however, a third option: there are instances where there are not only multiple independent variables involved, but also multiple dependent variables. And instead of multiple ANOVAS, we can use a MANOVA (Multivariate Analysis of Variance) to test for statistically significant differences – it is essentially the same issue that makes us use ANOVA instead of multiple *t*-tests: we try and keep the type 1 error as small as possible. MANOVAs, unfortunately, cannot easily be performed in Excel, so I limit the discussion here to explaining how to interpret the results, or to how to understand a discussion of a MANOVA should you come across it in the literature. If you need to perform a MANOVA yourself, you should think about using a different (or, as some people call it, 'proper') statistics software – I will introduce a few in the final section of this chapter.

As an introductory fictional example, let's once again use a teaching situation – easily understood, as most of us have been there at some point! Imagine a situation similar to the one we used when we discussed ANOVAs in Chapter Eight. There we used an example that looked whether different teaching types (our Independent Variables) have a significant impact on students' vocabulary retention (Dependent Variable) (Figure 10.3).

For a situation where we use a MANOVA, we will need a situation with two or move IVs *and* at least to DVs: for example, we can think of a situation where we would like to find out whether two (or more) different types of teaching have a significant impact on *both* students' listening and writing skills (Figure 10.4).

For our discussion of MANOVAs, we are using Purdie et al.'s (2002) study on 'Attitudes of Primary School Australian Aboriginal Children to their Linguistic Codes':

> In this study, 114 AE [Aboriginal English] (Nyungar) speakers were interviewed about their attitudes to AE and to SAE [Standard Australian English], and the attitudes they attributed to their teachers, Nyungar friends, and non-Nyungar peers in the context of the home, the classroom, and the school playground. (Purdie et al. 2002: 414)

As outlined in the above quote, part of the study focused on how Aboriginal children perceive the use of Aboriginal English (AE) and Standard Australian English, and what they thought about how their teachers' and

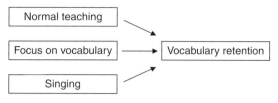

FIGURE 10.3 *ANOVA – 3 IVs, 1 DV.*

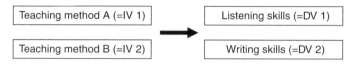

FIGURE 10.4 *MANOVA – 2 IVs, 2 DVs.*

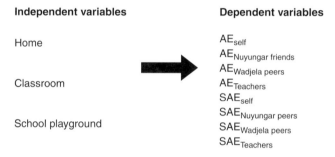

FIGURE 10.5 *MANOVA – 3 IVs, 8 DVs.*

Source: Purdie et al. (2002).

peers' perceived AE and SAE use across three different contexts. Our IVs in this case are hence the three contexts (home, classroom, school playground), and the DVs are the (attributed) perceptions: AE_{self} (e.g. how the children perceive AE), $AE_{Nuyungar\ friends}$ (how peers of the same ethnic group perceive AE), $AE_{Wadjela\ peers}$ (how peers of SAE origin perceive AE), $AE_{Teachers}$ (how teachers perceive AE); in addition, we get the same data for SAE (SAE_{self}, $SAE_{Nuyungar\ peers}$, $SAE_{Wadjela\ peers}$, $SAE_{Teachers}$). All in all, then, there are eight dependent variables over which the three contexts may or may not have an influence (Figure 10.5).

Following their MANOVA analysis, the authors conclude that:

[W]ith respect to context, there was a significant multivariate result involving self and Nyungar friends (F [8, 416] = 10.57, $p < 0.01$) but not for that involving Wadjela peers and teacher (F [4, 103] = 0.75, $p > 0.05$). (Purdie et al. 2002: 415)

In other words, the three different contexts – home, classroom and playground – make a significant difference in children's (attributed) perceptions:

> On the whole, the results indicate significant differences in the attitudes to AE and SAE of a group of Nyungar students. Students were generally positive about the use of AE at home, and in the playground, but negative about using SAE in those contexts. (ibid: 417)

MANOVA analyses are inherently complex and an in-depth discussion requires knowledge well beyond the scope of this book. However, as a 'quick and dirty' guideline, key to the interpretation of a MANOVA, as with so many tests we have looked at so far, is the significance value. As before, if the MANOVA provides a significance value of $p<0.05$, then we can be 95% confident that there is a real effect, as opposed to be a result that is a mathematical fluke (or $p<0.1$ for a 90% confidence level). As quoted above, Purdie et al.'s MANOVA has shown that we can be 99% confident that context has an effect on the perception of self and Nyungar friends, but we cannot be confident that this is the case for Wadjela peers and teachers, as their p-value exceeds the usual confidence level of 95%.

10.2. Using existing data: An intro to meta-analysis

10.2.1. Recycling and the search for 'true' effect

Let's look, once again, at the age of onset debate. I use this example not because I am obsessed with it (which I am – slightly), but because there is such a vast body of existing literature around that it is easy for you to find original studies and trace back their analyses. It is also, up to a point, pretty straightforward to understand. In a nutshell, the age of onset debate (also known as the Critical Period Hypothesis or, in its weaker form, Sensitive Period Hypothesis) suggests that the older a learner is at the time they start learning a second language, the less successful the outcome (or 'ultimate attainment') will be – older people don't learn languages (as) well (as young people). One way of exploring this phenomenon is to collect data from people's age of onset, measure their proficiency in a second language and carry out a correlation analysis (we ignore the fact that time of practice/ exposure to the language is also likely to play a role – we can do a partial correlation as discussed in Chapter Seven to sort that out). If there is a positive relationship between age of onset (AoO) and ultimate attainment (UA), the correlation coefficient r will be positive between 0 and 1; if the relationship is negative, the coefficient will be negative, somewhere between

0 and −1. We have seen in Chapter Seven that Johnson and Newport in their 1991 study found that the relationship between AoO and attainment was $r= -0.63$ – a strong negative relationship.

If we now argue that the authors have shown that the AoO debate holds true, we run into at least two problems:

1   J&N focused on only a particular type of second-language learner, namely native speakers of Chinese and Korean learning English as a second language.

2   Their main focus was on one particular syntactic phenomenon: subjacency.

In other words, what might be true for native speakers of Chinese/Korean acquiring (or not) subjacency in English is exactly that: a statement about native speakers of Chinese/Korean acquiring (or not) subjacency in English. What we cannot do is to generalize. If we are interested in the 'true' effect size, then we would need to not only look at all language combinations, but also all possible constructions within each constellation, and then run a correlation analysis on this massive data set. Suffice to say that most of us have neither the time, nor the energy, the resources nor the desire to actually do so.

10.2.2. Meta-analysis – first steps

Fortunately, help is at hand. While it is unlikely that any single author has looked at all language combinations and all possible syntactic constructions, when we survey the field we find that a lot of researchers have looked at a lot of different things related to the AoO debate. This leaves us with dozens, if not hundreds of individual and sometimes quite different findings. Glass, when discussing meta-analysis in educational research, laments the fragility of findings in educational research (Glass 1976: 3) and, similar to our discussion of the AoO debate, a high volume of output on the same or related topic. In addition, a series of related studies with near-identical setups may produce rather different results – a phenomenon also often observed in linguistic research.

One way to approach this problem is by means of a traditional literature review: a critical overview of previous studies. However, in the vast majority of cases, these reviews are mere discursive discussions, with the evaluation – and selection – of work included being at the subjective choice of the author. As a result, arguably, these reviews, as thorough as they may be, tend to be biased towards the author's own work (Glass, McGaw and Smith 1981). If, however, we are looking for the 'ultimate truth' (or, at least, the true effect size), then we need something more objective and robust, something that eliminates bias. And this is where statistical meta-analysis comes into play. Unlike the discursive literature reviews, meta-analysis is:

> a method for determining the overall effect of the relationship between variables by drawing together the findings from more than one, and often many more research studies. This is typically achieved through quantitative measurement and the use if statistical procedures. (Bryman 2004: 541)

Torgerson (2003) distinguishes between *systematic reviews* – essentially literature reviews in which, through careful selection and evaluation, bias is limited – and *meta-analyses*, '[t]he statistical synthesis of the data from separate but similar, i.e. comparable studies, leading to a quantitative summary of the pooled results' (2003: 8). Meta-analysis as an analytic approach has seen a 'meteoric increase' (Field 2001: 161) in the social sciences over the last three decades, with a variety of different approaches and methodological tools available to researchers. Because this is an introductory textbook, we focus on the most straightforward tools for conducting a meta-analysis. As before, turn to the 'Further reading' section at the end of this chapter if you would like to gain a deeper insight (and I strongly recommend you do!).

In order to achieve a maximum level of objectivity, simply pooling results from previous studies is not enough. Torgerson (2003), among others, suggests a seven-stage protocol for conducting a meta-analysis, with the actual synthesis, the statistical merging of results, only being the penultimate step. I have condensed them into six steps here.

1 Protocol: What goes for all statistical procedures of course also holds true for meta-analyses: rubbish in, rubbish out. Dumping large amounts of data into your spreadsheet will give you a result, but it is likely to be meaningless. Hence, as with any other kind of study, at the start of your meta-analysis stands the development of the theoretical, conceptual and methodological framework of the review. What is it you are looking it? How do you operationalize it? In our example, how do you define 'linguistic attainment'?

2 Establish inclusion and exclusion criteria: especially if there is a large body of previous research around, it is important to establish clear criteria that determine what is used and what isn't. You may want to focus on only a particular group of language(s), or a particular type of learner, or a particular type of data (e.g. experimental versus natural). Obviously, if your criteria are too strict, you might rule out too many studies, which in turn affects our search for a 'true' effect size.

3   Literature search: This is probably the biggest task. Based on the decisions we have made under (1) and (2), we search for all available previous work done on the topic. Torgerson (2003) recommends two reviewers at this initial screening stage, so as to ensure that inclusion/exclusion criteria are applied properly (bear in mind that it is objectivity we are looking for). In reality, especially if you are a student, it is likely to be tricky to find a second reviewer/screener.

4   Data extraction and appraisal: This is the point where we are extracting the data we are using for our actual statistical analysis. In the AoO debate, the key data usually comes in the form of (Pearson) correlation coefficients or, if the focus is on the comparison of groups (i.e. old versus young learners), t-test. Again, to make sure that this stage remains as objective as possible, two reviewers are recommended.

5   Synthesis of extracted data: This is the mathematical bit. I discuss this in Section 10.1.3.

6   Report: Unsurprisingly, the final stage consists of the writing-up of our results!

10.2.3. *Meta-analysis – doing the maths*

As with most things in research, there are various ways of conducting statistical meta-analyses. I will discuss here the method developed by Hunter and Schmidt (for a book-length discussion, see Hunter and Schmidt 2004: – not for the faint-hearted!). The Hunter-Schmidt method uses the Pearson correlation coefficient r as the effect size. If the studies in your pool do not use r (and quite a few don't), you can convert other effect sizes into r – see, for example, Field and Wright (2006). Hunter and Schmidt base their method on the assumption of random effect sizes – it assumes that different populations have different effect sizes.

Let's assume we have conducted an extensive literature search and screening on the topic of AoO, and we should have our data in a nice, neat table similar to the one below. Note that if we conducted a proper meta-analysis, the table would have to be a lot bigger, but this one will suffice for illustration purposes (see Table 10.1).

The Hunter-Schmidt method is based on the average-weighted effect size. This means that rather than just calculating the mean effect size (by calculating the mean r), the individual effect sizes are weighted according the sample size N. This avoids very small samples having a disproportionate effect on our 'true' effect size. Think back to the discussion of the arithmetic mean Chapter Six, where we have seen that the mean is, to an

TABLE 10.1 Summary of studies used for AoO meta-analysis

Author	Date	Study	Measures	Sample size	r
Johnson & Newport	1991	Critical period effects on universal properties of language: The status of subjacency in the acquisition of a second language.	Subjacency: Chinese learners of English	44	−0.63
Johnson & Newport	1989	Critical period effects in second-language acquisition: The influence of maturational state on the acquisition of English as a second language.	Grammaticality judgement task	46	−0.77
Birdsong & Molis	2001	On the evidence for maturational constraints in second-language acquisition.	Replication of J&N 1989 using Spanish L1ers of L2 English.	61	−0.77
Hyltenstam, & Abrahamsson	2003	Maturational Constraints in SLA.	Part 1: NS listener perception	195	−0.72
Hyltenstam & Abrahamsson	2003	Maturational Constraints in SLA.	Part 2: NS-likeness of NNSers, various measures	41	−0.38

extent, dependent on the sample size. If you look at Table 10.1, Johnson and Newport's 1991 study has a much smaller sample size (N=44) than Hyltenstam and Abrahamson's 2003 study with N=195. Simply calculating the mean between the two correlation coefficients would give undue weight to the much small J&N study.

The first step to do then is to multiply the effect size for each study with its sample size N; we also add up all Ns and all N^*rs as shown in Table 10.2.

TABLE 10.2 Multiply sample size N with effect size r

Author	Date	Sample size	r	$N*r$
Johnson & Newport	1991	44	−0.63	−27.72
Johnson & Newport	1989	46	−0.77	−35.42
Birdsong & Molis	2001	61	−0.77	−46.97
Hyltenstam & Abrahamsson	2003	195	−0.72	−140.4
Hyltenstam & Abrahamsson	2003	41	−0.38	−15.58
Sum		387		−266.09

As we can see from Table 10.2, the overall ample size of our pooled studies is 387; note that $N*r$ is meaningless, it is simply an interim step (so don't include it in your discussion!). To obtain our overall effect size – or more precisely, the overall weighted mean effect size – we simply divide the sum of $N*r$ by the overall sample size, so:

$$\bar{r} = \frac{\sum N*r}{N(total)} = \frac{-266.09}{387} = -0.6875$$

The interpretation of the weighted mean r works exactly like the interpretation of the non-pooled correlation coefficient: the 'true' effect size of $r= -0.6875$ indicated that we have a strong negative correlation between age of onset and L2 proficiency. In other words, the pooling of different studies looking at the relationship between AoO and proficiency gives us a more accurate picture of what is going on. The example is obviously based on a tiny sample of studies – for a real meta-analysis we would expect a lot more studies to be included – but do note that the weighted mean effect size of $r= -0.6875$ is stronger than the non-weighted mean effect size (e.g. simply calculated the arithmetic mean of all effect sizes of all studies): the non-weighted effect size is $r=-0.654$. If we project this difference onto a huge sample of studies, it becomes obvious that not weighing for sample size can dramatically affect our true effect size.

The next step is somewhat trickier: as with any correlation coefficient (or any effect size for that matter), we need to calculate the significance value. Andy Field's (1999) 'Bluffer's guide', from which the calculation of the mean r above is based, too, provides a reasonably straightforward step-by-step approach. According to Field, the calculation is 'based on taking the average effect size and adding or subtracting from it the square root of the estimated population variance multiplied by 1.96 (for a 95% confidence interval)' (1999: 6). In more digestible terms, follow these steps:

1   For each study, subtract the 'true' effect size r_{true} from the original effect size, and square the result:

$$(r - r_{\text{true}})^2$$

2   For each study, multiply the result from step 1 with the sample size for this study, so:

$$n(r - r_{\text{true}})^2$$

3   Add it all up and you should get a table like Table 10.3.

TABLE 10.3 Calculate confidence intervalls – step 3

Author	Sample size	r	Nr	$(r-r_{true})^2$	$n(r-(r_{true}))^2$
Johnson and Newport	44	−0.63	−27.72	0.00331443	0.145834783
Johnson and Newport	46	−0.77	−35.42	0.00679453	0.312548391
Birdsong & Molis	61	−0.77	−46.97	0.00679453	0.414466345
Hyltenstam, & Abrahamsson	195	−0.72	−140.4	0.00105164	0.205069056
Hyltenstam, & Abrahamsson	41	−0.38	−15.58	0.09459996	3.878598221
Sum	387		−266.09		4.956516796

4   Divide the sum of $n(r-(r_{true}))^2$ by the overall sample size. This gives us the *variance of the sample effect sizes*.

$$\sigma_r^2 = \frac{\sum n(r - r_{\text{true}})^2}{N} = \frac{4.9565}{387} = 0.0128$$

5   Calculate the *sampling error variance*; for this you also need to calculate the mean sample size (i.e. the mean size of all the samples). In our example, the mean sample size is $N_{\text{mean}} = 77.4$.

$$\sigma_e^2 = \frac{(1 - r_{\text{true}}^2)^2}{N_{\text{mean}} - 1} = \frac{(1 - 0.6875^2)^2}{77.4 - 1} = \frac{(1 - 0.4728)^2}{76.4} = \frac{0.278}{76.4} = 0.00364$$

6 Calculate the *variance in population effect size* by subtracting the sampling error variance (step 5) from the sample effect size variance (step 4):

$$\sigma_p^2 = \sigma_r^2 - \sigma_e^2 = 0.0128 - 0.00364 = 0.0092$$

7 Calculate the *upper and lower Credibility Interval* as follows. Note that the 1.96 is a given fixed value – it is not part of any of your calculations, so don't worry!

$$CredibilityInterval_{Upper} = r_{\text{true}} + 1.96\sqrt{\sigma_p^2} = -0.68 + 1.96\sqrt{0.0092} = -0.4999$$

$$CredibilityInterval_{Lower} = r_{\text{true}} - 1.96\sqrt{\sigma_p^2} = -0.68 - 1.96\sqrt{0.0092} = -0.8753$$

Our true effect size of r= –0.68 lies between these boundaries, so we can consider the result to be significant at a 95% confidence level. So, overall, we can say that our meta-analysis of the AoO debate indicated that there is indeed a strong negative correlation between age of onset and attainment, and that this relationship is statistically significant.

10.1.3. Meta-analysis – summary

In our example, it is well documented that there is a relationship between age and attainment, and that this relationship is likely to be negative. As such, the meta-analysis might enable us to get a more accurate picture. At the end of our discussion of meta-analysis we shall look at an example where the relationship is not as straightforward. So as not to make things too complicated, I will keep this abstract.

Imagine a situation where we are interested in whether there is a relationship between two variables A and B. Let's assume that a lot of other people have looked into this before, and having defined our criteria, selected our cases and extracted the data (see Section 10.2.2), we get a table looking like Table 10.4.

What strikes us straightaway is that unlike the AoO example, there does not seem to be a clear direction, with correlation coefficients ranging from strongly positive (Escargot 2006, *r*=0.84) to strongly negative (Deville 2005, *r*=–0.72). We also see that there is considerable difference in sample size.

TABLE 10.4 Meta-analysis – fictive example

Study	Sample size	r
Allen 2010	56	−0.25
Bergstrom 1978	187	0.18
Callum 2002	432	−0.25
Deville 2005	23	−0.72
Escargot 2006	232	0.84

Task 10.1

Before you read any further, calculate r_{true} and the confidence intervals for Table 10.4.

If everything has gone according to plan, you should have got a result of $r_{true}=0.097$, which is significant on a 95% confidence level. This is quite a striking result: although all individual studies in our made-up example have shown a relationship between A and B, the meta-analysis shows that the relationship is really only negligible, with the true effect size being quite small. And rather than creating a discursive argument around this, we now have a much more objective piece of evidence.

For obvious reasons, an introductory textbook can only ever provide a superficial glimpse at what are actually very complex processes, and this is certainly true for meta-analysis. Nevertheless, the above should provide you with a basic working knowledge of what meta-analysis is and how it works. The readings listed in the Further reading section at the end of this chapter suggest works that have looked at the issue in substantially more detail.

Further reading

Torgerson, Carol (2003), *Systematic Reviews*. London: Continuum.
     Carol Torgerson's book focuses on the systematic reviewing of existing research. It puts particular emphasis on issues to do to conceptualization and selection, but also dedicates a chapter to the pooling of quantitative data. It is a useful source for anyone conducting meta-analyses, be they statistical or discursive.

Hunter, John E. and Frank L. Schmidt (2004), *Methods of Meta-analysis: Correcting Error and Bias in Research Findings*. London: Sage Publications.
     If you like, this is at the other end of the spectrum from Torgerson's volume. Hunter and Schmidt's book looks, in great detail, at the different types of statistical meta-analyses. It is comprehensive, but as alluded to earlier, not

for the faint-hearted beginner: it requires substantial knowledge of statistical methods which go well beyond what you have read in this book.

Field, Andy P. and Daniel Wright (2006), 'A bluffer's guide to effect sizes', *PsyPAG Quarterly* 58, 9–23.
An annoying thing when conducting any kind of meta-analysis is the fact that different authors use different effect sizes, which makes comparison very difficult. Field and Wright's 'Bluffer's Guide' provides an accessible guide to how convert different effect sizes.

10.3. Excel revisited: Moving on

At various points in this book I have referred to Excel being somewhat limited, or indeed flawed, when it comes to certain statistical analyses. In fact, there are people who argue to steer clear of Excel altogether for statistics: Excel is a spreadsheet software, and it does well what the OED defines as such:

A program that allows any part of a rectangular array of positions or cells to be displayed on a computer screen, with the contents of any cell able to be specified either independently or in terms of the contents of other cells. (Oxford English Dictionary Online 2012)

So, it is good for organizing data and some simple mathematical operations, but for anything more statistical, it becomes problematic. What Excel does well is:

- Allows us to enter, sort and filter data quickly and efficiently.

- Allows us to create graphs and charts reasonably quickly and efficiently, although with its vast array of styles, do be careful that you do not fall into the style-before-substance trap.

- Does basic arithmetic (note that I avoid using the term 'statistic') operations, such as additions/subtraction, multiplication/division, calculation of absolute and relative frequencies.

- To a point, calculates measures of location (e.g. arithmetic mean, but even the median can be problematic) and dispersion.

- As it is part of the Microsoft Office suite, the look and feel are familiar to many users.

For the vast majority of entry-level statistics users Excel probably does not do too much harm for other statistical operations, as discussed throughout this book. If you need a quick and simple way of analysing data, maybe because you are an undergraduate or postgraduate student, of maybe because you simply want to get an idea of what your data looks like, it will do so job; sort of.

If, however, accuracy is at the essence (which, technically, it always ought to be!) or if your work requires more complex statistical methods, it is time to look elsewhere. In the next two sections, I will introduce two commonly used 'proper' statistic software package: SPSS and R.

10.3.1. SPSS

SPSS (an acronym of its original name, Statistical Package for the Social Sciences), or, more recently, IBM SPSS, has been around for more than two decades. As the (original) name implies, is popular tool in the social sciences and psychology. In fact, most undergraduate psychology courses (at least those I know, and that is quite a few) teach SPSS as part of their initial research method training.

The first thing to note is that SPSS is not a spreadsheet, although, irritatingly, when you first open it, it looks like one: the main interface looks like a table made up of cells. Do not make the mistake and try and treat it like a spreadsheet software – it will not work. To work with SPSS, you need to specify each individual variable: not only their name, but also their type (e.g. whether they are numerical, text-based, or something else) and their level of measurement. You can also specify 'missing values': it tells the software what to do if you do not have the data for a particular case/respondent – something Excel cannot do as easily. It is quite important that variables are specified correctly; SPSS is a powerful tool, but remember: rubbish in = rubbish out.

Unlike Excel, you cannot enter formulae directly into the spreadsheet (as SPSS isn't a spreadsheet!) but all functions can be accessed via numerous menus. In the past, there has been a tendency to move some functions to different menus from version to version, but by and large, the 'Analyze' menu gives you access to the main functions. Within it, the 'Descriptive statistics' gives you several options, among them 'Frequencies' and 'Descriptives'. The latter gives you access to the main descriptive statistics discussed in the early chapters of this book; the former does this, too, but also gives you the option to let the software create frequency tables. Depending on which version you use, you may need to click on the 'options' button first before you can select the tools you need – by now you will have figured out that quite a bit of clicking can be involved.

In version 20 of SPSS, you can find the following statistical tests in the 'Analyze' menu here:

Chapter 6:
Mean, median, mode, standard deviation, variance, range, frequency tables: → Descriptive statistics → Descriptive or Frequencies

Chapter 7:
Correlation analysis: Correlation analysis → Bivariate (for Pearson's and Spearman) or → Partial for partial correlation (partial correlation is a lot

easier to do using SPSS). Plus, for all correlation analyses, SPSS gives you the significance value straight away, so no need to look it up in the tables!

Regression analysis: → Regression → Linear

Chapter 8:

T-tests and Anova: → Compare means, then select the appropriate test

Chapter 9:

- Spearman Rank correlation and Kendall's tau : Correlation analysis → Bivariate, then tick the 'Spearman' box and/or 'Kendall's tau' box

- Mann Whitney U test, Wilcoxon Signed Rank test: → Nonparametric Tests, then select the appropriate option

Chapter 10:

MANOVA: → General linear model → Multivariate but I strongly suggest you read around the topic first!

Further reading

Good introductions to SPSS are:

Larson-Hall, Jenifer (2010), *A Guide to Doing Statistics in Second Language Research Using SPSS*. London: Routledge.

This is a thorough introduction to both SPSS as a software package and statistics for language researchers. With over 400 pages, it is comprehensive and there is little it has left out. As the title implies, the focus is on second-language acquisition but ultimately, the statistical tools discussed can of course be used for any subdiscipline.

Field, Andy P. (2009), *Discovering Statistics Using SPSS (and Sex, Drugs and Rock 'N' Roll)*. London: SAGE.

This is the third edition of Andy Field's intro to SPSS and statistics. Field is a psychology professor, hence examples, etc. are all based on psychology. It is comprehensive and accessibly written, and talks readers through show to use SPSS for different statistical tools. Lots of screenshots help readers to navigate their way through the software. This latest edition moves over the basics quite quickly, so make sure you are familiar with the basic issues first (by reading this book!) before moving onto Field's.

10.3.2. R

Especially in corpus linguistics, an area that has seen increasing popularity over the last decade or so, the software frequently used is called 'R': 'R is a language and environment for statistical computing and graphics' (www.r-project.org/). As such, R is not a statistics software like SPSS, or a spreadsheet software like Excel, it is actually a programming language. This means that you get a powerful tool that allows for complex statistical tests with a high degree of accuracy, but you do not get the easy-peasy click-and-hope-for-the-best interface of SPSS or Excel.

As a programming language, R uses a command line, that is, you need to tell it what to do by typing it in. In its simplest form, if we want R to add up three numbers, let's say 1, 2 and 3, we need to tell it to do so:

```
> 1+2+3              #press enter

[1] 6                #result displayed
```

A different way is to ask for the sum of the three numbers is to use the 'sum'-command:

```
> sum(1,2,3)         #press enter

[1] 6                #result displayed
```

We can (or must) specify variables through the command line, too. Imagine we have two variables, x and y, with five cases each, and the following values: for x, we have 1, 2, 3, 4, 5; for y we have 6, 7, 8, 9 and 10. We define these variables in R as follows:

> x <– $c(1,2,3,4,5)$ This tells R that variable x contains the values 1, 2, 3, 4 and 5

> y <– $c(6,7,8,9,10)$ This tells R that variable y contains the values 6, 7, 8, 9 and 10

This means that we can now carry on working with x and y, and R knows their values until we change them. So if, for example, we want to add up x and y, the command is:

> sum(x,y)

This will give us the correct response:

[1] 55

You can check this by entering:

>1+2+3+4+5+6+7+8+9+10

In R, it is very straightforward to create new variables based on existing ones, too. We can, for example, increase the values of x by 3 and call this new variable 'z', by simply telling R to do so:

> z <– $x+3$

If we then ask R to display the new variable, we will get

> z

[1] 4 5 6 7 8

If we want to calculate the arithmetic mean and standard deviation for x, we enter:

>mean(x)

[1] 3

> sd(x)

[1] 1.581139

Similarly, if we want to calculate the (Pearson) correlation coefficient between x and y, we tell R to do so:

>cor(x,y)

The answer is, unsurprisingly, 1 – there is a perfect correlation between x and y (because I have set it up that way!).

Further reading

Since this book does not deal with R, I have no intention of claiming to have given you an introduction to it – but hopefully you get a rough idea. Three popular introductions to using R is linguistics are:

Gries, Stefan T. (2009), *Statistics for Linguistics with r: A Practical Introduction.* De Gruyter Mouton.
    Gries' book pretty much does what it says on the tin: it is an introduction to *R* and an introduction to statistics. It includes a chapter solely dedicated to *R* as a program, which is useful for those who have never used it before. The remainder of the book contains various statistical tests and explanations as to how to conduct them using *R*.

Baayen, R. H. (2008), *Analyzing Linguistic Data: A Practical Introduction to Statistics Using R*. Cambridge: Cambridge University Press.
    Like Gries' volume, Baayen's book is both a good introduction to *R* and to statistics in general. The book comes with a set of data to play with, and a range of exercises, too.

Johnson, Keith (2009), *Quantitative Methods in Linguistics*. London: Wiley Blackwell.
    Johnson's book is primarily an introduction to statistics and uses *R* as the underlying software. It is particularly useful for those with a basic understanding of how *R* works in general already.

CHAPTER ELEVEN

Appendices and solutions

11.1. Excel functions

The following Excel functions are used in this book. Note that depending on the language version you have installed on your computer, you may have to replace the commas in the functions (e.g. in =frequency(DATA, bins_array) with semicolons, that is =frequency(DATA; bins_array).

Function	Description
Chapter 5	
=frequency(DATA, bins_array),	Returns the frequency distribution of a selected data range
=sum(DATA)	Calculates the sum of values in the selected data range, e.g. =sum(A1:A10) returns the sum of values in cells A1 to A10
Chapter 6	
=average(DATA)	Calculates the arithmetic mean of the selected data range
=median(DATA)	Calculates the median of the selected data range
=trimmean(DATA, per cent)	Calculates the trimmed mean for X per cent

Function	Description
=mode(DATA)	Calculates the mode of the selected data range. If multimodal, Excel will display the smallest value
=quartile(DATA, q)	Returns the value of the qth quartile
=percentile(DATA, p)	Returns the value of the pth percentile
=var(DATA)	Calculates the variance of the selected data range
=stdev(DATA)	Calculates the standard deviation of the selected data range
Chapter 7	
=chi-test(actual_range, expected_range)	Carries out a chi-squared test
=correl(array1, array2)	Calculates Pearson's *r* between 2 variables. If data is ranked, the function calculates Spearman's rho.
Chapter 8	
=t-test(array1, array2, tails, type)	Calculates the *t*-test. Note: Output indicates significance level only Type 1: paired sample Type 2: independent samples, equal variances Type 3: independent samples, unequal variances
=f-test(array1, array2)	Calculates the *F*-test to determine the difference in variances. 'Array 1' should be the variable with the higher variance. Output indicates significance level only
Chapter 9	
=rank(number,ref,[order])	Assigns rank to a particular score in the data. For order: '0' or omission: descending order any other value: ascending order
=R+((countif(range;R)−1)/2,	With 'R' being the original rank, and 'range' is the list of original ranks. Return the list of tied ranks
=abs(number)	Returns the absolute value of a number

11.2. Critical values for χ^2

Values given are *minimum values*: in order to be significant at a given level, χ^2 must be equal to or exceed the critical value.

df	0.1	0.05	0.01	0.001
1	2.706	3.841	6.635	10.83
2	4.605	5.991	9.21	13.92
3	6.251	7.815	11.34	16.27
4	7.779	9.488	13.28	18.47
5	9.236	11.07	15.09	20.52
6	10.64	12.59	16.81	22.46
7	12.02	14.07	18.48	24.32
8	13.36	15.51	20.09	26.12
9	14.68	16.92	21.67	27.88
10	15.99	18.31	23.21	29.59
11	17.28	19.68	24.73	31.26
12	18.55	21.03	26.22	32.91
13	19.81	22.36	27.69	34.53
14	21.06	23.68	29.14	36.12
15	22.31	25	30.58	37.7
16	23.54	26.3	32	39.25
17	24.77	27.59	33.41	40.79
18	25.99	28.87	34.81	42.31
19	27.2	30.14	36.19	43.82
20	28.41	31.41	37.57	45.31

11.3. Critical values for Pearson correlation

Values given are *minimum values*: in order to be significant at a given level, r must be equal to or exceed the critical value.

	1-tailed test			
	0.05	0.025	0.005	0.0005
	2-tailed test			
df	0.1	0.05	0.01	0.001
1	0.988	0.997	0.999	—
2	0.900	0.950	0.990	0.9999
3	0.805	0.878	0.9587	0.9911
4	0.729	0.811	0.9172	0.9741
5	0.669	0.754	0.875	0.9509
6	0.621	0.707	0.834	0.9241
7	0.582	0.666	0.798	0.898
8	0.549	0.632	0.765	0.872
9	0.521	0.602	0.735	0.847
10	0.497	0.576	0.708	0.823
11	0.476	0.553	0.684	0.801
12	0.457	0.532	0.661	0.780
13	0.441	0.514	0.641	0.760
14	0.426	0.497	0.623	0.742
15	0.412	0.482	0.606	0.725
16	0.400	0.468	0.590	0.708
17	0.389	0.456	0.575	0.693
18	0.378	0.444	0.561	0.679
19	0.369	0.433	0.549	0.665
20	0.360	0.423	0.537	0.652
25	0.232	0.381	0.487	0.597
30	0.296	0.349	0.449	0.554
35	0.275	0.325	0.418	0.519
40	0.257	0.304	0.393	0.49
45	0.243	0.288	0.372	0.465

	2-tailed test			
df	0.1	0.05	0.01	0.001
50	0.231	0.273	0.354	0.443
60	0.211	0.250	0.325	0.408
70	0.195	0.232	0.302	0.380
80	0.183	0.217	0.283	0.357
90	0.173	0.205	0.267	0.338
100	0.164	0.195	0.254	0.321

11.4. Critical values for Spearman's rho

Values given are *minimum values*: in order to be significant at a given level, rho must be equal to or exceed the critical value.

	1-tailed			
	0.05	0.025	0.01	0.005
	2-tailed			
N	0.1	0.05	0.02	0.01
5	0.900	1.000	1.000	—
6	0.829	0.886	0.943	1.000
7	0.714	0.786	0.893	0.929
8	0.643	0.738	0.833	0.881
9	0.600	0.683	0.783	0.833
10	0.564	0.648	0.745	0.818
11	0.523	0.623	0.763	0.794
12	0.497	0.591	0.703	0.780
13	0.475	0.566	0.673	0.746
14	0.457	0.545	0.646	0.716
15	0.441	0.525	0.623	0.689
16	0.425	0.507	0.601	0.666

	2-tailed test			
N	0.1	0.05	0.01	0.001
17	0.412	0.490	0.582	0.645
18	0.399	0.476	0.564	0.625
19	0.388	0.462	0.549	0.608
20	0.377	0.450	0.534	0.591
21	0.368	0.438	0.521	0.576
22	0.359	0.428	0.508	0.562
23	0.351	0.418	0.496	0.549
24	0.343	0.409	0.485	0.537
25	0.336	0.400	0.475	0.526
26	0.329	0.392	0.465	0.515
27	0.323	0.385	0.456	0.505
28	0.317	0.377	0.448	0.496
29	0.311	0.370	0.440	0.487
30	0.305	0.364	0.432	0.478

11.5. Critical values for Wilcoxon Signed Rank test

Values given are *maximum values*: in order to be significant at a given level, T must be equal to or less the critical value.

	0.05	0.025	0.01	0.005
N	0.1	0.05	0.02	0.01
5	1	—	—	—
6	2	1	—	—
7	4	2	0	
8	6	4	2	0

	0.05	**0.025**	**0.01**	**0.005**
N	**0.1**	**0.05**	**0.02**	**0.01**
9	8	6	3	2
10	11	8	5	3
11	14	11	7	5
12	17	14	10	7
13	21	17	13	10
14	26	21	16	13
15	30	25	20	16
16	36	30	24	19
17	41	35	28	23
18	47	40	33	28
19	54	56	38	32
20	60	52	43	37
21	68	59	49	43
22	75	66	56	49
23	83	73	62	55
24	92	81	69	61
25	101	90	77	68
26	110	98	85	76
27	120	107	93	84
28	130	117	101	92
29	141	127	111	100
30	152	137	120	109

11.6. Critical values for Mann–Whitney *U* test

Values given are *maximum values* for *U*: to be significant at a given level, *U* must be equal to or less the critical value. Upper value indicates 0.005 level 1-tailed (0.01, 2-tailed); lower value indicates $p=0.025$ 1-tailed ($p=0.05$, 2-tailed).

N2 ↓ \ N1 →	1	2	3	4	5	6	7	8	9	10	11	12	13	14	15	16	17	18	19	20
2	—	—	—	—	—	—	—	0	0	0	0	1	1	1	1	1	2	2	2	2
3	—	—	—	—	0	1	1	2	2	3	3	4	4	5	5	6	6	7	7	8
4	—	—	—	0	1	2	3	4	4	5	6	7	8	9	10	11	11	12	13	14
5	—	—	0	1	2	3	5	6	7	8	9	11	12	13	14	15	17	18	19	20
6	—	—	1	2	3	5	6	8	10	11	13	14	16	17	19	21	22	24	25	27
7	—	—	1	3	5	6	8	10	12	14	16	18	20	22	24	26	28	30	32	34
8	—	0	2	4	6	8	10	13	15	17	19	22	24	26	29	31	34	36	38	41
9	—	0	2	4	7	10	12	15	17	20	23	26	28	31	34	37	39	42	45	48
10	—	0	3	6	9	13	16	19	23	26	30	33	37	40	44	47	51	55	58	62

	1	2	3	4	5	6	7	8	9	10	11	12	13	14	15	16	17	18	19	20
11	—	—	0	2	5	7	10	13	16	18	21	24	27	30	33	36	39	42	45	48
	—	0	3	6	9	13	16	19	23	26	30	33	37	40	44	47	51	55	58	62
12	—	—	1	3	6	9	12	15	18	21	24	27	31	34	37	41	44	47	51	54
	—	1	4	7	11	14	18	22	26	29	33	37	41	45	49	53	57	61	65	69
13	—	—	1	3	7	10	13	17	20	24	27	31	34	38	42	45	49	53	57	60
	—	1	4	8	12	16	20	24	28	33	37	41	45	50	54	59	63	67	72	76
14	—	—	1	4	7	11	15	18	22	26	30	34	38	42	46	50	54	58	63	67
	—	1	5	9	13	17	22	26	31	36	40	45	50	55	59	64	69	74	78	83
15	—	—	2	5	8	12	16	20	24	29	33	37	42	46	51	55	60	64	69	73
	—	1	5	10	14	19	24	29	34	39	44	49	54	59	64	70	75	80	85	90
16	—	—	2	5	9	13	18	22	27	31	36	41	45	50	55	60	65	70	74	79
	—	1	6	11	15	21	26	31	37	42	47	53	59	64	70	75	81	86	92	98
17	—	—	2	6	10	15	19	24	29	34	39	44	49	54	60	65	70	75	81	86
	—	2	6	11	17	22	28	34	39	45	51	57	63	69	75	81	87	93	99	105
18	—	—	2	6	11	16	21	26	31	37	42	47	53	58	64	70	75	81	87	92
	—	2	7	12	18	24	30	36	42	48	55	61	67	74	80	86	93	99	106	112
19	—	—	3	7	12	17	22	28	33	39	45	51	57	63	69	74	81	87	93	99
	—	2	7	13	19	25	32	38	45	52	58	65	72	78	85	92	99	106	113	119
20	—	—	3	8	13	18	24	30	36	42	48	54	60	67	73	79	86	92	99	105
	—	2	8	14	20	27	34	41	48	55	62	69	76	83	90	98	105	112	119	127

11.7. Solutions to tasks and exercises (if not already discussed in the individual chapters)

11.7.1. Chapter Two

Exercise I: Variables

1   Identify whether the following outcomes are discrete or continuous.

  a   Continuous, as the taxi driver can spend any amount of time at traffic lights, for example 2 hours 23 minutes and 24 seconds or 3.4563 hours.

  b   Discrete: either workers are on strike or not – there cannot be any 'half-strikes'.

  c   Discrete: we cannot have a 0.7 left-handed person.

  d   Continuous: the cow can produce any amount of milk.

2   Levels of measurement

  a   Ordinal, as the ratings are in a semantic order, indicating decreasing quality. Interval *only* if the differences between individual ratings are defined as being equal (e.g. 10 points between each rating).

  b   Categorical/nominal: 'male' and 'female' are mere labels to describe a category; but there is no inherent order to them.

  c   Categorical: the number functions as a unique identifier (or label) for a person. Again, there is no ranking/order implied.

  d   Ratio: differences between two adjacent scores are always identical, and there is a natural zero point: 0 per cent means no one is studying linguistics.

11.7.2. Chapter Five

Task 5.1 Totals of individual clusters.

	BF simp	BF total	AO simp	AO total	Total simp	Grand total
/-st/	29	37	18	23	47	60
/-ft/	7	9	0	2	7	11
/-nt/	8	16	14	29	22	45

/-nd/	8	14	8	14	16	28
/-ld/	8	15	2	4	10	19
/-zd/	5	8	3	4	8	12
/-md/	2	3	0	1	2	4
Other	4	4	1	4	5	8
Total	71	106	46	81	117	187

It seems that, across both speakers, the /-st/ and /-nt/ cluster are the ones that show the highest degree of simplification, with 47 and 22 simplified clusters respectively. However, as these are absolute frequencies, they do not tell us the proportion of simplification. For a conclusive statement we need the respective relative frequencies (see Chapter Five, Section 5.2).

Task 5.2

Relative frequencies of simplified clusters.

	BF simp %	AO simp %
/-st/	78	78
/-ft/	78	0
/-nt/	50	48
/-nd/	57	57
/-ld/	53	50
/-zd/	63	75
/-md/	67	0
Other	100	25
Total	67	57

Among the many things we could say about the data, the most striking aspect is that BF's speech shows more simplified consonant clusters than AO's with 67% and 57% cluster simplification respectively.

Task 5.10

A quantitative analysis provides no evidence that the language of the female witnesses is more powerless than that of the male witnesses: both female and male witnesses produce 154 'powerless' features, out of a grand total of 308 – that is, 50%. If we look at the level of individual speakers, A shows the most powerless forms. To calculate the ration of powerless form per utterance, divide the total number of powerless forms by the number of interview answers. Again, there are some quite drastic differences between witnesses, but there is discernible gender difference. If anything, based on the ratios, males seem to produce a higher ration than women.

	Women			Men		
	A	B	C	D	E	F
Intensifiers	16	0	0	21	2	1
Hedges	19	2	3	2	5	0
Hesitation forms	52	20	13	26	27	11
Witness asks lawyer questions	2	0	0	0	0	0
Gestures	2	0	0	0	0	0
Polite forms	9	0	2	2	0	1
Use of 'Sir'	2	0	6	32	13	11
Quotes	1	5	0	0	0	0
# of answers in interview	90	32	136	61	73	52
Sum of all 'powerless' forms	103	27	24	83	47	24
Percentage of all 'powerless forms'	33%	9%	8%	27%	15%	8%
Sum of 'powerless' forms by gender		154			154	
Percentage of 'powerless forms by gender)		0.5			0.5	
Ratio of 'powerless' forms per answer	1.14	0.84	0.18	1.36	0.64	0.46
Ratio of 'powerless' forms per answer: gender differences		0.596899			0.827957	

11.7.3. *Chapter Six*

Task 6.3

Sort data and calculate mean:

● 25 52 56 57 58 59 60 62 63 65 70 79

$$\bar{x} = \frac{25+52+56+57+58+59+60+62+63+65+70+79}{12} = \frac{706}{12} = 58.8$$

Task 6.4

Measures of central location:

Mean $\bar{x}$ =19.25, median=18, mode=18.
Q1=15, Q2=18, Q3=22

You report could read similar to this:
The analysis of the course size for 20 courses (N=20) shows that the mean size is 19.25 students. The median indicates that half of the courses offered have 18 or more students enrolled on them. The smallest 25 per cent of all courses offered have 15 or fewer students enrolled, while the top 25 courses have student numbers in excess of 22.

Task 6.5

Standard Deviation for Norwich data
For the real data:

● $\bar{x} = 71$

● sum of squares:
$(31{-}71)^2 + (42{-}71)^2 + (87{-}71)^2 + (95{-}71)^2 + (100{-}71)^2$
$= (-40)^2 + (-29)^2 + (16)^2 + (24)^2 + (29)^2$
$= 1600 + 841 + 256 + 576 + 841 = 4114$

● N=5, $N-1$=4

● Divide sum of squares by $N-1$: 4114/4=1028.5. This is our variance σ^2.

● $\sigma = 32$

For the fictive data:

● $\bar{x} = 71$

● sum of squares:
$(68{-}71)^2 + (70{-}71)^2 + (71{-}71)^2 + (72{-}71)^2 + (74{-}71)^2$
$= (-3)^2 + (-1)^2 + (0)^2 + (1)^2 + (3)^2 = 9{+}1{+}0{+}1{+}9 = 20.$

- $N=5$, $N-1=4$
- Divide sum of squares by $N-1$: $20/4=5$. This is our variance σ^2
- $\sigma = 2.24$

11.7.4. *Chapter Seven*

Task 7.4

Probabilities – Syntactic variation

- With 428 utterances in the sample, and 155 of them produced by children, the probability of an utterance selected from the sample was produced by the child is

$$P(\text{child}) = \frac{155}{428} = 0.36$$

  Accordingly, $P(\text{caregiver}) = \frac{273}{428} = 0.64$.

- For agreement, we can calculate:

$$P(+\text{agr}) = \frac{349}{428} = 0.82 \text{ and } P(-\text{agr}) = \frac{79}{428} = 0.18$$

- The probability of an utterance selected from the sample to be produced by either a child or to show agreement violation, is

$$P(\text{child} \cup -\text{agr}) = P(\text{child}) + P(-\text{agr}) - P(\text{child} \cap -\text{agr})$$
$$= 0.36 + 0.18 - 0.06 = 0.49$$

  Note that $P(\text{child} \cap -\text{agr}) = \frac{24}{428} = 0.06$

- The probability of an utterance selected from the sample was produced by either a caregiver or shows agreement, is

$$P(\text{caregiver} \cup +\text{agr}) = P(\text{caregiver}) + P(+\text{agr}) - P(\text{caregiver} \cap +\text{agr})$$
$$= 0.64 + 0.82 - 0.51 = 0.94$$

  with $P(\text{caregiver} \cap +\text{agr}) = \frac{218}{428} = 0.51$

- An utterance shows agreement on the condition of being produced by a caregiver:

$$P(\text{caregiver} \mid +\text{agr}) = \frac{218}{273} = 0.80$$

Task 7.5

Chi-squared test

	Child	Caregiver	
+agr	126	223	349
−agr	29	50	79
	155	273	428

Using Excel, $p=0.2$. This is a non-significant result; it is unlikely that there is a relationship between the two variables 'agreement' and 'speaker type'. In other words, the variables seem to be independent from each other.

Manually:

$$\chi^2 = \frac{(131-126)^2}{126} + \frac{(24-29)^2}{29} + \frac{(118-123)^2}{123} + \frac{(55-50)^2}{50}$$
$$= 0.20 + 0.86 + 0.11 + 0.5 = 1.67$$

For df=1, this is well below the critical value for even p=0.1, which should equal to or larger than 2.7 – see table of critical values above.

Task 7.8

A short and far from exhaustive report on the data in task 7.7 could read like this:

The analysis of Extra et al.'s data provides some interesting insights. Particularly striking is the variation across the four linguistic dimensions: while proficiency across the 21 languages varies by 29 percentage points, with a minimum proficiency of 67% for Italian and a maximum of 96% for Turkish, the range of values for language choice varies considerably: for 88% of Somali speakers indicate that they speak Somali at home, but only 23% of Javanese speakers do so – a difference of 65 percentage points. Rather unsurprisingly, then, is the fact that Javanese scores the lowest overall vitality score with a mere 28%, compared with the 2 highest vitality scores: 72% for both Somali and Turkish.

A Pearson correlation including all 4 dimensions as well as the vitality index supports these finding: there is a strong and significant correlation between all four dimensions and linguistic vitality. Most notably, with $r=0.94$ and $r=0.95$, respectively, language choice and language dominance show an almost perfect correlation with vitality, followed by a similarly strong correlation between vitality and preference with $r=0.93$. Proficiency and vitality correlate with $r=0.83$. All correlation coefficient are significant on a level of $p<0.05$ (df=19). These results give raise the assumption that in particular the actual use of the language contributes positive to the vitality. The calculation of the R^2s shows that in particular linguistic choice and dominance contribute substantially to the variation in vitality, with $R^2=0.89$ and $R^2=0.9$, respectively.

Interestingly, though, despite their considerable impact on linguistic vitality, linguistic choice and dominance show low mean scores if compared to proficiency levels, with a mean proficiency score of $x=84.5\%$, but mean scores of choice and dominance at a mere $x=55.5$ and $x=32$. Dependent-sample t-tests show that the difference in scores between proficiency and choice, and proficiency and dominance are statistically significant on a level of $p<0.05$.

A brief checklist for data analysis:

1 Calculate all descriptive statistics, as in table below.

	Language proficiency	Language choice	Language dominance	Language preference	Language vitality
Min	67	23	6	16	28
Max	96	88	57	53	72
Range	29	65	51	37	44
Mean	84.52	55.52	31.95	37.90	53.71
STD	8.59	22.75	16.03	11.20	13.42

2 Look through your descriptive measure and identify anything noteworthy.

    a Are any of the descriptive measures 'off', that is, particularly high/low, or simple much different from what you had expected?

    b Do any of the variables show a particularly high variation, especially when compared to other variables?

3 Look for relationships between variables, by calculating correlation coefficients.

4 Based on the results of your correlation analysis and your descriptive measures, check the difference between individual variables for statistical significance; just because something is lower/higher does not mean it is of statistical significance – it might be a fluke. Use t-test of appropriate non-parametric measures.

5 Take all the results you have obtained so far. Look at them *critically*. What do they tell you? And, most importantly, how do they relate to your research question and your hypotheses? Remember: All the numbers and figures you receive are mere mathematical constructs – they only really make sense when you analyse them in the context of your theoretical and methodological framework!

6 Write up your results in such a way that the relationship between theoretical framework, data and data analysis forms a coherent unit. All three parts have to tell the same story – all too often, they appear independent from each other in reports, particularly when compiled by novices. Note: if there are any word limits, stick to them!

11.7.5. *Chapter 8*

Task 8.2

Run a t-test for all *independent* constellations of the data in Table 8.5.

t(EG_pre/CG_pre); *p*=0.94, 2-tailed. No significant difference between pre-test scores.

t(EG_post/CG_post); *p*=0.00, 1-tailed. As discussed in chapter.

t(EG_pre/CG_post); *p*=0.25, 2-tailed. Note that this is like comparing apples with pears and does not tell us anything useful.

Task 8.3

Create a bar chart with error bars for the dependent *t*-tests EG_pre/post and CG_pre/post. Interpret the result (refer Figure 11.1).

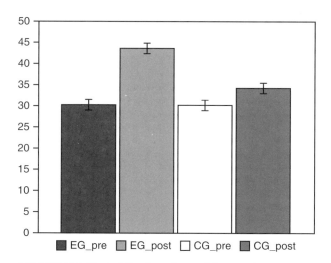

FIGURE 11.1 *Task 8.3 – bar chart with error bars.*

The bar chart with the error bars confirms our findings from the dependent t-test, as discussed in Chapter Eight: neither bar errors bars for the EG nor the CG overlap. We have seen that the scores for the experimental group are much higher in the post-stimulus condition, and accordingly the error bars are rather far apart. For the control group, the error bars are closer together, but again do not overlap, indicating a small but significant difference.

Task 8.5

Using a *t*-test assuming *unequal* (!) variance, first, analyse the difference between male and female performance. Is the answer as straightforward as it seems? What are potential pitfalls?

	Male	Female
Mean	19.25	21.43
Variance	18.15	2.17
Observations	7.00	5.00
Hypothesized Mean Difference	0.00	
df	8.00	
t Stat	−1.25	
P(T<=t) one-tail	0.12	
t Critical one-tail	1.86	
P(T<=t) two-tail	0.25	
t Critical two-tail	2.31	

For discussion, see Chapter Eight, Section 8.5.

Task 8.6

Remove HF and SA from the sample and re-calculate the *t*-statistic, this time assuming equal variance (as we have an equal number of men and women). Interpret the result with reference to your results from task 8.5.

	Male	Female
Mean	17.028	21.43
Variance	4.39702	2.17295
Observations	5	5
Pooled Variance	3.284985	
Hypothesized Mean Difference	0	
df	8	
t Stat	−3.840195613	
P(T<=t) one-tail	0.002472908	
t Critical one-tail	1.85954832	
P(T<=t) two-tail	0.004945817	
t Critical two-tail	2.306005626	

Task 8.9

Using a chi-squared test and the data on children's vocabulary acquisition, show that:

a the children *produce* significantly more IN than OUT words.

	IN	OUT	
Observed	33	12	45
Expected	22.5	22.5	45

For the chi-squared test, $p=0.00$, that is, the children produce significantly more IN than OUT words, showing a clear preference for word type in the domain of production.

b there is no difference between the two word types in the domain of comprehension.

	IN	OUT	
Observed	54	50	104
Expected	52	52	104

The result of the chi-squared test shows a significance level of $p=0.69$, so there in no statistical evidence that children's comprehension of IN words is better than of OUT words. In fact, the probability that the result is a fluke is almost 70 per cent.

Task 8.10

First and foremost, note that the count in two cells (female Churchgoers and female Rastafarians) is below 5 – this might lead to slight accuracies. You should acknowledge this in your report.

1 H_0: There is no association between gender and religious practices.

Expected values:

	Males	Females	
Christians	7	5	12
Churchgoers	6	4	10
Rastafarians	3	3	6
No religious affiliation	10	7	17
	26	19	45

If calculating the chi-square, you will find that p=0.55, which is highly insignificant. Hence, there is no association between gender and religious practices.

2 H_0: There is no difference between those with a religious affiliation and those without.

In a first step, pool the frequencies of all those with religious affiliation, independent from gender. Then calculate the expected frequencies.

	Affiliation	No affiliation	
Observed	28	17	45
Expected	22.5	22.5	45

For χ^2, p=0.10. This is a borderline case. We may want to argue that the number of those with a religious affiliation is statistically higher than those without, but the probability that the result is a fluke is as high as 10 per cent. It is up to your discretion.

3 H$_0$: There is an equal number of male and female Rastafarians in the sample.

	Male	Female	
Observed	5	1	6
Expected	3	3	6

For χ^2, p=0.10. Bear in mind the low frequencies in three of the four cells!

11.7.6. *Chapter Nine*

Task 9.2

Compare the Spearman with the Pearson coefficient.

As a general guideline, you should find that for most of the examples, the Spearman's rho indicates a stronger relationship than the Pearson's r; this is because we are working with rank, which will make our data more linear, hence pronouncing the relationship between the two variables. This obviously goes to the cost of the amount detail we receive. You should also find that the significance levels for the Spearman correlation are lower, that is, we can be more confident with the Spearman correlation.

NOTES

Chapter 6

1   This is one of the reasons why the arithmetic mean is called the mean – there are other 'averages' around.

Chapter 7

1   There will obviously be different degrees of obesity and severity of diabetes, but inevitably we need to draw a line where obesity starts and ends – see discussion in Chapter Two on measurement and operationalization.

2   This is also a highly insignificant result, hence a fluke. We shall ignore this here, as it is due to the extremely small size of the data set, and is for illustration purpose only.

BIBLIOGRAPHY

Baayen, R. H. (2008), *Analyzing Linguistic Data: A Practical Introduction to Statistics Using R*. Cambridge: Cambridge University Press.

Baker, P. (2006), *Using Corpora in Discourse Analysis*. London: Continuum.

Baquedano-Lopez, Patricia (2006), 'Literacy practices across learning contexts', in Alessandro Duranti (ed.), *A Companion to Linguistics Anthropology*. Oxford: Blackwell.

Baugh, Albert C. B and Cable, Thomas (2002), *A History of the English Language*. London: Pearson Education.

Bayley, Guy (2004), 'Real time and apparent time', in J. K. Chambers, Peter Trudgill and Natalie Schilling-Estes (eds), *Handbook of Language Variation and Change*, 312–22. Oxford: Blackwell.

Bergman, Manfred M. (2010), *Mixed-Method Research*. London: Sage.

Birdsong David and Molis, Michelle (2001), 'On the evidence for maturational constraints in second-language acquisition', *Journal of Memory and Language*, 44, 235–49.

Bourhis, Richard Yvon, Giles, Howard and Rosenthal, Doreen (1981), 'Notes on the construction of a subjective ethnolinguistic vitality questionnaire', *Journal of Multilingual and Multicultural Development*, 2, 145–55.

Brace, Nicola, Kemp, Richard and Snelgar, Rosemary (2003), *spss for Psychologists: A Guide to Data Analysis Using spss for Windows* (versions 9, 10 and 11). Basingstoke: Palgrave Macmillan.

Bryman, Alan (2004), *Social Research Methods*. Oxford: Oxford University Press.

Burton, Dawn (2000), *Research Training for Social Scientists: A Handbook for Postgraduate Researchers*. London: SAGE.

Butler, Christopher (1985), *Statistics in Linguistics*. Oxford: Blackwell.

Cambridge ESOL (2007), *IELTS Handbook 2007*. Cambridge: Cambridge ESOL.

Chambers, J. K. (2002), 'Patterns of variation including change', in J. K. Chambers, Peter Trudgill and Natalie Schilling-Estes (eds), *Handbook of Language Variation and Change*, 349–72. Oxford: Blackwell.

Clark, Eve V. (2003), *First Language Acquisition*. Cambridge: Cambridge University Press.

Clegg, Frances (1982), *Simple Statistics: A Course Book for the Social Sciences*. Cambridge: Cambridge University Press.

Cramer, Duncan (1998), *Fundamental Statistics for Social Research: Step-by-Step Calculations and Computer Techniques Using spss for Windows*. London: Routledge.

Cresswell, John W. and Vicki L. Plano Clark (2010), *Designing and Conducting Mixed-Method Research*. London: Sage.

Crystal, David (1999), *The Penguin Dictionary of Language*. London: Penguin.

Dörnyei, Zoltan (2007), *Research Methods in Applied Linguistics: Quantitative, Qualitative, and Mixed Methodologies*. Oxford: Oxford University Press.

Dörnyei, Zoltan and Ema Ushioda (2009), *Motivation, Language Identity and the l2 Self*. Bristol: Multilingual Matters.

Doughty, Catherine and Teresa Pica (1986), '"Information gap" tasks: Do they facilitate second language acquisition?', *TESOL Quarterly* 20, 305–25.

Du Plessis, Theodorus (2010), 'Bloemfontein/mangaung, "city on the move". Language management and transformation of a non-representative linguistic landscape', in Elana Shohamy, Eliezer Ben-Rafael and Monica Barni (eds), *Linguistic Langdscape in the City*, 74–95. Bristol: Multilingual Matters.

Duranti, Alessandro (1997), *Linguistic Anthropology*. Cambridge: Cambridge University Press.

Edwards, Viv (1986), *Language in a Black Community*. Clevedon: Multilingual Matters.

Extra, Guus, Yağmur, Kutlay and van der Avoird, Tim (2004), 'Methodological considerations', *Urban Multilingualism in Europe. Immigrant Minority Languages at Home and School*, 109–32. Clevedon: Multilingual Matters.

Fairclough, Norman (1988), *Language and Power*. Harlow: Longman.

— (1992), *Discourse and Social Change*. Cambridge: Polity.

— (1995), *Critical Discourse Analysis: The Critical Study of Language*. London: Longman.

Field, Andy P. (1999), 'a bluffer's guide to meta-analysis', *Newsletter of the Mathematical, Statistical and Computing Section of the British Psychological Society* 7, 16–25.

— (2000), *Discovering Statistics Using SPSS for Windows: Introducing Statistical Methods*. London: Sage.

— (2001), 'Meta-analysis of correlation coefficients: a Monte Carlo comparison of fixed-and random-effects methods', *Psychological Methods* 6, 161–80.

Foddy, William (1993), *Constructing Questions for Interviews and Questionnaires: Theory and Practice in Social Research*. Cambridge: Cambridge University Press.

Foley, William A. (1997), *Anthropological Linguistics: An Introduction*. Oxford: Blackwell Publishers.

Fowler, Floyd. J. (2002), *Survey Research Methods*. London: SAGE.

Frankel, Martin (2010), 'Sampling theory', in P. V. Marsden and J. D. Wright (eds), *Handbook of Survey Research*, 83–137. Bingley: Emerald Group Pub.

Füglein, Rosemarie (2000), '"Kanak Sprak"', Eine ethnolinguistische Untersuchung eines Sprachphänomens im Deutschen. Unpublished Diplomarbeit (dissertation). University of Bamberg.

Ganor, Boaz (2002), 'Defining terrorism: Is one man's terrorist another man's freedom fighter?' *Police Practice and Research* 3, 287–304.

Giles, H., R. Y. Bourhis and D. M. Taylor (1977), 'Towards a theory of language in ethnic group relations', in H. Giles (ed.), *Language, Ethnicity and Intergroup Relations*, 307–48. London: Academic Press.

Glass, Gene, V. (1976), 'Primary, secondary, and meta-analysis of research', *Educational Researcher* 5, 3–8.

Glass, Gene, V., Barry McGaw and Mary L. Smith (1981), *Meta-Analysis in Social Research*. London: Sage.

Gries, Stefan T. (2009), *Quantitative Corpus Linguistics with r : A Practical Introduction*. London: Routledge.

Hall, Suart (2007), 'The west and the rest: discourse and power', in T. Das Gupta, C. E. James, R. C. A. Maaka, G.-E. Galabuzi and C. Andersen (eds), *Race and Racialization: Essential Readings*, 56–64. Toronto: Canadian Scholars Press.

Hammersley, Martyn and Anna Traianou (2012), *Ethics in Qualitative Research: Controversies and Contexts*. London: SAGE.

Hardt-Mautner, Gerlinde (1995), '"Only Connect": Critical Discourse Analysis and Corpus Linguistics'. *UCREL Technical Papers*, vol. 6. Lancaster: Lancaster University.

Harvey, Greg (2003), *Excel 2003 for Dummies*. Hoboken, NJ: Wiley Pub.

Henry, Alison (2004), 'Variation and syntactic theory', in J. K. Chambers, Peter Trudgill and Natalie Schilling-Estes (eds), *Handbook of Language Variation and Change*, 312–22. Oxford: Blackwell.

Hirsh-Pasek, Kathy and Golinkoff, Roberta Michnick (1996), *The Origins of Grammar: Evidence from Early Language Comprehension*. Cambridge, MA: MIT Press.

Huff, Darrell (1991), *How to Lie with Statistics*. London: Penguin.

Hunter, John E. and Frank L. Schmidt (2004), *Methods of Meta-Analysis: Correcting Error and Bias in Research Findings*. London: Sage Publications.

Johnson, Jacqueline and Newport, Elissa L. (1989), 'Critical period effects in second language acquisition: The influence of maturational state on the acquisition of english as a second language', *Cognitive Psychology*, 21, 60–99.

— (1991), 'Critical period effects on universal properties of language: The status of subjacency in the acquisition of a second language', *Cognition* 39, 215–58.

Johnson, Keith (2008), *Quantitative Methods in Linguistics*. Oxford: Blackwell.

Johnson, Timothy, Kulesa, Patrick, Cho, Young Ik and Shavitt, Sharon (2005), 'The relation between culture and response styles. Evidence from 19 countries', *Journal of Cross-Cultural Psychology* 36, 264–77.

Johnstone, Barbara (2000), *Qualitative Methods in Sociolinguistics*. Oxford: Oxford University Press.

Keim, Inken (1984), *Untersuchungen zum Deutsch türkischer Arbeiter*. Tübingen: Gunter Narr.

Kennedy, Robert (1999), 'Is one person's terrorist another's freedom fighter? Western and Islamic approaches to "just war"compared', *Terrorism and Political Violence* 11, 1–21.

Labov, William (1963), 'The social motivation of a sound change', *Word*, 19, 273–309.

— (1972), *Sociolinguistic Patterns*. Philadelphia: University of Pennsylvania Press.

— (1977), *Language in the Inner City: Studies in the Black English Vernacular*. Oxford: Blackwell.

Lakoff, Robin Tolmach (1975), *Language and Woman's Place*. New York: Harper and Row.

LaPiere, Richard T. (1934), 'Attitudes vs. actions', *Social Forces* 13, 230–37.

Larson-Hall, Jenifer (2010), *A Guide to Doing Statistics in Second Language Research Using SPSS*. London: Routledge.

Lewis David Gareth (1967), *Statistical Methods in Education*. London: University of London Press.

Li, Xiaolong (1988), 'Effects of contextual cues on inferring and remembering meanings of new words', *Applied Linguistics* 9 (4), 402–13.

Litosseliti, Lia (2003), *Using Focus Groups in Research*. London: Continuum.

Macaulay, Ronald and Trevelyan, G. D. (1977), *Language, Social Class and Education: A Glasgow Study*. Edinburgh: Edinburgh University Press.

Martin, J. T. (2001), 'Cohesion and texture', in D. Schiffrin, D. Tannen and H. E. Hamilton (eds), *The Handbook of Discourse Analysis*, 35–53. London: Blackwell.

Milroy, Lesley (1987), *Language and Social Networks*. Oxford: Blackwell.

O'Barr, William M. and Bowman K. Atkins (1980), 'Women's language or powerless language', in S. McConnell-Ginet, R. Borker and N. Furman (eds), *Women and Language in Literature and Society*, 93–110. New York: Praeger.

Ping, Tay Li. (2005), 'does the survey response scale format matter?', Paper presented at IMTA – International Military Testing Association, Singapore.

Purdie, Nola, Rhonda. Oliver, Glenys Collard and Judith Rochecouste (2002), 'Attitudes of primary school Australian aboriginal children to their linguistic codes', *Journal of Language and Social Psychology* 21, 410–21.

Rasinger, Sebastian M. (2007), *Bengali-English in East London: A Study in Urban Multilingualism*. Oxford: Peter Lang Publishers.

Romaine, Suzanne (2000), *Language in Society. An Introduction to Sociolinguistics*. Oxford: Oxford University Press.

Sadighi, F. and Zare, S. (2006), 'Is listening comprehension influenced by the background knowledge of the learners? a case study of iranian efl learners', *The Linguistics Journal*, 1, 110–26.

Sapsford, Roger and Jupp, Victor (1996), *Data Collection and Analysis*. London: Sage.

Schnell, Rainer, Hill, Paul B. and Esser, Elke (2005), *Methoden der Empirischen Sozialforschung*. Munich: Oldenbourg.

Schwartz, Richard G. and Leonard, Laurence B. (1982), 'Do children pick and choose?', *Journal of Child Language*, 9, 319–36.

Sebba, Mark (1993), *London Jamaican: Language Systems in Interaction*. London: Longman.

Stern, H. H. (1983), *Fundamental Concepts of Language Teaching*. Oxford: Oxford University Press.

Tagliamonte, Sali (2006), *Analysing Sociolinguistic Variation*. Cambridge: Cambridge University Press.

Torgerson, Carole (2003), *Systematic Reviews*. London: Continuum.

Trudgill, Peter (1974), *The Social Differentiation of English in Norwich*. London: Cambridge University Press.

Wolfram, Watt (1969), *A Sociolinguistic Description of Detroit Negro Speech*. Washington, DC: Center For Applied Linguistics.

Woods, Anthony, Fletcher, Paul and Hughes, Arthur (1986), *Statistics in Language Studies*. Cambridge: Cambridge University Press.

Woods, Nicola (2000), 'New Zealand English across generations: An analysis of selected vowel and consonant variables', in Allan Bell and Koenraad Kuiper (eds), *New Zealand English*, 84–110. Wellington: Victoria University Press.

INDEX